Participants in the symposium entitled "Theories of Representation in American Indian Literatures: European and North American Perspectives." The symposium took place June 22–25, 1997, at the seventeenth-century Chateau de la Bretesche, near the town of Missillac in southern Brittany, France, and approximately two and a half hours from the port of St. Malo.

First row: A. LaVonne Brown Ruoff, Paula Gunn Allen, Willard A. Beling
Second row: David Murray, Kim Blaeser, Kathryn Shanley, Simone Pellerin
Third row: John Purdy, Bernadette Rigal-Cellard, Kathleen M. Sands, David Moore, Gretchen M. Bataille, Hartwig Isernhagen

Native American Representations

First Encounters,
Distorted Images, and
Literary Appropriations

EDITED BY
GRETCHEN M. BATAILLE

University of Nebraska Press, Lincoln and London

© 2001 by the University
of Nebraska Press
All rights reserved
Manufactured in the
United States of America
♾ Library of Congress
Cataloging-in-Publication
Data. Native American
representations : first
encounters, distorted
images, and literary
appropriations / edited
by Gretchen M. Bataille.
p.   cm.
Includes bibliographical
references and index.
ISBN 0-8302-1312-3
(cloth : alk. paper)
ISBN 0-8032-6188-8
(pbk. : alk. paper)
1. Indians of North
America – Public
opinion. 2. Public
opinion – United States.
3. Indians in literature.
4. American literature –
History and criticism.
5. Indians of North
America – Attitudes.
6. Indians in popular
culture. I. Bataille,
Gretchen M., 1944–
E98.P99 N38 2001
305.897′3–dc21
00-054475

Table of Contents

Acknowledgments

Any project of this size and complexity is successful only because of the efforts of many people working together. The impetus and primary support came from the Borchard Foundation in Los Angeles. For their enthusiastic support of this project from the beginning, I am grateful to Dr. Willard Beling, president of the Board of Directors of the Albert and Elaine Borchard Foundation and Mrs. Betty Beling, vice president of the Foundation. From my first discussions with them to the grand banquet at the French shore, they were full participants in the development of the proposal, in the entire symposium at Chateau de la Bretesche, and in the social events. This book is dedicated to them in recognition of their support.

Twelve scholars and two facilitators met in Brittany during June of 1997. Of the twelve scholars, all except Paula Gunn Allen, Simone Pellerin, and Kimberly Blaeser are represented in this collection. Ellen Nash served as organizer of all details before, during, and after the trip, and Greta Nash visually recorded the entire symposium, including a poetry reading and musical presentation that featured symposium participants. In the spring of 1998, Kathryn Shanley brought together many of the participants for further discussions at Cornell University. Jerold Ramsey participated in the Cornell conference, and his essay was added to the collection. Louis Owens, James Welch, Gordon Henry, Wolfgang Hochbruck, Neleye Delanoe, and Laura Coltelli were invited and unable to attend the 1997 symposium, but all of them offered advice and suggestions that contributed to the success of the endeavor. Louis Owens contributed an essay to the book that clearly articulates the focus of the collection.

Between the planning of the symposium and this final project, I have had the support of two institutions: University of California, Santa Barbara, and Washington State University. I am grateful to both institutions for the support I received from research assistants Noelle Williams at UCSB and Kristen Harpster and Bethany Blankenship at WSU. I am particularly appreciative of the sup-

port I received from Donna Clark at wsu, who had to do everything from figure out how to open "foreign" computer disks to following my nomadic colleagues from one institution to another or to sabbatical addresses. Now at the
University of North Carolina, I have had the support of Margaret Torbert and
Lisa Adamson in completing the final manuscript.

Finally, a project such as this is possible because of the many writers, scholars, and friends who remain interested in the history of Native Americans on
this continent and the representation of them throughout the world. In a
world where boundaries shift and sometimes disappear, the many distortions
and misrepresentations of Native Americans have remained and have gained
international presence and persistence. This collection demonstrates that
there are many writers and critics — American and European, Native American
and non-Natives — who continue to work to "set the record straight."

Gretchen M. Bataille
University of North Carolina
Chapel Hill, North Carolina

Native American Representations

Introduction

GRETCHEN M. BATAILLE

Columbus arrived in the New World in 1492, but America has yet to be discovered.

Jack McIver Weatherford, in *Indian Givers: How the Indians of the Americas Transformed the World*

On August 6, 1996, the *Wall Street Journal* (Aeppel A1, A6) had a front-page article about "tribes of foreigners" visiting Indian reservations, remarking that Germans are particularly taken with Native Americans. A Zurich tour company offers $3,200 package tours to Pine Ridge Reservation in South Dakota, and a Munich agency has a tour called Lakota Tipi and Travel. The *Journal* article describes a Japanese tourist being indoctrinated into the dress code of the sweat lodge before beginning his two-day fast on a hilltop for the "vision quest" part of his tour.

These stories are not isolated, nor is international interest in Native Americans unusual. Over 85,000 Germans belong to clubs devoted to learning about Indian tribes and cultures, this generation's version of the world created in the writings of nineteenth-century novelist Karl May, who wrote a series of novels about Old Shatterhead and his sidekick Winnetou, a fictional Apache chief. American interest in Native Americans is manifested in different ways and frequently in waves reflecting current politics, student unrest and protests, and, for literary scholars, various critical theories. The misrepresentation, commodification, and distortion of indigenous identities have existed from the moment of first contact.

The Norse in Newfoundland in 1004 are generally ignored in the history of European and Native relations because they simply killed those people who were in their way. They called the Native Americans *Skraelings*, a term that has been described as an untranslatable expletive. As a result, October 12, 1492, remains the official date of the first recorded "discovery" of America and the first documented interactions with the people of the New World. To label the Taino Indians, Christopher Columbus used the term *Indios*, variations of which have remained since the late 1400s. In his journals, Columbus wrote, "They should be good servants and very intelligent, for I have observed that they soon repeat anything that is said to them, and I believe that they would easily be made Christians, for they appear to me to have no religion." Later he added, "They have no religion and I think that they would be very quickly Christianized, for they have a very ready understanding" (Gill 3). When Columbus arrived, he carried two flags, the flag of Spain and the flag of the Catholic Church. He planted those flags where indigenous peoples for generations had planted corn, beans, chile peppers, and potatoes, and the systematic obliteration of Native American religion and sovereignty began.

Columbus had goals — for god, for glory, and for gold — but he was only the first of many to encounter the Native peoples and to describe those meetings through European eyes. Indians were brought to Europe for study and for exhibition, and Indians were displayed in Portugal as early as 1501. Several years later, in 1508, Canadian Indians were brought to France. Hernan Cortés brought Indians from Mexico to Spain in 1528 to perform, and in 1529 the German artist Christoph Weiditz created what may have been the first drawings of Indians in Europe. That same year some of the Indians brought to Europe by Cortes performed for Pope Clement VII.

Europeans were fascinated by the exotic New World and by the people who inhabited that world. Early explorers took back colorful birds and flowers as well as incredible stories about the inhabitants of the New World. Travel narratives as early as the 1500s depicted the Native American as a fierce, cannibalistic creature, and the woodcuts accompanying the stories portrayed the Indian as less than human — naked, violent, warlike, and, frequently, more animalistic than human. Early travelers heeded the warnings that they might be seduced into savagery by the demonic Indians, and accounts of unrestrained sexuality and immorality represented by images of nakedness influenced European attitudes.

By the late 1500s maps were appearing that portrayed "America" as a Native American woman in a bucolic and Eden-like setting or, conversely, as a hostile enemy carrying the body parts of white explorers. This duality was difficult to reconcile, but it presaged the ongoing ambivalence of the Europeans and later the Americans about the people of the New World. The story of Pocahontas introduced the Native woman as loyal to the white explorers who had invaded her tribal land, and the account gained wide circulation. The saga of the Native

American woman who was willing to give up her life for a white man continues to captivate audiences, if the Walt Disney movie is any indication.

Art and literature portrayed images that ranged from benign to hostile. Artists from John White to George Catlin, Alfred Jacob Miller, and Frederick Remington were fascinated by the Native Americans and frequently chose to portray them as domestic or even regal. In many cases, costumes and settings were more important than historical accuracy in the artistic depictions. In late-nineteenth-century literature, the captivity narratives had given way to dime novels and books with lurid covers and titles such as *The Death of Jane McCrea* and *The Murder of Lucinda*, tales that warned readers of menacing Indian males who would attack white women.

Clearly, contact between Europeans and Indians did not guarantee understanding. In 1693 William Penn remarked: "These poor people are under a dark night in things relating to religion, to be sure. . . . Yet they believe in God and immortality. . . . I am ready to believe them of the Jewish race, I mean of the stock of the Ten Tribes" (Gill 10). Cotton Mather saw the influence of the devil on American Indians: "The natives of the country now possessed by the New-Englanders had been forlorn and wretched heathens ever since their first herding here; and though we know not when or how those Indians first became inhabitants of this mighty continent, yet we may guess that probably the devil decoyed those miserable savages hither, in hopes that the gospel of the Lord Jesus Christ would never come here to destroy or disturb his absolute empire over them" (10). All these generalizations about Indian religion or the lack of it are clearly misleading and inaccurate; however, these early views are echoed in later assessments that perpetuated the idea that Native Americans lacked religion or spirituality.

The Native American presence moved easily from the printed page and portrait to the stage to became a stock figure in drama, with the roles played by whites, anticipating what was to become standard practice in the movies. Indians did get to "play themselves" in the popular Wild West shows, however. All of the shows had the same theme: the victory of the European — now American — over the Native Americans. The shows further spread the distorted image of Indians to Europe, and the images and storylines became the basis for the first films with Indian themes. The images of Native Americans that had been developing for nearly four hundred years were transferred to the screen in the early twentieth century, reaching an even wider audience than before.

The twentieth century began with visual images of Native Americans that had been evolving over four centuries. At the same time, Native American writers such as Charles Eastman, Gertrude Bonnin, and Simon Pokagon were writing about their lives and culture. It took nearly seventy more years, though, before Native writers were taken seriously by scholars, and then it was because N. Scott Momaday's 1968 novel *House Made of Dawn* had received the Pulitzer Prize. At a time frequently referred to as the "renaissance" of Native writing, critics, scholars, and students began to pay attention to Native American writers.

Throughout the years from first contact, if European countries did not have real-life Indians, their writers and artists created imaginary ones. In France, Chateaubriand created fictional Indians, and in Germany Karl May created Winnetou. "The Noble Savage" perpetuated the contradictions that had existed from the beginning, and eventually both Europe and America were struggling with images created and perpetuated by writers, artists, missionaries, explorers, and, in perhaps the most dramatic popular presentations, the creators of Wild West shows and movies.

The backdrop of centuries of misrepresentation has taken its toll. Woodcuts, paintings, explorers' journals, and missionary accounts provided early images to Europeans, and movies, western novels, and cartoons have perpetuated the myths and stereotypes. Germans live in tepees in the Black Forest, and children worldwide play with Pocahontas dolls with Barbie bodies.

Native Americans have been mythologized by anthropologists and ethnographers, by tourists and the tourist industry, and through art and literature. Both the popular media and scholars have participated in creating the "Indian that never was." Indian images reflected the creators of those images more than the people themselves, and the images have changed through time, with portrayals of vanishing Indians, primitives, half-breeds, squaws, warriors, and militants taking their turn in the foreground during various historical periods.

In her book about images of Indians in the Southwest, Leah Dilworth analyzes the politics of representation within the framework of collecting. Ethnographers, museum directors, dealers, tourists, and private collectors preserved those objects that, for them, represented Native American cultures. Similarly, Bohemians such as Mabel Dodge Luhan, Millicent Rogers, and Mary Austin sought to appropriate Indian culture and make it theirs in costume, lifestyle, or art. More recently Carlos Castaneda, Gary Snyder, Lynn Andrews, Jamake Highwater, and others in academia have done the same thing by appropriating ceremonies, languages, and history. These practices objectify Native peoples, resulting in strained relationships between the representer and the represented rather than any real communication (8).

Language, and our use or misuse of it, has frequently defined how Native Americans have been perceived. Naming itself has varied — Indians, Native

Americans, American Indians, Amerindians, Native Peoples, tribes, nations, The People, Diné, Anishanaabe, Tohono O'odam, Cherokee, Chippewa, or Ojibwa — to define the entire group or tribes or nations within the larger group. Dime novels and movies have defined Native Americans as "discovered" by Columbus, "lurking in the wilderness," "attacking wagon trains," "scalping pioneers," "savages" who hindered progress, and, usually, groups who would "vanish" along with the buffalo. Indians were called "braves" and "princesses"; they participated in "massacres" rather than "battles" and were frequently defined as "nomadic," "warlike," "primitive," and "simple." Vine Deloria Jr. wrote in *Custer Died for Your Sins* that historically African Americans were viewed as domestic animals whereas Native Americans have always been viewed as wild animals, providing justification for their extinction. A history textbook being used in the 1960s demonstrates that it was not just popular culture that was perpetuating the stereotypes: "To be sure, the Indians contributed something, but surprisingly little, to American history. . . . Indian contributions to American history have been so slight that one is justified in suggesting that they might be omitted entirely without appreciably altering the main trend of development. . . . American history began therefore not with the Indians but with the arrival of the first Europeans. . . . As compared with the meager contributions of the Indians, the English brought a complex, well-developed civilization" (Harlow 1–2).

A group of scholars responded to this history of inaccuracies in a chateau in France during the summer of 1997, and this collection of essays is the result of that symposium and a follow-up conference at Cornell University in the spring of 1998. The interest in Native Americans from tourists, scholars, students, and the media creates a dilemma for many literary critics. Movies and the popular press are more pervasive and influential than literary criticism, and the students we teach have been immersed in a culture of inaccuracies and stereotypes.

The authors from both sides of the Atlantic address a broad topic: "Native American Representations." The symposium, the conference, and these essays focus on issues of translation, of European and American perceptions of land and landscape, teaching approaches, and trans-Atlantic encounters for over five hundred years. The emphasis is on issues of representation. Who has represented Native Americans in the past? What images exist in various media on both sides of the Atlantic? Who controls the representation? What changes in representation have come about with increasing numbers of Native American writers and critics?

Edward Said asked in *Orientalism*: "How does one *represent* other cultures? What is *another* culture? Is the notion of a distinct culture (or race, religion, civilization) a useful one?" (324). The essays represented here explore ethical questions of appropriation and advocacy, of cultural sovereignty and respect for the "authentic" text. We kept in mind Said's warning to escape the temptation to define the "other" as if it is only a creation of our own culture and has no reality of its own.

This collection demonstrates some of the significant changes in reality and in academic awareness of Native studies in the United States and Europe. Native writers are communicating on their own behalf both in America and to an audience abroad. Increasingly, Native literature is being read in English as well as in translations into French, German, and Italian, and scholars throughout Europe are interested in both research and teaching that includes American indigenous literatures.

Beginning this collection, Native American writers Louis Owens and Kathryn Shanley introduce the subject from personal perspectives, drawing on their own experiences as well as their broad reading in critical theory and cultural appropriation. Both address the issues of misrepresentation that emanate from critical definitions. Owens explores the perspectives of the Asian version of "Indian" critics and their definitions of Native American literatures, while Shanley examines intentional deception such as that perpetuated by Jamake Highwater. David Moore, David Murray, and John Purdy focus on representation across many disciplines. They critique and take seriously the essentialist arguments for cultural nationalisms. Moore and Murray explore the commodification, ownership, and rights to cultural property. Purdy compares two Native American–produced films with Thomas King's novel *Green Grass, Running Water* and in the process demonstrates the visual and textual strategies used to counter stereotypes. In his film *Imagining Indians*, Hopi filmmaker Victor Masayesva plays on the theme of representation using movie history and white fascination with Indians to satirically make his point.

Jarold Ramsey, Kathleen Sands, and Bernadette Rigal-Cellard use specific literary texts to address representation, with Ramsey and Sands exploring the complex reciprocal negotiations that are necessary between cultures and languages as oral literatures move into print. Addressing the relationships between narrators and biographers demonstrates the distance that frequently occurs between the real and the unreal, the original voice and the reconstructed voice, and, for the purposes of this collection, the ambiguity of the final representations. Rigal-Cellard addresses what she calls the "hybridization of cultures" in Louis Owens's *The Sharpest Sight*.

Finally, Hartwig Isernhagen and A. LaVonne Brown Ruoff look at other ways of defining "representations." Isernhagen analyzes the American government view as expressed through the WPA papers and addresses private and public identities. Ruoff looks the other direction, describing how early Native Americans viewed Europeans and Euro-Americans. In her conclusion, Kathryn Shanley posits the issues that are not yet resolved and leads readers to the exploration of new directions in scholarship and criticism.

The historian Edmundo O'Gorman has said, "The native cultures of the newly found lands could not be recognized and respected in their own right, as an original way of realizing human ideals and values, but only for the meaning they might have in relation to Christian European culture." He describes America as being invented "in the image of its inventor" (qtd. in McQuade 11). It is this invention, this representation, this "sorting out" of the various images that these essays discuss. Myths about Indians and the West seem impenetrable by facts, and for many people who are not themselves Native American, the stereotypes and misrepresentation remain safer than reality.

Tonto is the one who started it all. He was the first really mainstream, pop culture Indian figure, the monosyllabic stoic Indian stereotype.

Sherman Alexie [Spokane/Coeur d'Alene],
in "The Many Lives of Sherman Alexie"

Can Amer Indians ever
be post-colonial? NO!

As If an Indian Were Really an Indian

Native American Voices and Postcolonial Theory

LOUIS OWENS

real Indian v. Indian (Amer)

It's very convenient, isn't it, that so much of what we perhaps loosely term post-colonial theory today is written by "real Indians" — with such names as Chakrabarty, Chakravorty, Gandhi, Bhabha, Mohanty, and so on — so that, in writing or speaking about indigenous Native American literature, we can, if we desire, quote without even changing noun or modifier, as if an Indian were really an Indian. I am myself neither a "real Indian" like Gayatri Chakravorty Spivak or Satya Mohanty, nor a theorist, but merely a teacher who also writes, a writer who also teaches — and my reflections should be taken in that context. I also wish to borrow a caution from the seminal postcolonial writer Frantz Fanon, who declares in *Black Skin, White Masks*, "Since I was born in the Antilles, my observations and my conclusions are valid only for the Antilles" (14). Following and narrowing Fanon's wise lead, I must say that in significant measure I am my own Antilles, and therefore my observations and conclusions are valid for only myself. As an American of deeply mixed heritage and somewhat unique upbringing, I speak on behalf of and from the perspective of no one else.

Edward Said has written about "*strategic location*, which is a way of describing the author's position in a text with regard to the ... material he writes about" (*Orientalism* 20). My own strategic location vis-à-vis what we have come to call Native American literature is a complicated and contingent one. Descended from Mississippi Choctaw and Oklahoma Cherokee peoples on both paternal and maternal sides, I am also Euro-American, with Irish and Cajun French ancestors. My strategic location, therefore, may be found in what I think of as a kind of frontier zone, which elsewhere I have referred to as "always unstable, multidirectional, hybridized, characterized by heteroglossia, and indeterminate" (*Mixedblood* 26). In this sense, my work, like that of many other writers identified as Native American, might in fact accurately be described as what postcolonial theorists have called "migrant" or "diasporic" writing. Although I spent my earliest years in Choctaw country in Mississippi, I do not write from the heart of a reservation site or community and was not raised within a traditional culture. It would not be incorrect to say, in fact, that today in the United States, urban centers and academic institutions have come to constitute a kind of diaspora for Native Americans who through many generations of displacement and orchestrated ethnocide are often far from their traditional homelands and cultural communities. Such a frontier/transcultural location is an inherently unstable position, from which it is difficult and undoubtedly erroneous to assume any kind of essential stance or strategy, despite many temptations to do so.

A commonality of issues, shared by all of us who work in the field of Native American literature, marks this unsettled zone of frontier, interstitial scholarship. Dipesh Chakrabarty has suggested that non-Western thought is consistently relegated to the status of what Foucault might term a "subjugated knowledge" or what others define as a "minor" or "deterritorialized" knowledge (Gandhi 43). Chakrabarty writes that although Third World historians "feel a need to refer to works in European history; historians of Europe do not feel any need to reciprocate. . . . We cannot even afford an equality or symmetry of ignorance at this level without taking the risk of appearing 'old fashioned' or 'out-dated' "(Chakrabarty 2). To Chakrabarty's lament, I would add that critics and teachers of Native American literature are in a similar position. We are very properly expected to have and exhibit a crucial knowledge of canonical European and Euro-American literature; if we fail to be familiar with Shakespeare, Chaucer, Proust, Flaubert, Dickinson, Faulkner, Eliot, Joyce, Pound, Yeats, Keats, Woolf, Tolstoy, Tennyson, and so forth — not to mention the latest poststructuralist theory — we are simply not taken seriously and probably will not earn a university degree in the first place. That, it is presumed, is the foundational knowledge, the "grand narrative of legitimation" in our particular field.

However, although I have a great fondness for and some knowledge of canonical Western literature, like Chakrabarty I have often noticed that the majority of my colleagues in various "English" departments around the United States know very little if anything about Native American literature, written or oral; nor do they often exhibit any symptom of feeling it to be incumbent upon them to gain such knowledge. It may be pleasant to believe, as Nancy J. Peterson, the guest editor of a recent issue of *Modern Fiction Studies*, declared, that "Native American literature has become part of the mainstream" (3), but despite incremental change over the past couple of decades, it would take only a few minutes in the English departments of most universities, even in the Southwest, the heart of supposed "Indian Country," to be disabused of such wishful thinking. In fact, surprisingly, it would not take much time spent browsing through contemporary critical/theoretical texts—including especially those we call postcolonial—to discover an even more complete erasure of Native American voices. It seems that Chakrabarty's "symmetry of ignorance" applies even less to postcolonial theorists' awareness of Native American voices than it does to mainstream academia. While Native American literature is gradually finding a niche within academia, one discovers predominantly an absence of Native American voices in works by major cultural theorists and respected writers. We find, for example, a surprising erasure of Native presence and voice in Toni Morrison's *Playing in the Dark*, in which this Nobel Prize–winning African American writer adopts the rhetoric of imperial discovery and cites Hemingway's "Tontos" as well as Melville's Pequod without ever noting an indigenous Native presence shadowing her figuration of blackness in America. The most extraordinary denigration of Native American voices is found, however, in Edward Said's *Culture and Imperialism*, where this celebrated father of postcolonial theory dismisses Native American writing in a single phrase as "that sad panorama produced by genocide and cultural amnesia which is beginning to be known as 'native American literature'" (304). We can add to this list Homi Bhabha's total silencing of indigenous Native Americans in his influential study *The Location of Culture*. Bhabha gives the impression of being acutely aware of a wide panoply of minority voices in this book, referencing Hispanic and black American writers, for instance, and extensively praising Morrison's *Beloved*, but nowhere, not even in a whispered aside, does he note the existence of a resistance literature arising from indigenous, colonized inhabitants of the Americas. How, one wonders, can this student of postcoloniality, difference, liminality, and what he terms "culture as a strategy of survival" (172) be utterly ignorant of or indifferent to such writers as N. Scott Momaday, James Welch, Leslie Silko, Louise Erdrich, Simon Ortiz, or, most incredibly, the Anishinaabe writer and theorist Gerald Vizenor? How, one wonders, can any serious student of the "indigenous or native narrative," the term Bhabha uses to define his subject, not read and deal with the radically indigenous theory of Vizenor? Imagine what lengths Bhabha and other postcolonial theorists would have to go to in order to come to terms with Vizenor's "trickster hermeneutics"—which effectively subsumes poststructuralist and postmodern theory into a Native American paradigm and discursive system — or the work of poet Luci Tapahonso, who writes in both Navajo and English from a position deeply embedded in her Diné culture while moving freely within the academic diaspora, liberating and appropriating villanelles, sestinas, and sonnets to a Navajo voice and epistemology. It is difficult to take seriously any cultural or critical theorist who is ignorant of this rapidly growing body of work, or who, if he or she is aware of it, clearly relegates it to a "minor," "subjugated," or "deterritorialized" knowledge worthy of only silence or erasure. Within this great silence, it comes as more of a surprise than it should to find Trinh Minh-Ha, in *Woman, Native, Other*, paying careful attention to Laguna Pueblo writer Leslie Marmon Silko's storytelling and then at least noting such Native American writers as Silko, Momaday, Joy Harjo, Vizenor, and Linda Hogan in a chapter from her 1991 essay collection, *When the Moon Waxes Red*.

As we argue for the recognition missing from such texts and, concomitantly, a place on the literary and academic stage, we must be wary of what Rey Chow has called the language of victimization and "self-subalternisation," which, Chow points out, "has become the assured means to authority and power" in the metropolis, a phenomenon Leela Gandhi refers to succinctly as the "professionalisation of the margin" (Gandhi 128), and Gerald Vizenor calls "aesthetic victimry." And we need to examine carefully those Native American texts that do make it somehow from the margin to, if not the center, at least an orbital relationship with the homogenizing gravity of that center. Citing her own frustrating experience at a white male–dominated academic conference as an example, Gayatri Spivak warns that "The putative center welcomes selective inhabitants of the margin in order to better exclude the margin." Spivak — a "real Indian" in America — quotes Adrienne Rich, who says, "This is the meaning of female tokenism: that power withheld from the vast majority of women is offered to the few, so that it may appear that any truly qualified woman can gain access to leadership, recognition, and reward" (Spivak 107).

In mentioning postcolonial theory and Native American literature in the same breath, we should also keep carefully in mind the fact that America does not participate in what is sometimes termed the "colonial aftermath" or postcolonial condition. There is no need in the United States for what has been called the "therapeutic retrieval of the colonial past" in postcolonial societies (Gandhi 5). In *The Wretched of the Earth*, Fanon wrote, "Two centuries ago, a former European colony decided to catch up with Europe. It succeeded so well that the United States of America became a monster, in which the taints, the sickness, and the inhumanity of Europe have grown to appalling dimensions" (313). Regardless of whether we share Fanon's harsh critique of the United States, I think it is crucial for us to remember that the American Revolution was not truly a war to throw off the yoke of colonization as is popularly imagined, but rather a family squabble among the colonizers to determine who would be in charge of the colonization of North America, who would control the land and the lives of the indigenous inhabitants. America never became postcolonial. The indigenous inhabitants of North America can stand any-

The Indian v Natives
(white men's construction)

where on the continent and look in every direction at a home usurped and colonized by strangers who, from the very beginning, laid claim not merely to the land and resources but to the very definition of the Natives. Although it may be true figuratively, as Fanon writes, that "it is the settler who has brought the native into existence and who perpetuates his existence" (*Wretched* 36), it is even more true, as Gerald Vizenor has argued, that the "Indian" is a colonial invention, a hyperreal construction. "The *indians*," Vizenor writes, "are the romantic absence of natives. . . . The *indian* is a simulation and loan word of dominance. . . . The *indian* is . . . the other in a vast mirror" (*Fugitive* 14, 35, 37).

In imagining the Indian, America imagines itself, and I know of no text that more brilliantly and efficiently illuminates America's self-imagining than Walt Whitman's poem "Facing West from California's Shores." Whitman speaks in his poem as and for America, and since it is a brief poem, it is worth quoting in its entirety:

> Facing west from California's shores,
> Inquiring, tireless, seeking what is yet unfound,
> I, a child, very old, over waves, towards the house of maternity, the land of migrations, look afar,
> Look off the shores of my Western sea, the circle almost circled;
> For starting westward from Hindustan, from the vales of Kashmere,
> From Asia, from the north, from the God, the sage, and the hero,
> From the south, from the flowery peninsulas and the spice islands,
> Long having wander'd since, round the earth having wander'd,
> Now I face home again, very pleas'd and joyous,
> (But where is what I started for so long ago?
> And why is it yet unfound?)

In her introduction to postcolonial theory, drawing upon Heidegger, Leela Gandhi writes that "the all-knowing and self-sufficient Cartesian subject violently negates material and historical alterity or Otherness in its narcissistic desire to always see the world in its own self-image" (39). In this extraordinary poem, Whitman articulates Euro-America's narcissistic desire to not merely negate indigenous Otherness and possess the American continent, but to go far beyond North America to "my" sea, "my" Hindustan, "my" Kashmere, "my" Asia, and so on. In her extraordinarily thorough "Translator's Preface" to Derrida's *Of Grammatology*, Spivak reminds us of Nietzsche's famous "will to power" and Nietzsche's explanation that "the so-called drive for knowledge can be traced back to a drive to appropriate and conquer" (xxii). The imperial, "inquiring" American of Whitman calls to mind not only this Nietzschean will to power but also Spivak's point that "the desire to explain might be a symptom of the desire to have a self that can control knowledge and world that can be known" and that "the possibility of explanation carried the presupposition of an explainable (even if not fully) universe and an explaining (even if imperfectly) subject. These presuppositions assure our being. Explaining, we exclude the possibility of the heterogeneous." Spivak concludes that "every explanation must secure and assure a certain kind of being-in-the-world, which might as well be called our politics" (*In Other* 104–6).

The Euro-American "child" of Whitman's remarkable poem claims possession of the womb of humanity in a great universalizing narcissism that subsumes everything in its tireless, inquiring quest after its own image, thereby excluding heterogeneity from the very womb, and it is pleased and joyous about the whole endeavor. Leela Gandhi writes that "In order for Europe to emerge as the site of civilisational plenitude, the colonised world had to be emptied of meaning" (15). Whitman brilliantly comprehends this grand gesture in the Americas, and in his final question he even more brilliantly registers the ultimate, haunting emptiness the colonizing consciousness faces at last, once it is forced to confront a world emptied of meaning outside of itself. Whitman's question — (But where is what I started for so long ago? / And why is it yet unfound?) — resonates not merely through the heart of America's own metanarrative, leaving the Jay Gatsby's of America alone and painfully perplexed, but through the rest of the world marked by European narcissism and expansion. In Whitman's poem, America, having completed a stunningly deadly, self-determinedly innocent waltz across the bodies and cultures of Native inhabitants, seeks to claim not just the territory of the world but also the womb of humanity, seeding its own consciousness alone within that embryonic place of origin. This self-willed, brutal child looks to the "house of maternity" beyond "Hindustan," "Kashmere," and all of Asia to legitimize its claim to primacy and thus legitimacy as the inheritor of all.

The large stride of Whitman's American child moves across and through hundreds of indigenous cultures. They are the Others who must be both subsumed and erased in a strange dance of repulsion and desire that has given rise to one of the longest sustained histories of genocide and ethnocide in the world as well as a fascinating drama in which the colonizer attempts to empty out and reoccupy not merely the geographical terrain but the constructed space of the indigenous Other. And if we doubt the place of the imagined Indian in America's imperial self-construction, we can turn to Scribner's *Concise Dictionary of American History*, which explains that "The experiences of the Indian agencies with people of a race, color, and culture wholly unlike our own have been of great value to United States officials dealing with similar peoples throughout the world" (Andrews 463).

Fanon has written that "Man is human only to the extent to which he tries to impose his existence on another man in order to be recognized by him." He adds, "In its immediacy, consciousness of self is simple being-for-itself. In order to win the certainty of oneself, the incorporation of the concept of recognition is essential" (*Black* 216, 217). European America holds a mirror and a mask up to the Native American. The tricky mirror is that Other presence that reflects the Euro-American consciousness back at itself, but the side of the mirror turned toward the Native is transparent, letting the Native see not his or her own reflection but the face of the Euro-American beyond the mirror. For the dominant culture, the Euro-American controlling this surveillance, the reflection provides merely a self-recognition that results in a kind of being-for-itself and, ultimately, as Fanon suggests, an utter absence of certainty of self. The Native, in turn, finds no reflection directed back from the center, no recognition of "being" from that direction.

The mask is one realized over centuries through Euro-America's construction of the "Indian" Other. In order to be recognized, and to thus have a voice that is heard by those in control of power, the Native must step into that mask and *be* the Indian constructed by white America. Paradoxically, of course, like the mirror, the mask merely shows the Euro-American to himself, since the masked Indian arises out of the European consciousness, leaving the Native behind the mask unseen, unrecognized for himself or herself. In short, to be seen and heard at all by the center — to not share the fate of Ralph Ellison's Invisible Man — the Native must pose as the absolute fake, the fabricated "Indian," like the dancing puppets in Ellison's novel.

If a fear of inauthenticity is the burden of postmodernity, as has been suggested by David Harvey in *The Condition of Postmodernity* among others, it is particularly the burden of the Euro-American seeking merely his self-reflection and even more so that of the indigenous American in the face of this hyperreal "Indian." In *Midnight's Children*, Salman Rushdie's character Saleem Sinai says, "above all things, I fear absurdity." Quoting Rushdie's character and reflecting on Sinai's predicament, Leela Gandhi writes that "the colonial aftermath is also fraught by anxieties and fears of failure which attend the need to satisfy the burden of expectation" (5). Not only does America contain no "colonial aftermath"; it also places no burden of expected achievement on the American Indian. On the contrary, for Native Americans the only burden of expectation is that he or she put on the constructed mask provided by the colonizer, and the mask is not merely a mirror but more crucially a static death mask, fashioned beforehand, to which the living person is expected to conform. He or she who steps behind the mask becomes the Vanishing American, a savage/noble, mystical, pitiable, romantic fabrication of the Euro-American

[margin notes, handwritten: "wearing the mask" / "becomes the Indian" / "in order to be heard"]

psyche fated to play out the epic role defined by Mikhail Bakhtin: "The epic and tragic hero," Bakhtin writes, "is the hero who by his very nature must perish. . . . Outside his destiny the epic and tragic hero is nothing; he is, therefore, a function of the plot fate assigns him; he cannot become the hero of another destiny or another plot" (36). While the "Indian" holds a special and crucial place within the American narrative, the Native who looks beyond his or her immediate community and culture for recognition finds primarily irrelevance and absurdity.

Frantz Fanon declares that "The town belonging to the colonized people, or at least the native town, the Negro village . . . the reservation, is a place of ill fame, peopled by men of evil repute. They are born there, it matters little where or how; they die there, it matters not where, not how. . . . The native town is a hungry town, starved of bread, of meat, of shoes, of coal, of light" (*Wretched* 39). Could this not be a description of Pine Ridge, South Dakota, today, a hungry reservation town and the poorest county in America, home to the very Plains Indians so celebrated in America's fantastic construction of Indianness, the aestheticized subjects of such romantic and insidious films as *Dances with Wolves*? Fanon writes: "For a colonized people the most essential value, because the most concrete, is first and foremost the land: the land which will bring them bread and, above all, dignity" (44). Above all, Native Americans have been deprived of land and of the dignity that derives from the profound and enduring relationship with homeland.

To understand this contemporary colonialism as it affects Native Americans, we need to recognize what Leela Gandhi, a "real Indian" writer and theorist, has called the "relationship of reciprocal antagonism and desire between coloniser and colonised." Gandhi suggests that "the battle lines *between* native and invader are replicated *within* native and invader" (4, 11–12). America's desire to control knowledge, to exclude the heterogeneous, and to assure a particular kind of being-in-the-world depends upon a total appropriation and internalization of this colonized space, and to achieve that end, America must make the heterogeneous Native somehow assimilable and concomitantly erasable. What better way to achieve that end than to invent the Indian as an Other that springs whole-formed from the Euro-American psyche? In *Black Skin, White Masks*, Fanon says simply that "what is often called the black soul is the white man's artifact" (14). It can be argued, and has been argued effectively by such Native American writers as Gerald Vizenor and Philip Deloria, that what is called the Indian is the white man's invention and artifact. In his book *Playing Indian*, Deloria documents exhaustively and persuasively America's obsession with first constructing the Indian as Other and then inhabiting that constructed Indianness as fully as possible. Deloria describes marvelous "Indian-ation" ceremonies in which white Americans induct one another into Indianness. In one such ceremony, a "spirit" voice intones, "The red men are my children. Long ago I saw in the future their destruction, and I was very sad." According to Deloria, the "spirit tells initiates that the only way to placate the mournful Indian shades is to preserve their memory and customs. The society's sachem then replies that the membership will accept the 'delightful task.' The ceremony concludes by offering the initiate complete redemption and a new life through mystic rebirth as an Indian child. 'Spirit,' prays the sachem, 'receive us as your children. Let us fill too the place of those who are gone'" (78).

Deloria comments: "Like all these boundary-crossing movements, however, Indianized quests for authenticity rested upon a contradictory foundation. In order to be authentic, Indians had to be located outside modern American societal boundaries. Because they were outside those boundaries, however, it became more difficult to get at them, to lay claim to the characteristics Indians had come to represent" (115). To extend Deloria's observation, I would also suggest that the artifactual "Indian," unlike the indigenous Native, could be easily gotten at because he or she was a pure product of America. Deloria also examines Natives who step into the Euro-American–constructed mask to play "cultural politics for social and political ends," actual indigenous Native Americans who "found themselves acting Indian, mimicking white mimickings of Indianness" (189). "If being a survivor of the pure, primitive old days meant authenticity, and if that in turn meant cultural power that might be translated to social ends, it made sense for a Seneca man to put on a Plains headdress, white America's marker of that archaic brand of authority" (189).

In the midst of such extraordinary torsions, where is the Native writer to locate herself or himself, and how is that writer to find or have a voice in a world articulated through another language or knowledge system? Raja Rao described the challenge faced by the indigenous artist who writes in a colonizer's language by saying, "One has to convey in a language that is not one's own the spirit that is one's own. . . . We cannot write like the English. We should not. We cannot write only as Indians" (Gandhi 150–51). Native Americans, with few exceptions, such as Navajo writers Luci Tapahonso and Rex Lee Jim, who write in both Navajo and English, do not have the option of writing and publishing in an indigenous language, and even more than those natives of India of whom Rao speaks, Native authors surely cannot "write only as Indians." After five hundred years of war, colonial infantilization and linguistic erasure, cultural denigration, and more, how and where does the Native writer discover a voice that may be heard at the metropolitan center?

Homi Bhabha, borrowing from V. S. Naipaul's *The Mimic Men*, writes of

"colonial mimicry," which, he declares, "conceals no presence or identity behind its mask" (*Location* 86). Leela Gandhi labels such mimicry the "sly
weapon of anti-colonial civility, an ambivalent mixture of deference and dis-
obedience" that "inaugurates the process of anti-colonial self-differentiation
through the logic of inappropriate appropriation" (149–50). In glossing Bhabha's formulation, Gandhi argues that "the most radical anti-colonial writers are 'mimic men'" and that "the paradigmatic moment of anti-colonial
counter-textuality is seen to begin with the first indecorous mixing of Western
genres with local content" (150). Gandhi's description of such counter-textual
mimicry would seem to apply well to such a work as Cherokee writer John Rollin Ridge's 1854 novel, *The Life and Adventures of Joaquín Murietta, the Celebrated California Bandit*, in which Ridge appropriates the genre of western romance to tell a deeply encoded story of colonial oppression and brutality.
Similarly, the native Okanagon writer Mourning Dove performed a brilliant
and clearly subversive act of appropriation in her 1927 novel, *Cogewea, the Half-
Blood: A Depiction of the Great Montana Cattle Range*, a novel that mimics the
classic western romance with indigenous mixed-bloods in the roles always reserved for Euro- American cowboys. But neither Ridge nor Mourning Dove
found acceptance in the centers that control textual production in America.
Ridge, the grandson of traditional Cherokee leader Major Ridge and the
founding editor of the *Sacramento Bee* newspaper in California, promptly vanished from the landscape of American literature to be rediscovered a century
later in a kind of ethnographical salvage operation. Mourning Dove found it
took not only collaboration with a white editor but also a dozen years and
money earned from her labor in apple orchards and hops fields to get *Cogewea*
published. Then it was forgotten for half a century until its discovery by Native
American scholars and feminist critics. Acceptance and recognition by American publishers and readers would not come for a Native American writer until
1969 when Kiowa author N. Scott Momaday won a Pulitzer Prize for his first
novel, *House Made of Dawn*. According to a member of the Pulitzer jury, an
award to the author of this novel "might be considered as a recognition of the
arrival on the American literary scene of a matured, sophisticated literary artist
from the original Americans" (Schubnell 93).

I want to focus briefly upon Momaday's historic accomplishment. And in
doing so, while keeping in mind that we are discussing a "colonial" rather than
"postcolonial" text, it may be helpful here to borrow from the critic Timothy
Brennan, who argues that the "privileged postcolonial text is typically accessible and responsive to the aesthetic and political taste of liberal metropolitan
readers. The principal pleasures of this cosmopolitan text accrue from its man-

aged exoticism. It is both 'inside' and 'outside' the West." Such texts provide a "familiar strangeness, a trauma by inches" (qtd. in Gandhi 162). Bhabha declares that "The desire to emerge as 'authentic' through mimicry— through a process of writing and repetition — is the final irony of partial representation" (*Location* 88). How does a colonial or postcolonial author — a collective whom I have earlier identified as "migrant" or diasporic in the postcolonial sense — achieve a text so accessible and responsive to metropolitan readers? Aijaz Ahmad suggests that "Among the migrants themselves, only the privileged can live a life of constant mobility and surplus pleasure, between Whitman and Warhol as it were. Most migrants tend to be poor and experience displacement not as cultural plenitude but as torment. . . . Postcoloniality is also, like most things, a matter of class" (Gandhi 164). It is not difficult to extrapolate from Ahmad's statement to the fact that most Native Americans live lives fashioned by generations of displacement with resulting impoverishment, suffering, and silence. While life for urban Native Americans can be difficult, the poorest and most desperate places in America are Native American reservations, populated by indigenous people who commonly live with as much as 85 percent unemployment, deplorable health care and even worse education, horrifying rates of alcohol and drug addiction, an epidemic of fetal alcohol syndrome, and the highest suicide rates and lowest life expectancy of any ethnic group in the nation — all the effects of profoundly institutionalized racism. It is apparently delightful to caricature Native Americans as sports mascots and in movies, but as long as the real people are hidden from sight on rural lands reserved for their containment, it is unnecessary for the dominant culture to even contemplate the Natives' quality of life. And before everyone protests, let me quote Jean-Paul Sartre, who wrote acutely in his preface to Fanon's *The Wretched of the Earth*, "Our worthiest souls contain racial prejudice" (21). How else could our worthiest souls live with Washington Redskins, Cleveland Indians, Atlanta Braves, Chief Wahoo, the Tomahawk Chop, and so on, all of which are merely the slightest indices of the far more profound currents that impoverish Native Americans in incalculable ways? Would we live so comfortably today with the New Jersey Jews, Newark Negroes, Cleveland Chicanos, Houston Honkies, Atlanta Asians, and so on? Entering the twenty-first century, would the city of Washington cheer a football team whose mascot scampered around at halftime in blackface or wearing a yarmulke and carrying a menorah? Again, Bhabha adds an interesting note here when he writes that "the discriminatory identities constructed across traditional cultural norms and classifications, the Simian Black, the Lying Asiatic— all these are *metonymies* of presence. They are strategies of desire" (90).

America has in large part at least recognized the impropriety of such racial stereotypes as those Bhabha describes — the "Simian Black" and the "lying" or "inscrutable" Asian — even if it has perhaps not relinquished them entirely. However, the same operative strategy of desire that for a very long time governed representation of other minority cultures clearly still controls Euro-American discourse representing the Native American Indian. Given the uncomfortable realities of most contemporary Native American lives, as we look around us in academia, I think it is perhaps time to recognize that what we are calling Native American literature is represented largely, if not exclusively, by the sorts of privileged texts Timothy Brennan describes and is created by those migrant or diasporic Natives who live lives of relatively privileged mobility and surplus pleasure. As a group, we published Native American authors have an impressively high rate of education, most possessing not merely a university degree but at least some graduate work if not an advanced degree. We may go back to our families and communities periodically or regularly; we may, like N. Scott Momaday, even be initiated into a traditional society within our tribal culture, but we are inescapably both institutionally privileged by access to Euro-American education and distinctly migrant in the sense that we possess a mobility denied to our less privileged relations.

The question remains: what must the colonial, or postcolonial, writer — in this case specifically the indigenous Native American, mixed-blood or full-blood — do to be allowed a voice like Shakespeare's cursing Caliban? Let us consider the Pulitzer Prize juror's words regarding Momaday's award for *House Made of Dawn*. What might such a statement as "the arrival on the American literary scene of a matured, sophisticated literary artist from the original Americans" possibly mean? I would suggest, as I have elsewhere, that these words indicate that an aboriginal writer has finally learned to write like the colonial center that determines legitimate discourse. Momaday so successfully mimicked the aesthetics of the center that he was allowed access. This — the evolution of the colonial subject to *something like* the level of the colonial master — fulfills the idealized, utopian colonial vision of reconstructing the colonial subject to reflect the colonizing gaze. To be heard at the center — to achieve both authenticity and recognition within the imperial gaze that controls dissemination of discourse — the Native must step into the mask and into Whitman's circle; and the more fully we enter that empowering circle, the more successful we may be. The most prosperous of such texts are both accessible to the aesthetic and political tastes of the metropolitan center and, perhaps more significantly, present to such readers a carefully managed exoticism that is entertaining but not discomfiting to the non-Native reader. Elsewhere I have called the most extreme versions of this publishing phenomenon "literary tourism." And, as I have also suggested in my book *Mixedblood Messages*, certainly N. Scott Momaday's Pulitzer Prize testifies to a Native American author's successful entry into that privileged circle. *House Made of Dawn*, with its very visible and pervasive indebtedness to classic modernist texts, is clearly "accessible and responsive to the aesthetic and political taste of liberal metropolitan readers." Just as clearly, Momaday's novel offers what Brennan calls a "managed exoticism." The Pueblo world of the protagonist, with its "familiar strangeness" and "trauma by inches," is never threatening or very discomfiting to its Euro-American readership, while it provides a convincing and colorful tour of Indian country, including titillating glimpses of Native ceremony and even witchcraft. With its exoticism packaged in familiar and therefore accessible formulas, carefully managed so as to admit the metropolitan reader while never implying that the painful difficulties illuminated within the text are the responsibility of that reader, clearly *House Made of Dawn* is both "inside" and "outside" the West.

To say all of the above is not to deny the aesthetic or artistic achievement or even the important political ramifications of Momaday's novel or many others that might be similarly described. *House Made of Dawn* is superbly subversive. Seen in this way, N. Scott Momaday becomes one of the "mimic men," to borrow V. S. Naipaul's term, who realize a genuinely appropriationist and subversive end by packaging a text in sufficient imperial wrappings as to get it past the palace guards into the royal Pulitzer chambers. It is an impressive achievement, yet an achievement requiring extensive education of its author — all the way to a doctorate from Stanford University — within the knowledge system of the metropolitan center as well as careful crafting to conform to that center's expectations. A peripatetic citizen of the U.S. Native American diaspora, a modern "migrant" intellectual and artist, Momaday — like all the rest of us who find ourselves in somewhat similar if less celebrated circumstances — has not only entered the trajectory of Whitman's circular journey but has internalized that circle. Momaday's "strategic location" vis-à-vis the Pueblo world he wrote about in his first novel, like the strategic location of most Native American writers, is surpassingly complex, shifting, hybridized, interstitial, and unstable.

Those of us working in the field of what we call Native American literature can and undoubtedly will chafe at the ignorance and erasure of Native American voices within the metropolitan center and within what at times appears to be the loyal opposition to that center called postcolonial theory. And we can, and undoubtedly will, continue to try to make our voices heard — to "give voice to the silent," as a recent academic conference termed the endeavor. However, such negotiations are never simple or free of cost. It seems that a necessary, if difficult, lesson for all of us may well be that in giving voice to the silent we unavoidably give voice to the forces that conspire to effect that silence. Finally, as we approach nearer to literate Euro-America, the circle within us may be almost circled, and like Whitman's America, we may be left asking, "But where is what I started for so long ago?"

I awake in a story told by my ancestors when they spoke a version of the very beginning, of how so long ago we climbed the backbone of these tortuous Americas. I listen to the splash of the Atlantic and Pacific and see Columbus land once more, over and over again. This is not a foreign country, but the land of our dreams.

Joy Harjo [Creek],
in *American Encounters*

The Indians America Loves to Love and Read

American Indian Identity
and Cultural Appropriation

KATHRYN SHANLEY

During that organizing time
and during that strike in 1961,
that jail full of Indians sure came in handy.
The jailer would even call in sick for you
and tell you which mines were hiring Indians.
The unions didn't have much of a chance,
and Grants just kept on booming.

  Simon Ortiz, "Indians Sure Come in Handy"

"At its most powerful," Seamus Deane writes, "colonialism is a process of radical dispossession." While many in the academy attend to theories of *post*colonialism, the process of which Deane speaks relentlessly maneuvers itself onward. In regard to American Indian cultures and histories, the implications of the adjective "radical," when attached to "dispossession," are being felt in ever expanding ways in the early twenty-first century; so much so that it is difficult for a Native critic to lay hold of a word such as *postcolonialism*. Deane goes on to say, "A colonized people is without a specific history and even, as in Ireland and other cases, without a specific language" (4). I believe him, or at least believe that the attempt to destroy a people's history and language figures centrally in destroying or subduing that people, in replacing one worldview with another if outright genocide is somehow unpalatable or impractical. Yet what does it mean to be "without a *specific* history . . . without a *specific* language"? In this context is "specific" a term of essentialist thinking? Does he mean having a history apart from that of colonization? How long does a people survive without a "specific" history or language? I argue here that we can identify neocolonial cultural appropriations, thefts of "cultural property," that expedite a people's being left "without" a specific history or language, and that such cultural appropriations inextricably belong to overall totalization efforts, the domination of indigenous peoples by the West, politically and ideologically.

Whether seen as "lack" or as voices in need of recognition, a colonized people's history and language must be heard in their own voices and terms. On the one hand, some theorists see the postcolonial subject (whom we can identify no matter whether we can agree on terms) as primarily related to a lack of exclusivity, a lack of possession, a loss. Thus, a denial of human wholeness results. On the other hand, some theorists recognize the postcolonial subject as possessing a history and language unique to his or her experience but requiring public voices that can be substantially heard — that is, a full narrative range of what it means for that people to be and for a person to be of that people. Perhaps this is where academics engaged in literary criticism and cultural studies can enter: to offer to be an audience and then to amplify those voices barely heard, or not heard at all without a committed audience. Then again, perhaps we ask theory to do something for us, to categorize and quantify in ways that its very language cannot reconcile with itself, let alone with the breadth and depth of human suffering it seeks to know, describe, and dispel. If nothing else, criticism and critical theory can invite indigenous peoples to the discussion and can extend to them the microphone, but issues of domination persist, even or especially in such gestures — that is the paradox of speaking from "centers" of intellectual "traditions" and from the perspectives and privileges of writing cultures.[1]

The prefix *post-* matters here in another way. Kwame Anthony Appiah, in his article "Is the Post- in Postmodernism the Post- in Postcolonial?" speaks of "postmodernism" as "a name for the rejection of that claim of exclusivity, a rejection that is almost always more playful, though not necessarily less serious, than the practice it aims to replace" (342). Hardly a more crucial theoretical question can be asked here than the one Appiah poses, since it is key to understanding the one world we inhabit together or, as he terms it, the "postmodern culture." He adds, "contemporary culture is ... transnational, postmodern culture is global — though that emphatically does not mean that it is the culture of every person in the world" (343). Indigenous voices amid other voices in Appiah's contemporary, postmodern culture (a perhaps useful illusion of media unity and global citizenship) should not be mistaken for those ventriloquized; Renato Rosaldo's term is useful here: "imperialist nostalgia," which is defined as "a pose of 'innocent yearning' [utilized] both to capture people's imaginations and to conceal its complicity with often brutal domination" (70). Somewhere in the timeless zone between the playful *post-* of postmodernism and the dispossessed *post-* of postcolonialism, Indians are — like Simon Ortiz's "handy" prisoners — being shuffled between the jail and the uranium mines, as their lands are being stripped and stripped away.

While American Indians struggle to regain power to determine their cultural identities and futures through economic, governmental, social, educational, and kinship refigurations, the "Indian" voices most popular in mainstream America are often those of would-be Indians, who reinscribe nineteenth-century, romantic images of "noble savages." Playing Indian has become an American pastime. Even when curricula attempt to expose Euro-American children to other cultures, they "are often taught about Indians [from] . . . the vantage point of an anthropological 'ethnographic present': a kind of timeless 'long ago and far away there once were Indians' " (Rosaldo 18). Learning to listen for ideologies in depictions and representations has not been easy for either popular or academic audiences. What follows are descriptions of two appropriative instances, one in fiction and one in "real life," that I hope will serve as a bracket for the 1970s end of appropriated contemporary Indianness. The 1970s represent the beginning of a renewed American interest in Things Indian, spawned by AIM activism and the rise of authors such as Vine Deloria Jr. and N. Scott Momaday. I conclude this essay with Indian voices that ought to provide a perspective on more contemporary times in an open-ended process.

In a humorous, staged confrontation between himself and his conscience, author Ken Kesey voices a reluctance to give up his attachment to what he terms his "stroke of genius, if not . . . masterstroke" — that is, Mr. Bromden, the Indian narrator in his popular 1970s novel *One Flew over the Cuckoo's Nest* (Comstock 75). The point of the encounter between author and conscience becomes clear when Kesey finally admits to "having never known an Indian before," and to his being "notified that a certain spirit was getting a little peeved at the telegraph operator for being so presumptuous as to take credit for messages coming in, as though the receiver were sending the signal" (75). W. Richard Comstock, in an article quoting the above passage, suggests that the messages are an aspect of the American cultural mind, that "something is happening to the consciousness of technological man that involves a continuing relation to the defeated native American antagonist" (76). Comstock's article centers on what "the man of technology" sees when he looks at the Native American, and vice versa, a binary that has had an obstinate and long life in American thought.

Two long-standing American cultural phenomena come together in the above drama: first, that pretending to be Indian or believing that it is possible to "know" what it means to be "Indian" is within the purview of most Americans; and second, that being preoccupied with national hypocrisies is also within the American experience — a preoccupation that rarely leads to genuine insight. Such a preoccupation with hypocrisy may be identified as Kesey's "certain spirit."

To limit my discussion to how such depictions serve America's evolving need for "the Indian" would be to eclipse Indian concerns and to duplicate the distortion — in other words, to focus on the problem without offering a vision of what is possible. My intent is to offer a broader perspective, however abbreviated and tentative, rather than definitive, of ways to begin defining Indianness. At the least, I hope the reader of this essay will gain a clearer understanding of the importance that images of Indians in popular culture ultimately have in determining the quality of the lived experience of American Indians and of the need for American Indian authors primarily, rather than non-Indians, to speak for themselves about that experience.[2]

In discussing popular culture and Indians, certain questions surface in clusters, questions about ethnic or cultural identity as it relates to art and literature, in general. Three such clusters of questions more or less congeal. First, what is *Indianness* today or, for that matter, at any point in history? What criteria do we use to determine Indianness? Is it enough that an author identifies himself or herself as Indian? How do we account for the differences within the category of "Indian" as they relate to tribal heritage or affiliation and language experience (for example, Indians who do not speak English or Spanish as their first language versus Indians who do)? Second, how do we locate Indianness in literary texts? What does the writing of fiction and poetry have to do with so-called traditional forms? Does the particular work in question need to contain mythic or historical references (for example, a reference to the individual's cultural heritage)? Can a non-Indian utilize Indian history and myth in creative writing as effectively as an Indian can? Would such literature, regardless of who writes it, be Indian literature? Third, how do the above questions reflect the political agendas of various Indian groups or individuals? How do they affect Indianists of dominant cultural institutions such as universities?

Following the lead of Robert Berkhofer Jr. in *The White Man's Indian*, I also use *Indian* as the polar "opposite" of *white* and as an indicator of a continuing power relationship; I intend to move beyond such binaries by showing how complicated definitions of "Indian" can be. To mix things up further, I use *Native* and *Native American* as well. (I apologize for my pragmatically narrow use of the term *American*, which for my purposes here includes only the continental United States.)[3] One further key term requires mentioning: ethnicity. According to Werner Sollors, *ethnicity* is a term coined by W. Lloyd Warner to describe the American national character in his *Yankee City Series*, "the well-known, five-volume community study of Newburyport, Massachusetts, which began to appear in 1941" (*Invention* 23). *Ethnicity*, as Sollors and others use the term, is impossibly broad, universalizing at its worst; I simply use it to connote "otherness" (as it has most commonly been used), rather than to refer to something we all have, like culture, something with specific content.[4]

In popular American culture, images of Indianness are always in contest; the term *Indianness* therefore requires historical contextualization. "The idea of the noble savage," Michael Castro tells us, in *Interpreting the Indian*, "has been traced back . . . to Greek antiquity" (xvi). Voyage accounts, popular in the sixteenth and seventeenth centuries, played heavily on the image in promoting "settlement and commercial exploitation" of America (xv). Moreover, Castro tells us:

The image [i]s central to the "Indian Death Song" poetry of the eighteenth and nineteenth centuries, of which Philip Freneau was a prominent practitioner; to Longfellow's immensely popular *Song of Hiawatha*, which can be seen as an epic culmination of that tradition; and to the widely read Leatherstocking novels of James Fenimore Cooper. Like the brutish stereotype, the noble one incarnated a central cultural myth — that of the Golden Age, in which the noble savage was pictured as living Adam-like in a higher (because unfallen) stage of development than his civilized counterpart. (xvi)

In other words, the necessity for a "noble savage" counterpart to the western European dates back at least to the Greeks; but through the ideological turns it takes on American soil, the image acquires unique symbolic dimensions, distinct to the historical enterprise of founding this nation. The Adam-like "innocence" of natives, an innocence used to replace "sinfulness" as America moved toward democracy (and hence, separation of church and state), dictated a unique emphasis on experience. After all, Euro-Americans did not want to become Indian any more than they wanted to remain European.

In order to achieve a blend, it became necessary for Americans, paradoxically, to claim *and* deny both ancestries. R. W. B. Lewis dubs this distinctly white and male hybrid "the American Adam," which he defined as "a radically new personality, the hero of the new adventure: an individual emancipated from history, *happily bereft of ancestry, untouched and undefiled by the usual inheritances of family and race*; an individual standing alone, self-reliant and self-propelling, ready to confront whatever awaited him with the aid of his own unique and inherent resources. . . . [In a phrase, he is] Adam before the Fall"[5] (5; emphasis added).

To disavow familial and "racial" influences, as Lewis's Adam does, is to postulate an identity beyond the heavily kinship-based foundations of tribal identity, while retaining another basic American Indian philosophy of individual distinction, at least inasmuch as Indian belief systems allow an experiential dimension that is significantly free of concepts like original sin. The power in and the importance of the way the "American experience" is privileged in this definition cannot be overestimated. The terms *self-made, self-reliant,* and *rugged* continue to describe a particularly American brand of individualism, the spirit of which is evident in the naming of American automobiles, recreation vehicles, and missiles. That myth of American individualism, being continually recycled, has most recently revisited us in the movies *Dances with Wolves, The Last of the Mohicans,* and *Pocahontas.* The American privileging of certain kinds of individualistic endeavors and experiences thus figures significantly in the current Indian wars — those conflicts centered around the making and enforcing of laws governing Indians on and around reservations, which can be so detrimental to Indian self-determination efforts, especially when resources such as hunting and fishing rights and land usage are at stake. (I do not take up the issue of Indian gaming here because it requires treatment beyond the limited space of this essay.)

Despite the sympathies for Indians that our literary and commercial media perpetuate, something peculiar happens when "Indian" ingenuity and independence (from sin and Christian restraint) become subsumed in an individual identity or in identities proffering American individualism. For example, a focus on right by "experience" disallows legal difference when entrepreneurs of Treaty Beer or Midwestern sportsmen and resort owners seek to prevent Indians from exercising their treaty rights. Since most Americans lack an understanding of what treaties guarantee Indians and why, they reduce Indian experience to the lowest common denominator, according it only the Euro-American sense of "rights" by experience. Non-Indian hunters are usually at odds with treaty hunting and fishing rights, because they feel equally entitled to all resources; tourist industries around the country use Indian lore and images to entice consumers and yet fight to prevent Indians from exercising their rights to be Indian — South Dakota serves as a prime example of this. When material gain is at issue, the battles become all the more vociferous.

Similarly, when the Supreme Court decided in the 1980s to defer to state laws in matters related to peyote use by Indians for religious purposes, the basic American value of freedom of religion took a back seat to the new morality espoused by the federal government on the individual's right (or lack thereof) to use drugs. In other words, experience as an aspect of the American ethos and identity is inextricably bound to the American habit of absorbing a false sense of American Native epistemology. That habit hardly translates into an understanding of actual American Indian history or philosophy, which is tribally or communally based, but instead shapes a damned-if-you-do-damned-if-you-don't dilemma for Indians — the double bind in which Indians find themselves when dealing with an ideologically, but not actually, sympathetic "other." It is a double bind that dangerously affects the American Indian literary realm.

Warning mechanisms such as Kesey's "certain spirit," telling his conscience that his presumptuous maneuvers have exceeded ethical limits, seem to have steadily weakened since the 1970s, as would-be shaman and would-be Indian writer alike have moved onto the lucrative turf of representing Indian life and truth. It has become fashionable to be Indian. That dilemma especially marks the instance of the real-life, self-created Indian Jamake Highwater. Hank Adams (Assiniboine) painstakingly documents in his 1984 article in *Akwesasne Notes* how Gregory Markopoulos, "son of American Greek immigrants," fabricated an Indian identity for himself (10–12). As Adams notes, Markopoulos's transformation to J. Marks to Jamake Highwater has been "simply a process of repackaging" his theatrical self in symbolic Indian garb and "winning the audience," and in that process he perpetrated "a fraud which has victimized American Indians, tribal communities and individuals" (11). Adams explains how such a thing could be allowed to happen: "Sophistry itself, and stereotypes, have aided in making Gregory Markopoulos the principal representative *for* Indians, Indian culture and Indian mentalities, to millions of Americans — Indian and non-Indian alike. Also considered a 'representative work of American Indians,' his text, *The Primal Mind: Vision and Reality in Indian America* (1981), has been distributed by the U.S. State Department to Third World countries overseas in several languages" (11). Moreover, before Highwater more or less got out of the "Indian business," he had not only been "reborn" as an "expert" on Indianness but had also been "'reborn' into money" (12). In less than a year between 1982 and 1983, Highwater received "more than $825,000 in grants and grant offers to his Primal Mind Foundation from the Corporation for Public Broadcasting" (12). And although a challenge to Highwater's claims to Indian heritage and expertise was drafted by a group of Indian leaders and sent to the Corporation for Public Broadcasting in 1983, with the reminder that it is "a federal offense to 'misrepresent any material fact in applying for federal grant' funds," the CPB was extremely reluctant to admit they had been fooled.

Finally, on February 16, 1984, *Washington Post* columnist Jack Anderson exposed Highwater, at the prompting of Indian intellectuals around the country, by pointing out the inconsistencies in Highwater's own claims regarding his birth date (which varied as much as ten years), his birthplace ("listed variously as Los Angeles, Canada, South Dakota, Montana, and Normandy, France"), his "bachelor's and master's degrees from the University of California at Berkeley, and a PhD from the University of Chicago," and his ethnic origins: "Highwater's father was either an 'illustrious motion picture director,' an 'alcoholic stunt man' or a rodeo clown, and died when the boy was 7 (or 9 or 10 or 13). His mother, according to Highwater's promotional materials and published interviews, either married a rich man or was destitute — or wasn't a Blackfoot at all, but a Cherokee who ran away at 15 to marry a Greek-born circus aerialist" (11). Although he has dropped his claims to Indian heritage in the promotional materials for his film *The Primal Mind*, he continues to claim (and in many respects can claim) expert knowledge on Indian art. Highwater should no longer represent Indians to America or, indeed, the world, but a confusion persists nonetheless.[6]

The issue then becomes, how do we determine who is an Indian author? And who is to determine this? On the one hand, there are so relatively few Indian leaders up against the media image machine, and even fewer who have the inclination or time to fight such hegemonic forces of misrepresentation. Nonetheless, much is at stake. To the grassroots activist, more pressing concerns related to basic survival — health, education, and welfare — receive first priority; ongoing legal battles and negotiations with state and federal governments preoccupy Indian leadership as well. Additionally, the issue of ethnic designation in American Indian writing, as it relates to literary works, is tricky enough, given the differences in critical skills between specialists and laypersons. Add to differences in literacy skills and reading tastes the problematic of non-Indian influences (that is, what gets published and taught in a profit economy), and we see not only how easily a Mr. Bromden or a Jamake Highwater can come into being, but we also intuit the absence of other, more (dare I say) authentic representations. On the other hand, artistic imagination cannot and should not be censored, categorized, or otherwise narrowly defined.

In *Being and Race: Black Writing Since 1970*, Charles Johnson explores the issue of artistic imagination as it relates to American black writing in ways that illuminate discussions of public taste and censorship relative to American Indian life and art. Establishing his argument against prescriptions for artistic production, Johnson writes: "Like fascist art in Germany during the 1930s, Negritude — all Kitsch — is a retreat from ambiguity, the complexity of Being occasioned by the conflict of interpretations, and a flight by the black artist from the agony of facing a universe silent as to its sense, where even black history (or all history) must be seen as an ensemble of experiences and documents difficult to read, indeed, as an experience capable of inexhaustible readings" (20).

While I would personally be reluctant to characterize Negritude simply as kitsch, Johnson's argument, cast in terms of both audience and artists, makes a compelling case against such nativist movements. Johnson primarily seeks to open black writing to a wider range of expression — to explorations and depictions of the fullness of black American experience. In doing so, he argues against "racial essentialism," a reading of beingness based on "race" — or more simply, on genetic difference. "But Negritude, in one incarnation or another," Johnson argues, becomes "one answer to the problem of controlling meaning," a problem he claims persists in contemporary black literary production (20). Not only does such a prescriptive dilemma exist for Indians; I would argue that it is intensified by the relatively small number of Indian writers, the American habit of loving its "Indian" (particularly as spiritual mascot or, in the case of writers, Indians loved one at a time), and by the very real impact images of Indians can have on the political sphere, where decisions are made that affect the quality of Indian lives.[7]

Regardless of our recognition of the impact false representations can have on lives and communities, we cannot ignore the philosophical appeal of (at least in moderated fashion) believing in art for art's sake and in the freedom of human imagination to think itself beyond constraints. The most imaginative, free-thinking individuals in any culture will not, and arguably should not, conform absolutely to others' (even their own people's) expectations. Different types of literature, moreover, fulfill different needs. As nearly as I can tell, many Indians love to read the fiction of W. P. Kinsella and Tony Hillerman, however stereotypical their works may be, perhaps because for Indians to see themselves depicted at all feels good for a change. But before all of this philosophizing leads to a conclusion of sorts — live and let live — I must circle back to Highwater and to the mythic values he seeks to emulate regarding art's Dionysian vein, but not to Highwater the individual so much as to what he can tell us about American spheres of influence — popular and academic.

In an article based on an interview with Highwater prior to Highwater's defrocking, David Jackson defends Highwater's right to create himself and his own ethnic identity; Jackson mingles his quotations from Highwater's writings with his own autobiographical reflection:

They [Indian people] consider him a "professional Indian," a pretentious, elitist intellectual. Having experienced similar criticism from blacks who felt I wasn't black enough for them, I know the pain and confusion such attacks bring. . . .

Highwater defended himself in an article, called "Second-Class Indians," he wrote for *American Indian Journal*. In it he challenged the self-righteous exclusivity of some reservation and other militant Indians. "*I am an Indian only because I say I am Indian,*" he wrote, "I am not enrolled on the reservation of my mother or father; I went to high school with non-Indians, and I don't have a bunch of aggressive relatives on a reservation who can back me up. I came by my heritage through the legacy of my mother and my own long efforts to reclaim an obscured identity." (38; emphasis added)

From Jackson's remarks, it should be clear that another sort of projection onto Indians is taking place: an identification with intragroup conflicts. But the confusion of Jackson's loyalties and the irony in Highwater's "obscured identity" aside, the issue adds up to much more than a man simply claiming that based on obscure blood links he can pronounce, "I am an Indian only because I say I am Indian," in order to make a place for himself in the world. Misrepresentations cost Indian peoples dearly. Not only do self-identifications such as Highwater's tie Indianness to bloodlines and biological, "essential" difference, but they provide unaware non-Indians with "chiefs" to represent a people, "chiefs" who have absolutely no ties to Indian communities and who tell many non-Indians what they like most to hear.

To many readers, the idea that Highwater's "invented" ethnicity costs Indian peoples dearly may seem like an exaggeration. To elaborate on that observation, it is crucial that I be explicit about why I have chosen to focus on Jamake Highwater thus far and to state, for the record, that although I hold the opinion that Highwater's claim to Indian heritage is fraudulent, that claim is not the primary issue here. His romanticized version of American Indian identity is the issue — an objection I would voice even if he were actually Indian. He has assumed a place for himself as the primary spokesperson for Indians, assumed it with an arrogance that belies a disrespect for American Indian communities.

Such disrespect misses the fact that, although American Indians remain on the bottom of the list of all disadvantaged groups in the United States, in terms of basic quality-of-life indicators, there *are* Indian intellectuals, educators, artists, writers, political activists, lawyers, and tribal leaders who are not "chosen" in the way Highwater has been to be the "Golden Indian," as Adams calls him. Neither would any one of them choose such a role. Instead, those individuals are rarely called upon to provide the many pictures of tribal and urban Indian life that would demonstrate the survival and continuance ("survivance" is Vizenor's term) of Indian peoples, of their evolving cultures.[8] Yet the sentiment against Highwater in Indian Country is not a question of his not having "a bunch of aggressive relatives on a reservation to back him up"; nor is it a question of a mean-spirited envy on the part of a people who refuse to recognize their "native son" as a prophet in his own country. Rather, the problem is that he has appropriated Indianness for his own gain and peddles it as artifact. He has little if any relationship to living Indian communities, even though before he began mixing up his own personal-origins narrative, many Indian individuals and communities treated him kindly (to their tribute), essentially welcoming him "home." People took him at his word, much as the Zunis took in anthropologist Frank Cushing during the 1870s and 1880s and made him a priest in their Bow society, when, in fact, "Cushing decided that he would do everything necessary to make the intimate acquaintance of the people" in order to obtain secret cultural information (Swiderski 178). American Indian leaders and intellectuals have learned a lesson about the confidence-man tactics of culture thieves since Cushing's time, a time when some felt the information gathered justified any means of procurement. Such genuine innocence or vulnerability on the part of the Zunis then and on the part of individuals in Indian communities now only makes such acts all the more reprehensible.

Although Indian cultural capital (ironically, one of the few marketable resources Indians consistently have) historically invites chicanery and fraud, I was nonetheless reluctant to accept Adams's evidence of Highwater's scam. For one thing, given the poor quality of the reproduction of the photographs in Adams's newspaper article — photographs meant to establish links between the identities of Gregory Markopoulos, J. Marks, and Jamake Highwater — questions remained in my mind about the extent of Highwater's confabulations. Many people find their way back to an identification with Indians and Indian causes after being, for example, adopted by non-Indian parents. I would never want to trivialize or otherwise undermine the difficult identity questions with which any person struggles. When I read Highwater's book, *Shadow Show*, however, my confusion over the photographs was cleared up. On page 56 of that publication, Highwater identifies himself as the man appearing with Robin Wagner, the famous set designer, taken at a time when Highwater admits he went by the name J. Marks.[9] The photograph (circa 1960) reveals Highwater, or Marks, with graying, slightly kinky, black hair, which greatly resembles the photographs of Gregory J. Markopoulos in Adams's article. To underline his chameleon abilities, this J. Marks contrasts sharply with the photograph (circa 1972) of Jamake Highwater on page 149 of the same text, in which he appears with straight, black hair and "Native" looking apparel. Moreover, "J. Marks" derives neatly from the middle of the name "Gregory [J. Mark]opolous," a point Adams makes. Many people went "ethnic" in the 1960s and 1970s, so the change in Highwater's appearance between the two photographs does not necessarily constitute anything peculiar or dishonest, but the link he himself creates between Markopoulous and Marks does — in effect, by his inviting comparisons with the Markopoulous photograph.

In *Shadow Show*, suggestively subtitled "An Autobiographical Insinuation," Highwater understandably takes great pains to avoid the controversy surrounding him; nevertheless, he stubbornly insinuates his righteousness in claiming or "inventing" any identity he chooses, when he says, "The imagination illuminates and, finally, defines our *only* reality — the only truth we can know. That light is a mythic lantern. And the world it illuminates for us is the realm of rituals by which we know ourselves and what we have been and what we are becoming"(233–34). Here Highwater denies the force of tradition and kinship so central to Indian community and identity, much as Lewis's American Adam would — "happily bereft of ancestry, untouched and undefiled by the usual inheritances of family and race" — and instead privileges a supreme belief in the imagination's power, "a mythic lantern," to illuminate a world where self-constructed ritual and identity reign. As Highwater states in *Shadow Show*, and as he insinuates throughout his stories of important people he has known, interviewed, or worked with, "I am not interested in reality. We are always told that we must put more reality into our dreams. But I wish to teach that it is more important for us to put dreams into our reality" (204). That he conceives of his work as "teachings" also comes across in this passage.

Quite fittingly, in *Shadow Show* Highwater begins the story of his life and achievements as an artist (as displaced as his story is from actual personal events and facts) with a quotation about "supreme fictions," from Wallace Stevens's *Opus Posthumous*: "The final belief is to believe in a fiction, which you know to be a fiction, there being nothing else, the exquisite truth is to know that it is a fiction and that you believe it willingly" (9). He goes on to preface anecdotes of his participation in various art scenes of the 1950s, '60s, '70s, and '80s, from San Francisco to New York to Europe, with an explanation without apology of what motivates him:

As a boy I was very badly burned. I still have the faint scars, which were a source of great self-consciousness when I was an adolescent, but I cannot recall the fire. That day has vanished — the place, the flames, even the agony. A first principle of Buddhism is: *Pain exists*. To escape things that are painful we must reinvent ourselves. Either we reinvent ourselves or we choose not to be anyone at all.

We must not feel guilty if we are among those who have managed to survive. (10–11)[10]

Highwater's metaphorical tale about the source of his personal pain and its transformation into a force shaping his identity resonates with the claim that opens his book: "I am a shadow . . . someone who was adopted as a child, at a time when adoption was still a covert matter" (9). Among his own conflicting accounts, we can possibly never know whether or not he was adopted without doing so through a legal encounter, but what he offers here as his confusion about his origins does not jibe with what he says elsewhere. Highwater states in *The Primal Mind* that because of the destitution of his family, he was put in a foster home at the age of ten — surely an age when memories of childhood are indelibly marked on one's memory (4). More importantly, it is difficult to comprehend why a man of such obvious talent (he writes well and has been involved with the American musical and theatrical avant garde for decades) would think that he could or should take on the identity he has — an Indian identity. He need *not* do so to achieve recognition as an authority on some aspect of American Indian art, literature, or culture. Many non-Indians have distinguished themselves among their peers and at the same time earned the respect of Indians for their efforts to record or interpret some truth about Indian history, language, or culture; other non-Indians have married into or otherwise entered kinship structures and have become permanent members of Native communities.

More puzzling yet is Highwater's clever deception in devising an authoritative voice (his spokesperson status), which is unethical by any standard. As one example of this deception, in his book *The Primal Mind*, he presents the material in Barbara Tedlock's influential scholarly article "The Clown's Way" (1975) in such a way as to make it sound like his own experience. He writes: "The sacred clown and his apparently antisocial behavior which is condoned in Indian ceremonies seems outrageous to Western people who believe it is savage for a culture to institutionalize behavior that seems to be psychotic and perverted. 'Many people who know about these things say that the clown is the most powerful,' an Apache has commented when asked about the comic role of the sacred clown in ceremonies. 'People think that the clown is just nothing, that he is just for fun. That is not so' " (1981, 174). If we compare Highwater's passage to the introduction of Tedlock's article, the usurpation becomes clear: "Sacred clowns, although they are often portrayed as merely providing comic relief in otherwise deadly serious ceremonies, are in reality close to the heart of American Indian religion" (105). The strong, moralizing tone Highwater adds with words such as "psychotic" and "perverted" echo his defiance in positing the value of "supreme fictions." But when Tedlock goes on to quote an Apache medicine man (interview by Morris Opler in the late 1930s or early 1940s), Highwater's usurpation borders on plagiarism: "People think that the clown is just for nothing, that he is just for fun. That is not so. When I make masked dancers and they do not set things right or can't find out something, I make that clown and he never fails. Many people who know about these things say that the clown is the most powerful" (105). From here he follows Tedlock's development of her thesis, alternating her documented examples of tribal clown figures with his own editorial comments and adding a few readings of his own. In his "Selected Bibliography," he does cite the text in which Barbara Tedlock's article appears but does so without specific reference to her article.

The above comparison should make it clear that when Highwater wrote *The Primal Mind*, he felt he could take license with archival materials and claim the experiences contained in them as if they originate from his own personal knowledge and insight. The authoritative voice he affects in the text results from his usurpation of others' research and from his questionable description of his life before age ten, when his Blackfeet/French mother was supposedly his principal tutor — a woman who "somehow retained much of the special *inclus-*

ivity which I identify with the very heart of the primal world" (xvi–viii). In other words, he presents himself as someone who understands the "primal world," his subject, well enough to speak with confidence on any aspect of it. His "authoritative" voice no doubt also derives from the fact that he quotes numerous Western writers and thinkers (such as Hannah Arendt, Carl Jung, Ernst Cassirer, and Maurice Merleau-Ponty) as an indispensable feature of his comparative approach and as a means of name-dropping.

A further irony I find in the Highwater inventions is that although interrogating the truthfulness of *The Primal Mind* was, for the most part, left to Indians themselves (where are our anthropologist friends when we need them?), many non-Indian scholars have gone to great lengths to "expose" so-called invented Indians — none other than Indian leaders and activists — who do not conform to their ideals of Indianness. As Vine Deloria Jr. writes, in his review of James Clifton's edited text, *The Invented Indian,*

The authors, for the most part, seem to be very disappointed that modern Indians do not act like the Indians of their undergraduate textbooks or the movies they enjoyed as children and they seem determined to attack contemporary expressions of Indian-ness as fraudulent and invalid because modern Indians fall short of their expectations. Part of the authors' goal is to excoriate Indians for not being their own ancestors and behaving as such. Indians in store-bought clothes have no romantic value whatsoever and are just pale imitations of "real" Indians and that is a good bit of the message of these essays. ("Comfortable" 399)

The two phenomena — that Highwater had been allowed to achieve the reputation he did as an "Indian" scholar, without his enterprise being significantly called into question, and that he chooses the verbs *to invent* or *to reinvent* to describe his quest for self-definition — are not coincidental. Both figure crucially in the current critical movements centered on ethnic literatures, as ethnic groups and individual authors from those groups assert separate identities for themselves, identities that are at the least oppositional to so-called mainstream American identity. However, an important dissimilarity exists between, on the one hand, groups such as Native Americans, African Americans, Asian Americans, Puerto Ricans, and Chicanos and, on the other hand, European immigrant groups. The difference is that racism and the particular histories of those groups in America have kept the former groups separate in distinct ways over a long period of time. Moreover, although no one would argue against the notion that groups reformulate their beliefs and objectives over time and under particular social pressures, *race*, as a historical rather than biological phenomenon, is not something one can *invent* (other than through fraud of some sort). *Racial* designations connote a historical and economic separation of the group from the mainstream on the basis of *race*, even when some individual members of the particular group in question may actually have a small amount of *racial* blood heritage tying those individuals to that community. Yet many scholars in current American ethnicity studies miss that distinction.

Werner Sollors, author of *Beyond Ethnicity* (1986) and editor of *The Invention of Ethnicity* (1989), takes the position that "it is most helpful not to be confused by the heavily charged term 'race' and to keep looking at race as one aspect of ethnicity" (*Beyond* 39). He eventually abandons the term *ethnicity* as well, when he states, "I propose that for the purposes of investigating group formation, inversion, boundary construction and social distancing, mythos of origins and fusions, cultural markers and empty symbols, we may be better served by the vocabulary of kinship and culture codes than by the cultural baggage that the word 'ethnicity' contains" (102). Although I agree with him that both terms, *race* and *ethnicity*, carry with them cultural baggage that often confuses rather than clarifies investigations of group formation and the like, it seems equally distorting to ignore the fact that racism maintains boundaries between historically *racially* designated groups and other Americans, through slavery, segregation, or what amounts to incarceration on reservations and that those boundaries figure essentially in the groups' culture codes. A blindness to the exclusion of Indian voices perpetuates the idea that non-Indians can speak better for Indians than Indians can speak for themselves, perhaps because the raw pain of loss expected from Indians would be unpalatable. In fact, in Sollors's *Beyond Ethnicity* the chapter devoted to Indians focuses almost exclusively on non-Indians' views of Indians in the nineteenth century, yet he does not question that he has not learned of any Indian writers and scholars, even though Indians have been publishing in English at least since 1772.[11]

Sollors is nonetheless amply aware of the way Euro-Americans have invented an ethnic identity around the Indian presence in their history. In writing of the "standard dying-Indian speech[es]" popular at the end of plays in the early nineteenth century — speeches that he describes as being "full of disdain," he concludes that "[t]hey were part of a presumptuous reconstruction of American kinship" (*Beyond* 125). Sollors might have deepened his argument had he read Vine Deloria Jr.'s book *Custer Died for Your Sins*. Deloria humorously comments on how frequently non-Indians told him, when he was executive director of the National Congress of American Indians, that they have Indian heritage, always through a Cherokee grandmother, a tribe they locate variously "from Maine to Washington State" (10–11). Deloria is not alone in that experience; most Indians know what it feels like to have people approach us, gushing over the fact that they, too, have Indian ancestry, and also to know that such exuberant individuals have no idea what it is like to be Indian where and when Indians are despised. In many places where legal contests over Indian rights, resources, and lands occur, "loving" Indians is the last thing on many white people's minds.

Sollors later notes that "the popular image of the Indian exists in a web of subdued love relationships" (*Beyond* 127). A "presumptuous reconstruction of American kinship" indeed undergirds American identity—the Indian male dies in defeat, while the Indian female lives on to bestow an aristocratic, truly American heritage on Euro-Americans through intermarriage; then she too disappears into a family's history (*Beyond* 125). The gender issues related to assuming Indian identity further complicate the picture.[12]

I spoke earlier of how pretending to be Indian or believing that it is possible to "know" what it means to be "Indian" is something Americans believe to be within their purview, and I stated that being preoccupied with national hypocrisies is also an essential aspect of the American experience. The "disdain" on the part of defeated Indian chiefs to which Sollors refers falls within that latter preoccupation of thought, while the former American pretense is evident in what he describes as "a web of subdued love relationships": "From Pocahontas to the hundreds of stories—supposedly of Indian origin, but invariably products of the Euro-American imagination—which are associated with America's many lovers' leaps, Indians remain connected with love in the American imagination and, more specifically, with the imagery of chivalric courtly love of the European Middle Ages" (*Beyond* 127). Understanding how those two facets of American imagination work would, I believe, lead to the genuine insight Americans need in deciphering the difference between an Indian person who can instruct them and one (or a pretend one) who is mirroring their own distorted images back to them.

After nearly five hundred years of contact with Native Americans, Euro-Americans continue to retreat from the ambiguity inherent in recognizing how difficult it is to determine who or what one is observing and how one affects someone or something by observation. As Charles Johnson says, a people's history must be seen "as an experience capable of inexhaustible readings," if we mean to vivify our lives with that people's art (20). Meanwhile, it is important to conceive of the constraints put upon Indian communities in their being defined by the judicial system as well as by popular culture media and academia.[13]

A confusion of definitions of historical or contemporary Indian life plagues scholarship on Indians.[14] As Sharon O'Brien notes, attempts to explain and define the relationship between the United States and tribal governments have been the subject of over one thousand law articles and many major studies. Shunning the suggestion that its rulings are based on racial criteria, the Supreme Court has held that the U.S. government maintains a *political* relationship with America's tribal peoples. Nevertheless, another branch of our tripartite governance structure, the legislature, seems to hold a different perspective on how to define Indians: as of 1978 "federal legislation contained thirty-three definitions of Indians," many of them based on "racial" bloodlines, rather than on political community or history. The difference between judicial and legislative views seems to be equivalent to the difference between fiduciary principles (the government's trust relationship to Indians based on treaties) and fiscal principles (the government's legislative allocation of those treaty responsibilities). Therein lies an essential lesson in why it is important not to subsume "race" into the larger category of "ethnicity." "Race" in the sort of pseudo-scientific terms of the nineteenth century's eugenics movements — that is, as blood quantum — functions to erase some Indians and bury others under a mound of red tape. In the 1800s, competency hearings, in which blood quantum played an important role, were frequently held to determine whether an Indian person should be seen as capable of becoming the farmer that policymakers hoped he would be. The evidence at such hearings, perhaps something as simple as the fact that the individual had gotten a haircut in the style of white men or was believed to have a white ancestor, was often enough to issue a fee patent to him on his allotted land — land that he would subsequently lose for failure to pay taxes. Today the government uses blood quantum as a requirement for awards, services, and benefits; in some cases, the Indian Health Service requires DNA evidence to establish paternity in order to qualify the children of unmarried couples for benefits. Added to that, under many tribal enrollment policies, if a tribal person's parents are from different nations, but the individual cannot document at least one-quarter blood quantum in one parent's nation, he or she cannot be counted as being Indian at all. A last point on the subject of legal Indian identity: over one hundred tribes have yet to complete the lengthy and expensive process required to establish recognition as tribes.

Although the trust relationship between the U.S. and tribal governments requires that the U.S. government act in the best interests of Indians (with Indians being a quasi-sovereign political entity), the rights of Indian peoples to be separate and to remain Indian are undermined by policies that define them by "race." When Euro-Americans "reinvent" themselves through false autobiographical intimations or through fictional representations, this wishful thinking (at its best) or deception (at its worst) runs parallel to unrelentingly assimilationist policies on the part of the federal government, whether the goals to assimilate Indians are short-term or long-term.

"Racial essentialism" is not the means of determining who is an Indian; the cultural identity of a writer claiming to be Indian must depend on both community recognition and self-declaration. What that often means, unfortunately, is that Indian writers are forced to reveal details of their personal lives and histories in ways not expected of other writers. Even at that, scholars who attempt to reconstruct the traditional American literary canon may not know how to deal with the question of who is truly an Indian writer. As laudable as their shared vision of and hope for change may be, they often quite understandably lack a shared knowledge of the ethnic groups whose literatures they hope to include in the new canon. Ill-defined beginnings characterize reform movements, of course; but, as Werner Sollors suggests, the time has come for a closer examination of what we propose to change, how, and why: "Literary critics easily succumb to the danger of resorting to an implicit 'good vibes' methodology (which approaches ethnic literature with well-intentioned optimism, though sometimes with moral indignation as its underpinning), grounding close readings of texts on static notions of descent and on primordial, organicist, sometimes even biological—but in all cases largely unquestioned— concepts of ethnic-group membership" (*Beyond* 11). In the past twenty years, the emergence of a significant number of Indian writers enables us to move away from "static notions of descent" and to open the perception of the field to a plethora of voices, *without* gutting the political imperatives of Indian peoples themselves.

Any definition of American Indian identity obviously must begin with Indians themselves, and as I said earlier, it is not a simple matter, given tribal diversity, the ruins of colonialism, intermarriage, language extinction, and so forth. Definitions of any human community can never adequately contain the multiplicities, the inexhaustible readings of a collective of individual lives — yet each needs to accommodate the other, the individual and the community. In *Manifest Manners*, Gerald Vizenor warns about the difficulty in finding and keeping the balance: "Nationalism is the most monotonous simulation of dominance in first person pronouns of tribal consciousness. . . . The concerted creations of tribal cultures are in continuous translations as stories, and the situation of hermeneutics remains the same in simulations; the silence of heard stories in translations, and the absence of the heard, antecedes a presence in the shadows of names" (60). Spoken from a trickster persona, Vizenor's words nonetheless leave us (Native and non-Native) in an uneasy place, asking as he does for the full texture of the tribal fabric. He weaves together here more words than we can easily grasp and later more questions than he answers, but this one, from the middle, speaks to me: "What are the real names, nouns, and pronouns heard in the field of tribal consciousness?" There are, in other words, important distinctions to be made for the sake of representation of a people or peoples — the "real" world inhabited by Native Americans — more than for the identities of its citizens, the sum being greater than its parts: the difference between the "tribal identities . . . heard in names and stories" and the individual who believes he can name himself, declare himself Indian.[15]

Two books — Joseph Bruchac III's *Survival This Way: Interviews with American Indian Poets* and Brian Swann and Arnold Krupat's *I Tell You Now: Autobiographical Essays by Native American Writers* — offer intriguing perspectives on how contemporary American Indian authors see themselves, as writers and as individuals of indigenous American heritage.[16] One such writer is Mary TallMountain, now deceased, whose mother and brother died of tuberculosis; she was adopted by non-Indians and eventually taken away from her Alaskan homeland. She presents an agonized view of the importance of searching for her roots, of reclaiming the grounds of her identity:

The spirits in the graveyard can't show me where my mother lies, and I will not let them persuade me to return here. But I know who I am. Marginal person, misfit, mutant; nevertheless I am of this country, these people. I have used their strengths. I have wrestled to the earth their weaknesses that have echoed in me . . . [I] recall with startling clarity and longing every detail of the land, the river, the people . . . Alaska is my talisman, my strength, my spirit's home. Despite loss and disillusion, I count myself rich, fertile, and magical.

I tell you now. You *can* go home again. (Krupat and Swann 12–13)

In the larger context of TallMountain's struggles and sorrows, her statement stands for the importance of being rooted in a culture — something all the more acutely felt and grieved when it has been lost. Some tribal groups (and individuals) welcome their lost "brethren" home, whereas some do not. But TallMountain does not create for herself an identity or "invent" a place for herself. Rather, her reclaiming of a place for herself in the world is dynamic and living, replete with grief and hope and based on a heritage rooted in the particular history of an Alaskan Native community. Whether or not she had chosen to stay there, and whether or not they would have her belong among them, her story merges with their stories. There is a difference between claiming an *identity* and seeking to *represent* a people to the larger world.

The writer Elizabeth Cook-Lynn is a Crow Creek Dakota who, unlike Mary TallMountain, was not taken away from her family and homeland; she grew up in an extended Dakota family in South Dakota, where she was born. Cook-Lynn addresses some of what it means to her to be an Indian writer, when she states, "I do not speak for my people" (58). She gives two reasons: in addition to guarding against the "tendency . . . [some poets have] to think too much of themselves," she shuns "the idea that poets can speak for others" (58). Her statement of why this is true is the most cogent, honest answer I have encountered: "[T]he idea that we can speak for the dispossessed, the weak, the voiceless, is indeed one of the great burdens of contemporary American Indian poets today. . . . The frank truth is that I don't know very many poets who say, 'I speak for my people.' It is not only unwise; it is probably impossible, and it is very surely arrogant, for *We Are Self-Appointed* and the self-appointedness of what we do indicates that the responsibility is ours and ours alone" (58). What is the difference between Cook-Lynn's sense of being "self-appointed" and Jamake Highwater's? Cook-Lynn addresses an "opposite" concern, when she goes on to distinguish between poets such as herself and "'real' poets of our tribes, the men and women who sit at the drum and sing the old songs and create new ones" (58). While she sees the "real" poets as the ones tied to the oral tradition community, she nevertheless discerns a place for herself in the range of a people's literature, "that it is the responsibility of a poet like me to 'consecrate' history and event, survival and joy and sorrow, the significance of ancestors and the unborn" (59). Written to contextualize her poem "A Poet's Lament: Concerning the Massacre of American Indians at Wounded Knee," the aforegoing quotations amply mark the distinction between a deeply felt responsibility toward the lived history of a community of people she calls "home" and the "primal" mind espoused by would-be Indians.

Other American Indian writers take up the issue of "race" as a concept guiding the government's treatment of Indians, having more to do with money allocation than with human identity or belonging. Carter Revard presents facts of reservation life that might surprise non-Indian readers who imagine that "real" Indians look more or less like Sitting Bull rather than like Revard. (An Indian friend told me recently of meeting Creek woman who holds a leadership position in her tribe and who speaks Creek as her first language; she is blond and blue-eyed.) Carter Revard knows that he should make his origins clear to "east-of-the-Hudson friends of the Indian," when he declares: "I was born 'on the res' in the Agency town. . . . Better stress that for [those] . . . who would like to know that a child of the wild who doesn't look much Indian was actually born on an Indian reservation and lived among the Indians when he was growing up" (69). Americans generally know very little about reservations, the history of reservation inception, their governance, their economics, or their "racial" makeup, for to know these things one would have to learn something of U.S. policy toward Indians, most likely in history courses, or at least how significant pieces of legislation like the Dawes Act and the Indian Reorganization Act have shaped contemporary Indian community life. Revard throws questions at his reader, questions he knows exist beneath the surface of discussions of Indianness, and then he answers them without flinching. But the anger and pain of having to account for who you are is there, as it is in many Indian writings, autobiographical and otherwise. People who are visually identifiable as being Indian may face a somewhat different set of questions, but the underlying ignorance and racism remains the same.

Despite the humiliation inherent in such declarations, they are nonetheless part of an ethos among Indian writers who recognize the sensitivity of the issues surrounding fraudulent claims and confabulations, cultural genocide, and cultural thievery. Indian writers can go on to write about a teapot or a blue balloon or a day at the Field Museum of Natural History, but they must situate themselves in relation to Indian people. Does that mean that being an American Indian writer is, of necessity, being political? In my opinion, the answer is yes, in part — it is ideological, as are all things in America — and, in the sense that colonialism and racism produce a double consciousness in the oppressed, Indian people who have known the legacy of America's racist history will develop a double consciousness to preserve their right to be Indian. At least Ken Kesey got that part right in his creation of Mr. Bromden, the "schizophrenic" Indian.

But unlike Revard, Cook-Lynn, TallMountain, or a host of other Indian writers responsive to Indian communities, Kesey misses the point entirely of what it means to be Indian, as does Highwater when he lets Carlos Castaneda off the hook for deceiving his reading public as well as his dissertation committee. Castaneda claimed to have gained essential truths from Yaqui elders and fabricated the sources of information in his Ph.D. thesis. Highwater asserts that *all* Castaneda did was "evolve a set of metaphors out of Western Mentality that conveys something of the fundamentally historical and sociological otherness of Indians." He concludes, in Castaneda's defense, that his "work may not be truthful but it is meaningful, and that is ultimately what counts about any work of art or any philosophy" (*Shadow* xx). To claim art can be art without being truthful is akin to claiming a people can exist without having a *specific* language or history. And that is where we began: at the juncture between colonialism's process of radical dispossession and cultural appropriations of things Indian. Learning to read "real Indians" in American cultural art media requires a subtlety of mind, a clarity of purpose, and a willingness to hear "the silence of heard stories in translations." Those who are willing to accept an "art" that does not cherish truth deserve what they get.

NOTES

This essay originally appeared in *American Indian Quarterly* 21.4 (1997): 675–702 and appears here by permission of the University of Nebraska Press, copyright 1997 University of Nebraska Press. Special thanks to Simon Ottenberg, professor emeritus of anthropology at the University of Washington, for inviting me to present an early form of this essay in his seminar, Ethnicity and the Arts, University of Washington, 1989, and for his close reading of that manuscript. Thanks to the University of California, Irvine, Humanities Center for inviting me to present a paper on this topic; and special thanks to David L. and Richard O. Moore for their careful and constructive readings. Despite all the fine help I have received, errors may persist; they are mine and mine alone.

1. The dilemma of the postcolonial critic is described well by Graham Huggan, in his writing about Canadian and Australian postcolonial discourse:

> Postcolonial critical theory—much of it inspired by the various French post-structuralisms—proves, at best, to be a double-edged sword; for while on the one hand it clearly allied itself to the material practice of an anticolonial struggle, on the other it presents itself as a carefully nuanced understanding of the constraints of human agency. And nowhere is this dilemma clearer than in approaches toward "the Native," who risks being seen as a differential signifier—as a symbolic marker of the split within (white) settler cultural identity—rather than as a socially constructed subject with his/her own embattled history (131–32).

Huggan's words "nowhere is this dilemma clearer" point toward a sense of the extreme "othering" under which Natives and Native topics suffer. The subject position of the Native critic, then, becomes all the more problematic.

2. I recognize that particular media moguls have been attempting lately to produce programming about American Indian life and with American Indian input. Most of the programming, however, centers on nineteenth-century Indian life, particularly the so-called Indian Wars. Even the episode in the Turner series on Native Americans based on the best-selling autobiography *Lakota Woman*, recounting activist years of the 1960s and 1970s in Lakota country, harkens back to the nineteenth century nonetheless. It is a visual representation of an as-told-to autobiography, Mary Crow Dog's life story told to Richard Erdoes, who taped and transcribed interviews, arranged them according to his own sense of narrative, and supplemented them with historical background materials. Moreover, although it was written in the 1970s, the text was not published until the 1990s, when its radical politics and its woman's voice were more likely to find a broad audience—its potential for causing a stir had greatly diminished over twenty years. The actual text was apparently not changed from when it was first written, and its peculiar publication circumstance was not explained until the publication of its sequel, *Ohitika Woman*.

3. Establishing a working vocabulary for any topic that deals with ideological issues can be problematic. As I develop my argument, I trust that the meanings of terms will deepen by contextual use.

4. Although I recognize that *ethnicity* may be an inappropriate (if not erroneous) designation for segments of the Indian population, I use the term because it engages the current debates around *race* and *ethnicity*, particularly as those debates impact groups or "nations" within nations who get generalized under it.

5. John Patrick Diggins, in *The Promise of Pragmatism*, locates the goal of American Experience in the future, in a way that ties back to the concepts and impulses behind manifest destiny, as philosophy and as policy, though he does not make that historical or political connection:

> All three modernist propositions, despite their obvious political differences, pre-suppose that the meaning and significance of the present await the future, that nature is responsive to human initiative, that the philosopher's responsibility is to be effective and useful rather than to search for preexisting ideas to which the mind must be congruent, and that objects take on meaning and value only when undergoing change. With pragmatism in particular, the use of experience only prepares us for further experience, without experience itself being immediately self-illuminating or self-rewarding. The assumption that truth and value are produced in future action rather than revealed in present reflection holds out the promise of success, and as such pragmatism becomes not so much a philosophy as a story of the upward movement of life, a hopeful vision that appeals to America's romantic imagination. . . . Pragmatism advises us to "beat on" and not allow ourselves to be "borne back ceaselessly into the past." (20)

6. One reason I am focusing so intently on Highwater is that, although the dubious-ness of his connections to an Indian heritage may be well-known in Indian Country, no substantial archival record exists outside of the newspaper accounts, a layer or two away from easy access, because they are on microfiche. Gerald Vizenor makes passing reference to him in *Manifest Manners*.

7. Several years ago, the editors of *Indian Country Today* ran a series of three articles directed at individuals whose Indian heritage they felt they could call into question. I did not applaud that effort, although I found it perfectly understandable, because it is so difficult to judge the quality and substance of another person's life. Many of the individuals mentioned have contributed significantly to American Indian Studies topics and identify with Indian life in thoroughgoing ways. But I know well the sentiment of being fed up with on-the-bandwagon Indians. Unemployment on some reservations runs as high as 70 percent in the winter, less in the summer because of fire-fighting crews. Although some people go about spouting platitudes about Indians' connected-ness with nature, parents are unable to put decent food on the table for their children or experience much pride in having prospects for meaningful work or work at all. Moreover, there is obviously a direct correlation between the darkness of one's skin and the level of achievement likely in education and industry.

8. An extremely peculiar and controversial example of someone pretending an American Indian identity is that of Forrest Carter, author of *The Education of Little Tree*. As Dan T. Carter (no relation) reports in a *New York Times* article on October 4, 1991 (at which point a half million copies had been sold, and the book was on the *New York Times* bestseller list), Forrest Carter had changed his name from Asa Carter, obscuring his connection to George Wallace and other racist and fascist politicians and organizations. Purportedly, the name Forrest derived from Nathan Bedford Forrest, the person "who founded the original Ku Klux Klan (KKK)" (Browder, *Slippery* 1). Of Forrest Carter's book, Browder writes that it was a "means of reinventing and rehabilitating himself from his public past as a white supremacist" (112).

9. Another odd discrepancy I discovered is that if Markopoulous *is* J. Marks and if J. Marks is Highwater, then Highwater did not go to high school in California with Susan Sontag as he claims in *Shadow Show*.

10. Buddhism does not teach that we need to "escape things that are painful" by reinventing ourselves, or that not to reinvent ourselves means not being "anyone at all." On the contrary, Buddhists hold that we grow through suffering.

11. See A. LaVonne Ruoff's account of Indian writing in English ("History," particularly pages 62–63).

12. Entry into mainstream American culture differs by gender as well as "race." In the popular culture paradigm, the Indian male must be defeated or die, while (or so that) the Indian female can become intimately involved with the white male. Either that or some sort of trading of women takes place between men. Crossing racial lines for sexual liaison gets legitimated by white male consent and sanction, with women of all colors "belonging" to the white male.

13. I do not believe that Johnson is saying no definite meaning can be identified or located; rather, he says that we must dislodge our characters and subjects from the victim role and restore the full range of possible human agency to them.

14. Also see my article "Bloodties and Blasphemy: American Indian Women and the Problem of History" in *Is Academic Feminism Dead: Theory in Practice* (New York: New York UP, 2000) 204–32.

15. The "Indian" that the American Indian writer declares himself (or herself) to be must be read sometimes against the grain of what one might expect. As Scott B. Vickers notes, in *Native American Identities*, "[Louis] Owens is particularly insightful in noting that the major semiological and thematic thrust of modern Indian writing lies in the writer's appropriation of an alien language to recast the themes and plots heretofore assigned Indian characters by Anglo writers" and "emphatically [make of] the Indian the hero of other destinies, other plots" (132).

16. Arnold Krupat and Brian Swann have just released another volume of contemporary Native American writers' autobiographical writings, entitled *Here First*.

It was the white people who had nothing; it was the white people who were suffering as thieves do, never able to forget that their pride was wrapped in something stolen, something that never had been, and could never be, theirs.

Leslie Marmon Silko [Laguna Pueblo], in *Ceremony*

Return of the Buffalo

Cultural Representation as Cultural Property

DAVID L. MOORE

We are a people of permission.

Frank Brown [Hieltsuk Nation], in *Canoe Nation Newsletter*

I tried to make it a point to learn the English language, write it, and think in it, while at the same time trying to present some aspects of Mesquakie culture — without dealing with sensitive material.

Ray A. Young Bear [Mesquakie], in *Survival This Way*

As the party of inclusion, we take special pride in our country's emergence as the world's largest and most successful multiethnic, multiracial republic. We condemn antisemitism, racism, homophobia, bigotry and negative stereotyping of all kinds. We must help all Americans understand the diversity of our cultural heritage.

From the Democratic Party Platform, 1992

Competing as "the party of inclusion" must be 1990s discourse for the Latinate eighteenth-century American ideal of *e pluribus unum*. If, indeed, America would view itself as the "most successful" crown of community atop a millennium of Crusades, conquests, and colonizations, there remain limits in our national consciousness of "negative stereotyping of all kinds." Clearly one of those limits is the tired vanishing Indian, whose *pluribus* nature has never found a welcome in the *unum*. Yet the vanishing Indian continues paradoxically to haunt the halls of power, and it is such a haunting quality that I wish to address here as a context for shifts in representation of Indians.

For instance, President Clinton's national touring "Dialogue on Race" initially omitted Native Americans from the pantheon of America's oppressed minorities, an omission corrected only after protest. Tacit approval of manifest destiny animates not only American boosterism, but much of American self-critique as well, whose "inclusive" desires, like the Democratic Party platform above, so often erase diversity in the name of American community. The fact that so many Native American writers are publishing stories and poems today suggests the possibility of a cultural shift in America's concept of community as radical and as incomprehensible as the return of the buffalo.[1] Native literary formulations around the Ghost Dance and the return of the buffalo begin to suggest patterns by which Americans might conceive of *e pluribus unum* as community built on difference rather than on making differences vanish.

Many contemporary Native writers use the sacred buffalo image to signal such a shift. Linda Hogan, Chickasaw, has a poem, "Return: Buffalo," whose title is an imperative invocation. In her piece, the buffalo calf, "a round, naked thing," returns power to face decimation and white guilt (265–67). Ward Churchill, Cherokee, has written an essay entitled "Generations of Resistance: American Indian Poetry and the Ghost Dance Spirit," a spirit that affirms the buffalo's return. Leslie Silko features a lecture on the return of the buffalo in her novel *Almanac of the Dead*.

If a number of Native writers, including Hogan, Churchill, Silko, James Welch, Gerald Vizenor, and many others, are invoking the return of the buffalo, many of their readers, both Native and non-Native, remain quietly nonplussed: Is this new buffalo imagery "mere" metaphor? Is this a joke? A fantasy? Nostalgia? Idealistic rambling at the keyboard? Quixotic belles lettres? Atavistic political rant? Anti-American vigilantism? Visionary bravado? Romance? Prophecy? A pitifully desperate gesture? Another Ghost Dance?

The Ghost Dancers' visions of returning buffalo were both dismissed and feared in the 1880s as dangerous hallucinations of a doomed race. Stories such as the following, glossed with a twentieth-century non-Indian historian's light sarcasm, only served then and now to strengthen that skeptical reading. A Sioux delegation in the 1880s is traveling back from Nevada to South Dakota, back from a pilgrimage where they had seen Wovoka, the Paiute prophet of the Ghost Dance. Ralph K. Andrist writes, "When they were returning home, they had come on an encampment of the dead of their tribe and had visited with old friends for some time. On continuing their journey, they found a herd of buffalo (these buffalo had apparently returned from the dead for the occasion, too), and had killed one and feasted on its meat; head, hoofs, and tail were left lying as Wovoka had instructed them, and as they walked off, had reassembled into a new buffalo" (340–41). The historian's parenthetical comment that "these buffalo had apparently returned from the dead for the occasion, too," derives its sarcastic rhetorical force from a matrix of cultural boundaries, notably a founding split between matter and spirit. This binary parlays into an evolutionary paradigm of present and past, specifically into a progressive premise that no buffalo could have survived, that buffalo were a thing of the past. Thus any return of the buffalo must be merely a Ghost Dance of mystification.

Yet to revise such linear historiographic assumptions of loss leads to further questions about how to represent historical change. Is the claim of Vizenor's trickster discourse, for instance, a more than false optimism when he, like Ward Churchill, describes contemporary Native writing as "the new ghost dance literature" of "liberation"? Is a claim to "tribal survivance" after the American genocide an ethically inadequate "fidelity to trauma," to use Dominick LaCapra's term? Is a literary claim to cultural "survivance" too easy for history, or for historical "facts"? The loss of the buffalo is America's symbol for that genocide of Native Americans. What does it mean when Native Americans begin to deny the finality of that loss? How is it possible after the unspeakable slaughter of the buffalo to speak of their return?

Behind these ethical questions are further questions of representation. Who is to represent Indians? How do different representations affect history and the survivance of contemporary Native communities? How do Indians represent their own losses, their own survival? Who owns images of Indians? And how do revisionary images of Indians affect America's national narrative? These representations, with their political and economic resonances, become questions of cultural property and, ultimately, questions of land.

As Winona LaDuke writes about the 1996 state-sanctioned slaughter of Yellowstone Buffalo in Montana, "Underneath is a deeper question, the conflict between two very divergent world views of the region — the mythology of America, and the reality of the land. Those divergent paradigms play out in an ongoing intergenerational drama." LaDuke contrasts "the economics of a dying mythology" of American agrarianism with the long-term "foundation of an actual buffalo commons — that vision of the Ghost Dance" (19). She summons Great Plains demographics from the 1980 and 1990 censuses to lend credence to a possibility of the buffalo's return: "While non-Indians are moving out of the Great Plains [due largely to the failure of beef farming], Indian populations are growing in that same region, with the highest birthrate in the country" (18). The politics and economics of returning buffalo embody the Native artistic claim to represent history after the dominance of colonial narratives. It is a question of progressive versus cyclic narratives.

The dissonance between those narratives continues in the new turn-of-the-century Indian wars. In January of 1999, Mel Russo of Seneca County and Connie Tallcot of Cayuga County, respective county chairs for the New York State Citizens for Equitable Resolution of the Cayuga Land Claim in the Finger Lakes, wrote a letter critical of the Cayuga claims and of the U.S. government's handling of the dispute. Characterizing white property owners as "real Americans" being "harassed with the threat of eviction" by "the Indians" supported by the federal government, they wrote:

Why is our (?) U.S. government strengthening the position of the Indians by suing, threatening and intimidating its taxpaying, hardworking, patriotic citizens? . . . Now, to create a better negotiating posture, the Indians are calling for eviction of innocent citizens all over New York state. It is important for each of us to write to our elected and appointed federal officials to stop this nonsense of harassing property owners who have a 200-year history to the valid conveyance of title to their property. (Russo 9A)

Various responding letters to the editors of area newspapers expressed liberal dismay: "If Russo and Tallcot are so insistent on placing Native Americans on one side of the divide, and 'real Americans' on the other side, then I want to say publicly that I am on the side of 'unreal Americans'" (Pernal 9A). "After reading their shameful diatribe, I want to contact my elected officials and let them know that I hope they will do whatever is within their power to help the various Indian nations with their land claims" (Potter 9A).

Whether or not these positions, expressed in the liberal hideout of Ithaca, New York, are conveyed to other government representatives, Governor George Pataki has announced that he will marshal the full authority of the State of New York to oppose Indian land claims and the U.S. government in the courts, to protect New York land owners, who by this functional definition do not include New York Indians.[2] Property is white. Perhaps if the Cayugas, the Oneidas, or other New York tribes do reclaim the land east of Buffalo, it indeed might be turned over to the buffalo once again. Such a scenario and its zealous opposition need to be accounted for. Since some forty-one tribes nationally are actively rebuilding herds in the Intertribal Bison Cooperative, and since western tribes and environmentalists like LaDuke are pursuing a High Plains "Buffalo Commons," such fears of competing use of property are not entirely unreasonable.

In the 1980s, the Agriculture Department in President Reagan's administration quietly announced that the effort to raise beef cattle on the High Plains had been a hundred-year mistake. LaDuke's analysis of prospects for the return of the buffalo incorporates this conservative claim. Buffalo, being more self-subsistent, are more cost-effective. The prospect of a returning buffalo economy continues to grow. Recently the *New Yorker* ran an article entitled "Cash Cow: It's Buffalo, the Other Red Meat." Wade Graham wrote, "The demand for breeding stock and meat (not to mention hides, skulls, and stuffed heads for curios) is so high, in fact, that bison can sell for five times the amount that cattle bring, and the overall herd is literally growing as fast as it can, since all females are being kept for reproduction. The economics are so compelling that many farmers have begun to reseed their land with native prairie grasses — reversing the botanical course of American history" (96–98). Whether breeding and cultivation, not to mention commercial slaughter, would prove beneficial to buffalo herds remains an open question. The prospect of partial reversals, however, seems to be a given, while the irrational violence by the Montana Department of Livestock only serves to amplify the stakes. They insist on slaughtering buffalo that wander outside of Yellowstone Park. The state maintains official reluctance to treat the buffalo as originary wildlife rather than as livestock threatening cattle interests. The fleeting evidence of brucellosis contamination to cattle is apparently an excuse for the ponderous economic competition implied in the return of the buffalo. There is no scientific evidence of such contamination in the field.

As compelling as these economic and biological prospects might seem, even if measured by their oppositions, they only begin to follow the efforts of the Ghost Dancers and the contemporary "ghost dance literature" to dream the world into harmony. Literary allusions to the survival and revitalization of herds of American bison test any reader of American Indian literatures to trace key dynamics, both aesthetic and ethical, textual and contextual, of that literature as it strives to envision cracks of reversal in the linear engine of history and manifest destiny. For centuries, Native writers have returned to complex modes of cultural survival against the reductive mentalities of colonial invasion. Field logics of cyclic interchange have made indigenous agency visible to colonized peoples if not to their colonizers intoxicated by the violence of dualities. Many postmodern readers have indeed grown used to such deconstruction of opposites, the "blurring of boundaries," the vital complexities between and around traditional binaries.

Although old categories have been breaking down, many "mainstream" Euro-American modes of thinking about Native cultures remain committed to an evolutionary paradigm, which equates civilization with property and technology against "the wilderness." A linear evolutionary view is founded in turn on notions of pure, static cultures and on what James Clifford calls "a Puritan taboo on mixing beliefs and bodies" (*Predicament* 344). The current controversy over Indian gaming casinos is shot with accusations about how "un-Indian" it all is. Certainly internal community discussions of cultural values around gaming raise crucial questions, but I am referring here to the external criticisms based on generations of Hollywood images. Donald Trump testified in congressional hearings against Indian gaming by claiming that his Pequot competitors, owners of Foxwoods Casino, one of the most lucrative in North America, simply do not "look Indian." This is not to underplay serious questions about Indian cultural values in gaming economics, yet in critiques of Indian gaming the temporal split between culture and nature, or to use the nineteenth-century discourse, "civilization and savage," still permeates a so-called postmodern America. In the academy, critics of Native American literature still rely on dualistic "frontier" metaphors. In the media, enterprising Indians are an anachronism. When the venerable buffalo symbol ambles "back" into the picture, such an affront to history, such an intractable breakdown of binaries, seems silly, perhaps kitsch, but not radical. The buffalo, like the Indian, is relegated to the past in America's national narrative, and any attempt to rewrite the buffalo into America's present or future must be absurd. To cite Andrist again, returning buffalo "apparently returned from the dead for the occasion." Indeed, the return of the buffalo, precisely because it seems so outrageous to most readers, has become one of the more audacious evocations for Native writers to convey complexities of survival and to reclaim representation of their cultures.

Professional readers who interpret Native literatures for an academic living have a peculiar ethical relation to the ways they erase or make visible those complexities. Professional readings help to define Native literary expression and experience in print, in the classroom, in the courts, in Congress, and even eventually in Native communities. Cultural representations in criticism of Native American literature become implicated in the political substance of that literature.[3] Literary politics, ultimately, comes down to questions of cultural property, for if representation effectively is culture, and if culture effectively is property, then cultural representation is cultural property.[4] To work through this set of relations is to arrive at a critical ethics. To explore that ethics in practice, I trace some further literary functions of the return of the buffalo, quintessential embodiment of High Plains and other Native cultural property.

The three epigraphs introducing this discussion map a set of broad cross-cultural questions. Frank Brown's proclamation, "We are a people of permission," given at Qatuwas in Bella Bella, British Columbia, refers to protocols among Northwest canoe nations regarding permission to enter each other's harbors. It reflects the assumption of many Native culture bearers that their stories, their images, are a form of property, like their land and water, and that there are protocols for proper and improper ways to exchange cultural materials. Ray A. Young Bear's attention to "sensitive material" carries that assumption into an autobiographical voice and focuses the notion of property on cultural representation. The excerpt from the 1992 Democratic Party Platform takes pride in an America in which such cultural exchange is assumed to be problem-free. Yet what happens when the buffalo roams into that crossfire? Do Americans and Native Americans still read the buffalo in ways as divergent as in the nineteenth century?

Linda Hogan's poem "Return: Buffalo" tries to probe a cross-cultural psychology around a sacred symbol of cultural information, an evocative psychological imagery of the buffalo that begins to suggest ways to approach sacred information across cultures. Gerald Vizenor and Leslie Silko represent the Ghost Dance and the return of the buffalo in virtually apocalyptic terms. James Welch reaches a remarkable simultaneity of divergent cultural and historical perspectives. Before discussing these test cases for imagery of the return of the buffalo, I need to lay out questions of cultural property and critical theory that constitute a few acres of the larger literary ground on which those buffalo roam.

Scruples over literary permission have long been institutionalized in the publishing world, which employs full-time "permissions editors" to check copyright of material not in the public domain. That more "available" public domain, however, has been defined as including ethnographic material, which often is identified with colonized cultures, whose knowledge, because of communal authorship, has not been subject to copyright in the Euro-American legal system. Much attention has been paid to the fact that European and Euro-American "intellectual property" has carried an individualistic stamp. The very notion of *cultural* property requires mental gymnastics that stretch the Western legal code so wedded to colonialist and capitalist structures of individual title.[5] The racial and racist formulations that accompany these notions translate into an equation between whiteness and property. Although these linkages between race, property, capital, and the academy have been examined, they have rarely been looked at in terms of Native American ethics or literary materials.[6]

As the academy identifies its goal of generating "productive citizens," circulation between information, education, and capitalism becomes more transparent. Robert Hutchins, former president of the University of Chicago, writes, "An educational system directed to economic growth will regard the people as instruments of production and teach them to regard themselves as such." Human instruments of production might regard knowledge, in turn, instrumentally as a commodity, increasingly as data. The "free flow of information" becomes, in this epistemological territory, as free for the taking as were the rivers and streams. In a colonial structure, such "free exchange" of knowledge frequently flows in a mercantile direction at the expense of the colonized.[7] The United Nations Information Centre for Australia, New Zealand, and the South

Pacific has written, "The legends, songs and lore of indigenous peoples, passed orally for many generations, are written, recorded and sold by others."[8]

The assumed free exchange of accurate knowledge has taken on, over centuries, the status of an inalienable right, associated closely in the United States with the First Amendment right of free speech, translated by academics into academic freedom. Paula Gunn Allen contrasts an epistemological protocol of caution and respect in Native communities with an academic way of knowing, which poses "a different set of values," "one which requires learning all and telling all in the interests of knowledge, objectivity, and freedom" ("Special" 382). The advent of computerized information and a subsequent commodification of knowledge as data have merely amplified such cultural values.

Yet in its ideal view of itself, the academy, even in its current multicultural upheavals, is driven by a "thirst for knowledge," a "love of science," a "passion for learning," which are assumed to be essential to the human condition and thereby open to all human conditions. For example, Cornell University's 1997–98 catalog description for its College of Arts and Sciences carries this notion of free information to a level of intellectual boosterism: "The richness of the curriculum is extraordinary; there is no course that all students must take, and there are nearly two thousand from which they may choose" (347). The student sets sail on a sea of knowledge, conquistador marching to the City of Gold. Logos must conquer chaos, as America's founding binary in John Winthrop's "citee on a hill" must make civilization conquer the wilderness.

When colonizing eyes, projecting an ethos of free information, analytical rigor, and exacting formulations of knowledge, "discover" their other, this discourse of taming the wilderness, of chaos and order, has required eventual ethnographic definitions of the other in the name of missionary, military, and colonial strategies that feed back into scholastic knowledge. Gerald Vizenor, in "The Ruins of Representation," refers to this process as "the cruelties of paracolonial historicism" (12). Colonial survival reifies rational survival, and vice versa, by ostensible control of the unknown.[9] The need to know becomes the right to know, linked with the right of conquest. Colonial survival and domination become confused. I am exploring here a different need, lying on both sides of the colonial divide but especially visible in Native American literature. This ethos fosters a different kind of academic rigor attentive to the values in uncertainty, in ignorance, in lack of domination, even in fallibility, not as anathema but as a welcome element in a mode of communication that would tolerate the unknown in a continuing, pragmatic process.

The dimly emerging awareness of cultural property ethics among humanities scholars blinks its way out of the libraries after a generation of dialogue on the topic among social scientists doing fieldwork in actual communities. The self-reflexive anthropology of George Marcus, Clifford Geertz, James Clifford, and others, whether it does indeed signal an academic paradigm shift, has shaken up the various disciplines of indigenous studies to try to avoid refixing the colonial gaze through the scholarly lens.[10] *American Indian Quarterly* devoted a special issue, entitled "Writing about (Writing about) American Indians," in winter 1996 to historical treatments of Native topics.[11] That issue establishes an ethical groundwork for ethnohistory that makes room for Native voices. A parallel volume of the *American Indian Quarterly* for literary treatments of Native issues, entitled "Cultural Property in American Indian Literature: Representation and Interpretation," came out in summer of 1998. That collection of essays looks at applications of ethical principles of literary scholarship to specific questions of Native cultural property, questions such as authenticity and difference, collaboration and copyright, individual and collective authorship, private and public representation. Whether or not these new academic efforts may be functions of an institutional conscience, they have begun to suggest radical, sometimes seemingly chaotic, departures from the norm that decenter enduring academic power structures.

Indigenous assertions of cultural property challenge that norm in particularly painful ways. What could be more nightmarishly chaotic to a white physical anthropologist, because of ethical intrusions into objective science, than to see Native bones returned from a laboratory to the ground? What could be more nightmarish to a white English professor than to be told by a Native student that she has no right to elucidate a particular tribal story in class? In a form of literary repatriation, the student claims that the story belongs back on its Native ground. What nightmare could more disrupt the American dream than the repatriation of the buffalo?

Repatriation of Native bones is the prototypical claim to cultural property and to limits on interpretation and representation in the name of cultural survival and continuity. The Native American Graves Protection and Repatriation Act of 1990, by instituting means for Native nations to reclaim bones and artifacts from museums, took remarkable steps to legally structure cultural difference. Such a retrospective denial of a certain exchange, where bones and stories belong in a specific tribal space not open to universities' encyclopedic volumes of time, are affirmations of a pluralist view of culture itself against the evolutionary paradigm. Such a denial of free exchange rests on an assertion of untranslatable difference. Jean-Francois Lyotard's *Le Differend* is tangentially useful here, especially to show how a context of cultural property helps to make that sense of difference more visible. The representation of cultural difference takes on new dynamics when its purposes include protection of cultural property.

Lyotard combines semiotics and politics in his definition of *le differend*. Although he is discussing linguistic representations of memories and claims about the Jewish Holocaust, the parallels in representing an American genocide are noteworthy. How can one adequately represent unspeakable losses in the European Holocaust or in the extended genocide and oppression of Native America? Again, the "vanishing Indian" remains the tacit discursive moniker, despite political correctness, in the media, the courts, the Congress, and the classroom, against which Native writers must speak. Unspeakable difference, or the differend, can become a radical rhetorical claim and response. Lyotard defines the term: "A case of differend between two parties takes place when the 'regulation' of the conflict that opposes them is done in the idiom of one of the parties while the wrong suffered by the other is not signified in that idiom" (9). They are not "speaking the same language," one an a priori discourse of manifest destiny, the other an even prior discourse of tribal sovereignty or community.

Lyotard's definition focuses a primary problematic for Indian writers in the way America's regulative discourse of the "vanishing Indian" offers no idiom for either the suffering or the survival of Indian communities and identities. America's recidivist investment in manifest destiny in the press and the publishing world, and in Hollywood, does not allow for descriptions of American Indian cultural struggle, much less tribal sovereignty. The differend begins to describe a context in which Indian writers then must make choices about cultural property, some of which the writers do not wish to signify or represent. Texts thus become shot with the syntax of a differend, strategically communicative of cultural information, silence, and cross-cultural negotiation. The return of the buffalo emerges as a prime example of this differend, insisting on survival of a power that is incomprehensible in the American idiom. In one epigraph introducing this essay, Young Bear, Mesquakie poet and novelist, points to a constant of silence in Native writing. He makes a choice to avoid "dealing with sensitive material" such as ceremonial or private clan information. Out of that silence emerge images like the buffalo.

In Lyotard's terms this critical process has political resonance: "To give the differend its due is to institute new addressees, new addressors, new significations, and new referents in order for the wrong to find an expression and for the plaintiff to cease being a victim" (*Differend* 13). Not only does conventional discourse continue to erase the wrongs suffered by Native Americans as "manifest destiny," but it has no room to register continuing cultural differences, which it reads as "vanishing" if not always already "vanished." Reading text and context for what Lyotard calls "new phrase families or new genres of discourse" (13) leads readers to a number of systems of signification in Indian literatures that elude victimization, especially to a sense that what has been considered vanished may instead have remained concealed. As Young Bear writes, the "Angels of Circumspection" expect his people to follow "the cardinal tenet" (not always lived up to by Young Bear's fictional characters), which is "to refrain from providing detailed words of Black Eagle Child Star-Medicine songs to the *wa be ski na me ska tti ki*, white-complexioned people" (263).

Such an affirmation of difference may be quite different from Lyotard's specific historical intentions that describe silence as negative: "The differend is the unstable state and instant of language wherein something which must be able to be put into phrases cannot yet be. This state includes silence, which is a negative phrase, but it also calls upon phrases which are in principle possible" (13). The model of a positive or desirable differend in Native literature, which because of such cardinal tenets and other constraints on cultural property does not desire to be put into phrases, is certainly not Lyotard's, who assumes that the gap, the aporia, the differend, longs for expression. Lyotard writes, "What is at stake in literature, in a philosophy, in a politics perhaps, is to bear witness to differends by finding idioms for them. . . . In the differend, something 'asks' to be put into phrases, and suffers from the wrong of not being able to be put into phrases right away" (13). In contrast, we can see in some Native literary approaches to cultural property a differend, a cultural difference with no translatable language, which not only accepts but affirms its own silence. If one postmodern holy grail is representation, the silence of a positive differend may speak the other postmodern holy word: difference.

One could say that this particular cross-cultural application of Lyotard's differend challenges his notion that the differend signifies a negation, but that would be too reductive. The point is that under different historical circumstances, Europe under fascism or the Americas under colonialism, similar patterns of representation, such as aporias described by the differend, generate different possibilities for reading and expression. Indeed, the danger is in transferring the model too easily from one set of historical circumstances to another, as Lyotard's admonitions elsewhere against metanarratives suggest. The crux is not to read the differend as the horrible vacuum that a reductive theory of Holocaust might suggest.[12]

The prospects for a kind of freedom through the differend translate into a certain positive postmodernism that writers as diverse as Vizenor, Hogan, Silko, and Welch envision in their various ways as well. In their cultural landscapes, slippery signs become tools or weapons, "wordarrows" of survival. Lyotard refers to an "honorable postmodernity" (*Differend* xiii), which might avoid both the nihilism of ideal uncertainty and the oppression of metanarratives, by recognizing the differend and then by looking for alternative forms of representation to bridge or to navigate that acknowledged gap. For a number of Native writers, the gap itself, the differend, becomes a valid semiotic, a "new signification" or a "new genre of discourse" in a postcolonial language.[13] Writers can manipulate those gaps to both reveal and conceal cultural property. This positive differend can prove a useful critical term for understanding evocative allusions to cultural property, such as Ghost Dance visions of buffalo, where the sacred is both unspoken and yet evoked by textual lacunae. The buffalo speaks for itself. A careful connotation can offer an articulate aporia, and the adequate representation of difference can remain silent on the need for explanations.

Difference might thus affirm itself as much through cultural silence as through description or proclamation. Such affirmations call for a new way of reading that would alter academic institutions. Encyclopedic aspirations might moderate themselves by recognition of cultural and historical limitations; universal claims might balanced with specific genealogies; definitive and reductive pronouncements might give way to exploratory respect. Whether focusing on cultural content or on processes of permission, attention to cultural property may have the effect of affirming cultural difference against universalizing tendencies, and thus may make more visible the dynamics of cultural survival in the discourse of Native literary studies.

Although corn, salmon, deer, caribou, whales, and other critters have provided the sacred subsistence of various tribes, the ultimate symbol of Native survival and defeat in the American unconscious is the "buffalo," or American Bison. Perhaps General Philip Sheridan said this best: "Let them kill, skin, and sell until the buffalo is destroyed . . . it is the only way to bring lasting peace and allow civilization to advance (Miller and Faux 8). In spite of an American cultural ideology of erasure, a more than nostalgic virtual America remains "where the buffalo roam," as the virtual American remains "the Indian."

In the pop cultural hands of dramatist Buffalo Bill Cody, in the hands of novelists Zane Grey or Louie L'Amour, or in the hands of Hollywood from D. W. Griffith to Kevin Costner, the buffalo is the sign of America's self-contradictory fantasy: both to possess and to destroy the American land and its original peoples. America's "high culture" of transcendentalism shares in this contradiction as well. In Thoreau's paean to America, "Walking," for example, he follows his manifesto, "in Wildness is the preservation of the World" (613), with supporting praise for a neighbor farmer "who intends to put a girdling ditch round the whole [swamp] in the course of forty months, and so redeem it by the magic of his spade" (618). This civilized swamp does not erase Thoreau's ideal "Dismal Swamp," the wildness of which he has just preferred to "the most beautiful garden that ever human art contrived" (616). The Concord monk's agrarianism may indeed see no contradiction in both revering and tilling the land. He describes farm work as connecting the farmer to the land toward the ultimate American fantasy of being more indigenous than the Indian: "It is said to be the task of the American 'to work the virgin soil,' and that 'agriculture here already assumes proportions unknown everywhere else.' I think that the farmer displaces the Indian even because he redeems the meadow, and so makes himself stronger and in some respects more natural" (617). Thoreau envisions this natural strength in context of a battle, with the ostensible enemy as wild nature itself, discreetly erasing the human indigenes who would put up active resistance: "The weapons with which we have gained our most important victories, which should be handed down as heirlooms from father to son, are not the sword and the lance, but the bushwhack, the turf-cutter, the spade, and the boghoe, rusted with the blood of many a meadow, and begrimed with the dust of many a hard-fought field" (618).

The Indian body on and in the land must be not only erased but also emasculated in this passage, where the warrior image pours into a single fatalistic reference to "the blood of many a meadow." Thereby, the buffalo, who would have grazed that meadow and who is to become the flip side of the Indian-head nickel, marks America's currency for emasculation and castration of the continent. In the cowboy's myth of the West, which Thoreau asserts "is but another name for the Wild" (612), the buffalo must be replaced by the castrated Texas longhorn steer, whose hyperextended phallic horns compensate America's testicle envy for the buffalo's eternal *cohones*. Subsequently, by the force of American agrarianism, the longhorn must be replaced by the Hereford beef and the Holstein dairy cow, as the cowboy must be by the farmer and his wife, in a land of the free and a home freed from the brave.[14]

Thus runs the highly racialized and highly gendered national narrative of erasure, of civilization as assimilation. Meanwhile, the projected testosterone anxieties of that narrative remain entirely unaware of the feminine qualities that various Native cultures attribute to the image of the buffalo, notably in the Lakotas' White Buffalo Calf Woman, who is the source of their sacred pipe, ceremonial life, and social structure.

In the hands of what Cherokee literary critic Jace Weaver calls "communitist" Native writers, the buffalo does not represent merely America's prelapsarian Adamic male nostalgia.[15] Instead, it becomes a positive differend — witness to and symbol of a silence across difference that is key to the survival of Native communities and their cultural property. That difference resonates with gendered and ritualistic power to nurture and survive as people. To Native writers from particular traditions, the buffalo remains sacred. Their literary references to the return of the buffalo reflect on both American readership and Native American cultural expression. The buffalo, like the land, can represent the past and the future of Native American cultural property, and how readers read those representations can reflect their recognition or lack of recognition of not only cultural property issues in relation to Native literatures but also the dynamics of survival that those literatures both articulate and reserve for silence.

The return of the buffalo, and of the Ghost Dance that invoked that return, are as radically revisionary of the American national narrative as is the notion of tribal sovereignty coexisting in a nation state like the United States. The implications of that historical revision are another reason for their silence in the literature. In 1831, when Supreme Court Chief Justice John Marshall circumlocuted the phrase "domestic dependent nations," he was forced into that language by the historical, legal, and practical reality of tribal sovereignty (even though the court decision *Cherokee Nation v. Georgia* worked against the tribe in that moment). Tribal sovereignty is the principle at the heart of the nineteenth-century Ghost Dance and the twentieth-century literary evocation of the return of the buffalo.

Tribal sovereignty as an economic and political principle survives as an open question in the literature and in the newspapers.[16] A key political dynamic as the millennium turns is the multiple negotiations between different ethnic groups and national states worldwide. Witness Yugoslavia. At this writing, the Serbs, the Kosovo Albanians, and NATO have failed in their negotiations and have reverted to military action over Kosovo autonomy. On another front with similar ancient military history, Scotland has had its parliament reinstated in negotiation with England after centuries of colonial hiatus and contestation. Wales is standing in line. A recent *New York Times Magazine* (February 21, 1999) highlights a historic moment. Is this "the end of Britain?" asks the cover article by Andrew Sullivan.[17] Tibet waits on China. The European Community waits on Denmark and Britain. On every continent, the millennial dream of a "united states" strives for balance between national and local powers. In this open sense of history and postcolonial change, Native writers continue to raise the question of tribal sovereignty.

That question is beginning to lose its monolithic stature, as well as its borrowed connotations from American and British law, with their feudal, hierarchical heritage. A binary colonial mind moving into nationalism could never conceive of a multicultural state, only a melting pot of erasure and assimilation. Perhaps an imperial sovereignty cannot understand a national sovereignty because the imperial impulse is absolute whereas the national impulse is relative. Indeed, in neither an earlier period of "international relations" nor in the emerging "global capitalism" was there ever a supremacy in sovereignty.[18]

Tribal nations rarely claimed imperial sovereignty over other nations.[19] Tribal sovereignty always was and still is defined as self-determination, a sense of nationhood or "peoplehood," as Vine Deloria Jr. (Yankton Sioux) puts it. This inability of American imperial sovereignty to comprehend tribal sovereignty is the problem of American conformity and assimilation against American pluralism.

However, gradual negotiations between American tribes and towns, counties, and states are beginning to sculpt "tribal sovereignty" into a twenty-first-century, postcolonial notion out of its fifteenth-century, colonial and precontact implacability. As the millennium turns and as some tribes assert economic and political power, there are numerous examples of emerging coexistent models. At Salamanca, New York, for instance, the Senecas have negotiated a renewed lease for the white town on the edge of their Allegheny Reservation after the town's ninety-nine-year lease ran out in the mid-1990s. In the Black Hills of South Dakota, the Sioux, after succeeding in the courts with their land claim but refusing Congress's monetary compensation, have clarified that their goal is not to evict private property owners, but to convert state and public lands, a large portion of their sacred Paha Sapa, into a Great Sioux National Park. The Mashantucket Pequots, with their newfound political strength built on economic development through gaming, are exploring their historical land rights. In New York, the current Oneida, Cayuga, and Seneca Grand Island land claims have emerged with challenges to the status quo of the vanishing Indian. Oren Lyons, a faithkeeper of the Onondaga Nation, also in New York, was cited in the *Syracuse Post Standard* in reference to an Onondaga land claim: "the chiefs are already involved in quiet negotiations with the Metropolitan Development Association about projects that would benefit both communities. Most important, Lyons said, his people understand how it feels to get thrown off your own land — and he said the Onondagas won't do that to someone else" (qtd. in *Syracuse Post Standard* B1, B5). These New York negotiations are founded also on centuries of intergovernmental experience between the state and the Iroquois Confederacy. If the League of Six Nations was a model for the American Constitution in a number of formative ways, it was not only in its democratic foundations and in its separation of powers but in its federated autonomy of nation states, its coexistent tribal sovereignties, as well.[20]

At the end of the twentieth century, that sovereignty became not a static entrenchment of in-group power, but, as Osage scholar Robert Warrior analyzes Vine Deloria Jr.'s view, a process: "Through this process-centered definition of sovereignty, Deloria is able to avoid making a declaration of what contemporary American Indian communities are or are not. . . . His straightforward warning against making the rhetoric of sovereignty and tradition a final rather than a beginning step remains an important reminder to those who engage in community, federal, and other Indian work" (91, 97). This flexible theory fits a historical moment in which more than five hundred separate tribal groups continue in widely divergent cultural and economic conditions. With various populations, resources, and levels of cultural and language continuity, tribal sovereignty can apply only as an organic process to each tribe's chosen balances. Indeed, this focused and tribally specific rather than pan-tribal approach to sovereignty affirms the "tribal" particularity, the difference, which is Native sovereignty's political and cultural goal. Thus Deloria's notion of tribal and local sovereignty "is oriented primarily toward the existence and continuance of the group" (*We Talk* 123).

Jace Weaver writes that this politic of group survival becomes "representational sovereignty" in the work of Native writers, against five centuries of colonial misrepresentation. "By (re)presenting the Indian, they are asserting Native representational sovereignty. It is a declaration that the Native is self-defining" (163). Yet the rhetoric of "definition," whether imposed by self or other, can upstage that politics of "process" that Deloria foregrounds. Vizenor's survivance, like Deloria's process, operates by a communal ability to sustain change and exchange, even while his "new ghost dance literature" invokes one of the most dramatic movements of self-definition in America. If we look closely at the dynamics of the Ghost Dance and at Native literary allusions to that long tradition of the return of the buffalo, we find principles of cultural exchange that conceive of current negotiations between sovereign federal nation and sovereign tribal nation, between authority and difference, between the universal and the particular, between self and other. The "new ghost dance literature" might conceive of tribal sovereignty *within* what America calls *e pluribus unum*. It begins to conceive of a functional "pluribus" that would redefine America's ideal "unum" by building on, rather than eradicating, robust difference.

Michael Elliott points out that the historical Ghost Dance held within it the very solutions that nineteenth-century American ethnographers, the American government, and the American army thought were problems. A colonial myopia often has projected "the Indian problem" onto its others. Elliott explains how James Mooney, sympathetic author of the Bureau of American Ethnology's 1896 best-selling *The Ghost Dance Religion and the Sioux Outbreak of 1890*, "shows us the reality of the Lakota suffering, but dismisses the possibility that the teachings of the Ghost Dance could have been part of a solution to the problems facing the Lakotas rather than, as the Army understood it, the problem itself" (221). Some ethnologists and government policymakers can see now, after a century of retrospect focused by Native critiques like Deloria's, that, again, "The responsibility which sovereignty creates is oriented primarily toward the existence and continuance of the group," and that the problem in 1890 was not the Ghost Dancers' efforts to reestablish their communities under colonial circumstances but those very colonial efforts to assimilate and erase Indian communities from a definition of American democracy and community. In a fascinating discussion of the ideology of "friends of the Indian," linked with American literary realism of the fin de siecle, Elliott explains,

As *realists*, they believed that they could take a hard-nosed look at U.S.-Native relations and devise more effective strategies for the survival of indigenous peoples by recognizing the economic issues at the heart of their understanding of the *real*. Working under the premise that the real was connected to a certain kind of suffering and to a particular relationship with property, the realist reformers' efforts to learn "what the real Indian is" were intimately connected to their contention that assimilation, rather than tribal sovereignty or revitalization, held the only possible solution to "the Indian question." (202)

Against white cultural notions of property, Elliott suggests that "tribal sovereignty or revitalization" of Indian communities might have been the solution a century prior to their emergence now as de facto prerequisites to the health of Native communities.[21] The different historical circumstances of the late nineteenth and twentieth centuries make such a comparison a larger question for a different study, yet the principle of sovereignty remains. Native sovereignty was as invisible to colonial eyes in the 1890s as in the 1990s, even while Ghost Dancers then and a "new ghost dance literature" now have tried to keep tribal sovereignty clearly in their view.

Gerald Vizenor describes the elusive energies of Native literature to survive, and his context for a "new ghost dance literature" is revealing: "The tribal characters dance with tricksters, birds, and animals, a stature that would trace the natural reason, coherent memories, transformations, and shadows in traditional stories. The shadows and language of tribal poets and novelists could be the new ghost dance literature, the shadow literature of liberation that enlivens tribal survivance" ("Ruins" 27–28). Vizenor's neologism *survivance* throws off the traces of tragic victimhood in *survival* and finds an acceptable tribal stature with *continuance* against *dominance*. Through contemporary writers' linkages and usages of oral traditional materials and forms, transforming "the shadows and language" into liberating stories of survivance, the literature imagines agency and cultural continuity.

Thus the Ghost Dance of the buffalo cultures and others holds within it prophetic principles of cultural exchange at the turn of the millennial century. Although individual and tribal differences over interpretations of Ghost Dance politics and philosophy have accompanied the movement since its beginning, writers such as McNickle, Hogan, Vizenor, Silko, and Welch articulate those principles in radical ways that might encompass both the exclusionary and inclusionary, the oppositional and alternative approaches. Tribal sovereignty might exclude or include non-Native presence on the land. By Oren Lyons's comments at Onondaga, it is inclusive. In literary treatments, these pluralistic principles form a matrix, a poetics, a methodology, a pragmatic process, which redefines and recontextualizes colonial polarities. These polarities map not only the academy but the white man's burden as well, beginning at logos/ chaos, trekking through civilization/wilderness, and marking the "boundary" between white/Indian. For the purposes of the following readings, I focus on various efflorescences of the binary in static and dynamic, or "pure" and "impure," culture in McNickle, in present and past in Hogan, in spirituality and agency in Silko, and finally in a complex blend of cultural narratives in Welch.

The Tewa anthropologist Alfonso Ortiz wrote an afterword to D'Arcy McNickle's (pre)historical novel *Runner in the Sun*, clarifying his new approach to polarized thinking about culture that had characterized the first century of ethnography. As Gerald Vizenor describes the problem, "The anthropologist would celebrate theories over imagination; in this sense, academic evidence was a euphemism for linguistic colonization of tribal memories and trickster narratives" (*Trickster* xiv). Both McNickle and Ortiz were indigenous professional anthropologists. Ortiz's literary analysis of McNickle, the Flathead Indian novelist, suggests that it never was necessary to define indigenous cultures out of imperialist nostalgia as pure and unchanging, in need of "salvage anthropology" to protect them from change, to protect pure culture from impurities over time. Together McNickle and Ortiz suggest that survival of cultural property can include alteration and adaptation of that property. As Ortiz writes,

McNickle demonstrates a continuity in Indian life and values from ancient times until the present, but his main concern, clearly, was the living Indian societies of his time and beyond. In telling of the first Americans he has pointed repeatedly to modern Indian societies as if to say that as long as Indians survive there is no reason for despair. They are the living embodiment of the peaceful ways of the ancient Americans and they retain for present and future generations the greater gift we once "let lie . . . the gift of peace on earth." (241)

Yet that utopian view is not static. Nor is it teleologically utopian. Rather, it is cyclic or emergent. In the terms of the novel, where an ancient Sonoran tribe faces starvation unless they replace their sacred strain of corn and import a new drought-resistant strain from the Aztecs far to the south, survival of the culture depends on change. Ortiz is suggesting that the Aztec civilization plays the role of colonizer in McNickle's allegory among the early Sonorans. Ortiz points to the binary: "Utter destruction looms as a possibility, and change provides the only possible solution. Besides change, there is another factor, culture, the role of which we have inadequately appreciated in determining Indian actions" (244). And on this set of apparent opposites in the novel, Ortiz shows how McNickle then builds a pragmatics of cultural continuity. He refers tellingly to McNickle's earlier novels set in contemporary colonized conflicts:

From the interaction of these two factors, change and culture, arises the problem of acculturation, or culture change, which he dealt with in a different way, first in *The Surrounded*, and later in *Wind from an Enemy Sky*. In both novels tragedy is the obvious consequence of a mistaken notion of acculturation, one which assumes that it is entirely a one-way process. The problem D'Arcy presents us with in *Runner* is the same, dealt with differently. Salt [the protagonist] is the prototype of the modern Indian, for whom the only hope lies in change. He sets out on a journey, a process which can lead to knowledge and wisdom. Like Salt, the modern Indian must know the alien culture that surrounds him in order to get what he needs for his survival. In the first two novels we find the consequences of this process as it is erroneously understood by many. In *Runner* we find a statement of what it should be, a "creative process in which there is selection, rejection, and modification or adaptation of elements." (244–45)

By a cultural act of political deconstruction, McNickle offers an alternative to the colonial view of acculturation as a one-way process. The colonial Other engages power assumed to reside only in the colonial self. The colonial view assumes the centralized power of the colonial *metropole*, of capital dominating its markets. Indeed, as Ortiz suggests above, the tragic plots of McNickle's earlier novels tend to reify that view of purity and impurity, of colonized powerlessness and colonizing power. Here in McNickle's later novel, however, he envisions a different kind of exchange, one that does not centralize power but decenters it in a positive pragmatics of Foucauldian capillary distribution of power.

If power is not a one-way street, Native writers can also redistribute powerlessness across the colonial divide in the name of reversing the present and past. In the poem "Return: Buffalo," Linda Hogan evokes the reemerging domination of the buffalo over the soul of both the Indian and the white. Because the buffalo is a colonial symbol of "the past," her affirmation of its haunting presence drives a wedge in the founding split of America from its own history, that gendered myth of the American Adam. The buffalo's present return is a final marker of colonial impotence, of a failure of American exceptionalism, of the deluded impossibility of the five-hundred-year project to "vanish" the Indian. Hogan begins by describing a nineteenth-century photograph of a hill of buffalo bones and by excavating the religious underpinnings of civilization's domination of the wilderness:

> One man made a ladder
> of stacked-up yellow bones
> to climb the dead
> toward his own salvation.
> he wanted light and fire, wanted
> to reach and be close to his god.
> But his god was the one
> who opened his shirt
> and revealed the scar of mortal climbing. (265)

She goes on to blend the scar of Christ's suffering with her own people's scar of memory of the decimated buffalo:

> It is a brother
> who heard the bellowing cry of sacred hills
> when nothing was there
> but stories and rocks. (266)

Hogan brings the imagery back to the Ghost Dance with an ironic loss and skepticism that set up the prophetic climax:

> It was what ghost dancers heard
> in their dream
> of bringing buffalo down from the sky
> as if a song and prayer
> were paths life would follow back
> to land. (266)

Toward a finale, she envisions a struggling buffalo emerging from the hunted corpses, in a spiritual dimension of survival alluding to Ghost Dancers' dreaming trances:

> and one was not dead
> or it had come back from there,
> walked out of the dark mountains
> of rotted flesh and bony fur,
> like a prophet

coming out from the hills
with a vision
too unholy to tell. (266)

Like Black Elk's Ghost Dance dream, or like the vision on the "yellow paper" in James Welch's *Fools Crow*, this buffalo travels in dream to the lands of the whites and "the future," only to return home with a message "too unholy to tell." "It must have traveled the endless journey / of fear" to return from "the far reaches / where men believed the world was flat," where they believed in "the pitiless fire" of hell and therefore had no real belief in the cyclic turns of life and death, of resurrection, of the return of the buffalo, as in the final lines about the coming invaders:

... and they must have thought
how life came together
was a casual matter,
war a righteous sin,
and betrayal
wasn't a round, naked thing
that would come back to them
one day. (267)

The white man's betrayal of life cycles must come round in the form of a baby buffalo, like a returning baby Jesus, the "Return: Buffalo" of Hogan's title, again making the opening link between Christian and Native imagery. The sacred return mixes ambiguously with historical, environmental, and ethical repercussions, while it reverses the power dynamics of the victors' history. The buffalo's return reverses the symbolic annihilation of Native cultural property.

Articulating these reversals, Leslie Silko, toward the end of her epic novel *Almanac of the Dead*, elucidates some of the dynamics of the Ghost Dance itself to reverse the tragic narrative that both Indians and non-Indians have been telling of that movement. Through layers of ironic play on the New Age movement, she sets up one of her prophets, Wilson Weasel Tail, to address the International Holistic Healers Convention. After he begins, one of the narrators, Lecha, is "impressed with the silence Weasel Tail had created in the main ballroom. 'Naturopaths,' holistic healers, herbalists, the guys with the orgone boxes and pyramids — all of them had locked up their cashboxes and closed their booths to listen to Weasel Tail talk" (723). He refers to a fictionalized James Mooney after he launches one of the most painful questions in Indian history:

"Today I wish to address the question as to whether the spirits of the ancestors in some way failed our people when the prophets called them to the Ghost Dance," Weasel Tail began.

"Moody and other anthropologists alleged the Ghost Dance disappeared because the people became disillusioned when the ghost shirts did not stop bullets and the Europeans did not vanish overnight. But it was the Europeans, not the Native Americans, who had expected results overnight; the anthropologists, who feverishly sought magic objects to postpone their own deaths, had misunderstood the power of the ghost shirts. Bullets of lead belong to the everyday world; ghost shirts belong to the realm of spirits and dreams. The ghost shirts gave the dancers spiritual protection while the white men dreamed of shirts that repelled bullets because they feared death." [quotation of Weasel Tail ends; narration begins]

Moody and the others had never understood the Ghost Dance was to reunite living people with the spirits of beloved ancestors lost in the five-hundred-year war. (722)

The question of whether this is a "spiritual" retreat from political agency dissolves by the end of *Almanac*, when the Native people of Chiapas begin their march north into the United States to enact the Ghost Dance vision: "they seek nothing less than the return of all tribal lands" (15). Silko is not negating political agency but is infusing it, or deconstructing it, with a nonbinary affirmation of spiritual power.

In her earlier novel *Ceremony*, she pointed to a liberating requirement, both spiritual and political, for non-Native America to face the buffalo. Rather than replay the oppositional binaries of history, a polarized violence that Silko mythologizes as "the witchery," the whites could reexamine their so-called manifest destiny as the projection of destructive forces. It is a complex revision of history, worth a larger quotation:

The liars had fooled everyone, white people and Indians alike; as long as the people believed the lies, they would never be able to see what had been done to them or what they were doing to each other. . . . If the white people never looked beyond the lie, to see that theirs was a nation built on stolen land, then they would never be able to understand how they had been used by the witchery; they would never know that they were still being manipulated by those who knew how to stir the ingredients together: white thievery and injustice boiling up the anger and hatred that would finally destroy the world: the starving against the fat, the colored against the white. The destroyers had only to set it into motion, and sit back to count the casualties. But it was more than a body count; the lies devoured white hearts, and for more than two hundred years white people had worked to fill their emptiness; they tried to glut the hollowness with patriotic wars and with great technology and the wealth it brought. And always they had been fooling themselves, and they knew it. (191)

The white man's binaries built on nature *versus* culture apparently serve only to desiccate culture against a more powerful earth. Thus the *Almanac of the Dead* can quote prophecy: "Ancient prophecies foretold the arrival of Europeans in the Americas. The ancient prophecies also foretell the disappearance of all things European" (14). Silko rallies indigenous people to a kind of radical patience.[22] Her view straddles a differend that maps time and space on the land in terms quite longer and stronger than terms of colonial invasion. Cultural property remains as long as the people remain on the land.

The disappearance of all things European depends on the eradication of an ideal linear history and its binaries of past and future, civilization and wilderness, in favor of not only a longer view but also a pragmatic and continually changing present. A return of the buffalo invokes this different history as an invocation of a different future. Rather than a metanarrative of manifest destiny, there continue to be specific moments when pragmatic possibilities for community can arise on the buffalo commons. In James Welch's novel *Fools Crow* those imperial forces of "history" contend over the protagonist's vision for Blackfeet survival. The protagonist of the title mourns over the future suffering of his people revealed to him on the "yellow paper" by the sacred Feather Woman. The irony and poignancy of the ending of the novel derive from its simultaneous evocation of both the reductive, linear, and fatal history of colonization and the complex, circular, and vital history of cultural survival, "it was as it should be":

When they were finished with the long ceremony, Mik-api lit the pipe and offered the smoke again to the sacred beings, as well as the four directions. After his offering to the Thunder Chief, the people smoked and prayed for good health, abundance and the ability to fulfill vows. They prayed for long summer grass, bushes thick with berries, all the things that grow in the ground-of-many-gifts. They prayed that the blackhorns would be thick all around them and nourish them as they had nourished the before-people. Far from the fires of the camps, out on the rain-dark prairies, in the swales and washes, on the rolling hills, the rivers of great animals moved. Their backs were dark with rain and the rain gathered and trickled down their shaggy heads. Some grazed, some slept. Some had begun to molt. Their dark horns glistened in the rain as they stood guard over the sleeping calves. The blackhorns had returned and, all around, it was as it should be. (388–89)

In this finale Welch envisions the buffalo in intimate detail, just as he has envisioned the buffalo culture of the 1870s Blackfeet in detail. This shaggy nineteenth-century foreground grazes on the twentieth-century reader's unrepresented background of loss and an impending "vision too unholy to tell." As a contemporary act of cultural representation, this passage may be read on the one hand as merely ironic, where the retrospective gaze of a linear, disastrous history sits ominously behind the affirmative surface of the words. The buffalo were soon decimated, so how could it possibly be "as it should be"? On the other hand, the moment may be read as a poignant embodiment of cultural affirmation, carefully layering and foregrounding that detailed vision over the claims of a retrospective colonial fatalism. "It was as it should be" because the circle turns, because history and cultural change might not be linear. Readers are invited to choose between these options, like Silko's different readings of the Ghost Dance. The instant, full of molting and regeneration, evokes the longer view of history, "Their dark horns glistened in the rain as they stood guard over the sleeping calves."

Welch invokes an American and Native American icon that evidently survives not only in ideology but also as culture, as property, and as presence on the land. These ways of representing and interpreting buffalo images do more than make visible a possibility of Native cultural survival. Not only do these writers give those representations back to their peoples, but they construct a way of seeing the buffalo and the American land that details the representational myopia of centuries of polarized history. That cultural myopia is the imperial gaze that would read Native representations, like Native lands, as property in the public domain. By reclaiming that representational property, Native writers are redefining the possibilities of American history.

NOTES

1. Kenneth Lincoln's *Native American Renaissance* celebrates that literary efflorescence, while other critics, for instance, A. LaVonne Brown Ruoff in *American Indian Literatures* or Helen Jaskowski in *Early Native American Writing*, have emphasized the point that Native publications have steadily proceeded since the colonial era.

2. Readers may know that the federal government still has fiduciary responsibility to protect trust resources of Native Americans as individual wards and as its "domestic dependent nations," even against states such as New York.

3. See the *Tribal College Journal* special issue entitled "Cultural Property Rights." "Copyright Law and Traditional Indigenous Knowledge of First Nations Peoples: A Resource and Information Guide" is available for US$10 from the Association of Aboriginal Post-Secondary Institutions: AAPSI, Education Resource Centre, 2nd Floor, 2280-B Louie Drive, Westbank BC, Canada V4T IY2; phone, 604–768–5488; fax, 604–768–5496; e-mail, *aapsierc@silk.net*. See also James D. Nason; Murray L. Wax; Vine Deloria Jr. ("Commentary: Research, Redskins, Reality"); and Devon A. Mihesuah. In October 1994, the Arizona–Sonora Desert Museum in Tucson, Arizona, held a conference entitled "Native American Intellectual Property Rights" and compiled a survey on ethical conflicts relating to Native American knowledge, beliefs, and resources in Arizona. Interested readers might also wish to contact the Pueblo Indian Study and Research Center in Albuquerque, New Mexico. For a broad perspective see Robert A. Williams, esp. pp. 6–7.

4. See my introduction (Moore 545–54) to a special issue of *American Indian Quar-*

terly on cultural property and my essay "Rough Knowledge and Radical Understanding" (633–62) in that volume.

5. For discussion of this legal evolution, see, for instance, Fikret Berkes; see also the special issue of *Cultural Survival Quarterly* entitled "Voices from the Commons: Evolving Relations of Property and Management." See also Jane Gaines for a poststructuralist, literary critical exploration of questions of individual and corporate ownership, the right to privacy versus the right to publicity, and the legal and cultural status of media images.

6. See also a probing article of the interrelations of racial identity and property in American legal discourse by Cheryl I. Harris: "Even as legal segregation was overturned, whiteness as property continued to serve as a barrier to effective change as the system of racial classification operated to protect entrenched power" (1709).

7. See, for instance, Vine Deloria Jr. on the exploitations by anthropologists of Indian traditions in *Custer Died for Your Sins*.

8. "In 1984, the World Council of Indigenous Peoples, an association of indigenous organizations from various countries, adopted the Declaration of Principles of Indigenous Rights. Principle 13 of the document affirms that 'the original rights to their material culture, including archaeological sites, artifacts, designs, technology and works of art lie with the indigenous people.' Though this declaration demonstrates one way in which indigenous peoples have tried to articulate and assert their rights, it carries little political weight and is considered inadequate in its ability to protect these rights" (United Nations Information Centre). The Society for Critical Exchange, Guilford House, Case Western Reserve University, sponsored a 1993 conference in Bellagio, Italy, on "Intellectual Property and the Construction of Authorship." The Bellagio Declaration, which emerged from that conference, articulates these issues clearly. Papers from that conference are slated for publication in a volume tentatively titled "Cultural Agency/Cultural Authority: Politics and Poetics of Intellectual Property in the Post-Colonial Era." See also Martha Woodmansee and Peter Jaszi. See also Shelton H. Davis.

9. Another obvious dimension to this dynamic, beyond the scope of this essay, is the Euro-American projection by missionaries, conquistadors, anthropologists, and Hollywood directors of their own cultural primitivist impulses onto Native cultures. See, for instance, Leah Dilworth or the classic studies by Berkhofer and Pearce.

10. For a discussion of some of this history, see, for instance, H. David Brumble III and Karl Kroeber. See also Bonnie Glass-Coffin.

11. Devon A. Mihesuah ("Voices"). A telling statement in Mihesuah's epilogue to this volume of the *American Indian Quarterly* blends the theory and practice of research and cultural property rights: "The Institutional Review Board at Northern Arizona University has recognized this problem and is asking researchers why they chose their projects and if the findings will benefit tribes or the authors" (98).

12. It should be noted, however, that Lyotard's *The Differend* and his later *Lessons on*

the *Analytic of the Sublime*, a commentary on Kant's "Critique of Judgment," connect the differend to the sublime, as I am here connecting it to the silence surrounding the sacred. In a further parallel to my dialogical argument, Lyotard also claims, in a section of *Sublime* entitled "Attempt to Resolve the Differend through a 'Dialectic,'" that "A dialectical reading . . . has no access to a sublime that is subjectively felt by thought as differend" (131).

13. Again see my essay "Rough Knowledge and Radical Understanding" for a discussion of this different semiotic in Native American literatures.

14. Compare the heterosexual male fantasies described in R. W. B. Lewis's *The American Adam* with the homoerotic male fantasies of the West in Leslie Fiedler's *Love and Death in the American Novel*.

15. "Communitism is related to Vizenor's 'survivance,' Warrior's 'intellectual sovereignty,' and Georges Sioui's 'autohistory.' . . . Literature is communitist to the extent that it has a proactive commitment to Native community, including what I term the 'wider community' of Creation itself. In communities that have too often been fractured and rendered dysfunctional by the effects of more than 500 years of colonialism, to promote communitist values means to participate in the healing of the grief and sense of exile felt by Native communities and the pained individuals in them" (Weaver xiii).

16. Fergus M. Bordewich's *Killing the White Man's Indian* is an often skeptical look at the resurgence of tribal sovereignty as a politic in Indian Country. For a broad historical perspective, see Ward Churchill (Tragedy).

17. Current discourse on the topic of local autonomies coins the term "devolution" to describe the erosion of empire and the return of colonial power from the *metropole* to the territories. For example, a short editorial published in the *Los Angeles Times*, headlined "The Theory of Devolution," stated that "The challenge for British Prime Minister Tony Blair and the devolution elections earlier this month in Scotland and Wales was how to preserve the United Kingdom under a formula fair to all." This language reveals the cultural contradictions that require a backward prefix *de-* to reify the "evolutionary" view of colonial history by giving its revolutionary, even cyclic, momentum a negative spin. This discursive confusion leads to remarkably polarized rhetorical valences, as in a description of Blair's willingness to cede powers to a local assembly in Northern Ireland to advance the peace process as "a step toward devolution."

18. Arnold Krupat, in *The Turn to the Native*, addresses this historical phenomenon of relative sovereignty from a different perspective: "Lest this seem to denigrate Native Americans' desire in these regards, it should be said that in the present moment of transnational capitalism, no state or nation has sovereignty in the strong sense of the dictionary definition" (15). He cites Vine Deloria Jr. and Clifford M. Lytle's *The Nations Within* (329) in this regard as the authors summon Monaco, Liechtenstein, and Luxembourg as examples of relative sovereignties.

19. The additional power of tribal confederations such as the Iroquois was built largely on relative [national] sovereignties that formed a model for American states' rights.

20. See Jose Barreiro.

21. The Indian Self-Determination Act was passed in January 1975, and in spite of its legislative title it maintains clear federal controls on tribal sovereignty. The Indian Gaming Act of 1988 included further erosion of tribal sovereignty in relation to states.

22. See my article "Silko's Blood Sacrifice."

These people [tourists] would look and every once in awhile they'd pick up something but in a strange way I think they were interested in us, too. But nobody ever really looked at each other. It was a strange, strange encounter.

Rena Swentzell [Santa Clara Pueblo], in
Inventing the Southwest: The Fred Harvey Company and Native American Art

Representation and Cultural Sovereignty

Some Case Studies

DAVID MURRAY

Representations are what we all live by and with, not only as scholars but also as citizens and members of communities, but the dangers involved in the control of representation are as great, if not always as evident, as the need for representation itself. One difficulty lies in the double role of representation. At one level it means the recording or copying of something, as in an aesthetic or documentary account. The process is therefore one of "standing for" something else. At another level, though, it means "standing-for," or speaking for, a person or whole community as in the sense of political representation. In both cases the constant danger is of the representative replacing or obscuring what is meant to be visible "through" it — and in so doing threatening a whole complex of ideas that rely on being able to keep a clear distinction between what is real or one's own and what is represented, clustered around the idea of the proper (property, propriety, appropriation, and ultimately sovereignty).

The effect of the deconstructive critique of this view of representation has been to question whether it is ever possible to conceive of a world prior to representations and to stress the instability of a representation's relation as "supplement" to what it represents — both an addition and a replacement. Taken seriously, this critique may lead us to reexamine some of the distinctions on which discussions of proper representation as well as cultural appropriation have been based.[1] Given the way in which Native Americans as individuals and communities have been misrepresented, politically and culturally, over many years, and given the current importance of cultural and political self-representation and self-determination, it is not surprising that the present diverse range of writings that constitute Indian literatures are the site of continuing debate over what is, or should be, representative. This essay explores the linked ideas of cultural representation, appropriation, and authority through a number of rather diverse examples.

One of the clearest and most uncompromising positions on the need for

American Indian writers to be aware of their representative role is that of Eliza-beth Cook-Lynn. In her essay "American Indian Fiction Writers," significantly subtitled "Cosmopolitanism, Nationalism, the Third World, and First Nation Sovereignty," she voices her misgivings about the failure of most Indian writers to match in their writings the political efforts being made by Indian nations "to defend sovereign definition in the new world" (*Why* 82). For Indian writers the body of nationalist material made up of myth, history, and earlier cultural ex-pressions "must form the body of the critical discourse that functions in the name of the people; the presence of the Indian nation as cultural force" (85). Instead, according to Cook-Lynn, we have the demoralizing cosmopolitanism of so many contemporary writers, whose popularity with mainstream America seems related to their presentation of Indians as "gatherings of exiles, emi-grants, and refugees, strangers to themselves and their lands, pawns in the con-trol of white manipulators, mixedbloods searching for identity" (86).

Cook-Lynn's approach makes a direct connection between political and cultural sovereignty, and she wants to protect and nurture "the myths and metaphors of sovereign nationalism," which need to operate as "the so-called gold standard against which everything can be judged" (84). For this to hap-pen, a degree of protectionism, an insistence on boundaries, is necessary as a bulwark against the forces of cosmopolitanism. The economic metaphor of the gold standard is revealing. For Cook-Lynn there needs to be a fixed standard of value by which things can be judged — in this case the nation and the national interest, as opposed to the relative or exchange value created by circulation across economies or cultures. Cook-Lynn's bold line here throws into very clear relief the differences between a socially engaged and committed literature and a free-floating or cosmopolitan aesthetic. It seems to me unfortunate that the deeply unfashionable nature of Marxist approaches has restricted and dis-torted a still very necessary debate over realism and other literary forms, with the result that to describe her approach as in the tradition of Lukacs and social realism will sound to many, especially in America, like a pejorative dismissal, but in many respects this is still one of the few Western traditions that offers any sustained examination of the role of the artist other than as a free-floating creator.[2] One of the key issues has always been that of control and of who has the authority to exert it, whether cultural or political. In other words, who con-stitutes the representative body that has the authority to control representa-tion? Cook-Lynn regrets that "Indigenous peoples are no longer in charge of what is imagined about them, and this means that they can no longer freely imagine themselves as they once were and as they might become" (143).

The problem term here, I think, is "no longer," in that it can be seen in two different contexts. It may be true that indigenous people now have less control over their own self-representations, but when did any group have complete control over how others imagined or represented them? And what right would they have to do so? This raises the crucial question of boundaries and the proper limits of cultural property and sovereignty, a theme explored by many Indian writers in ways opposed to Cook-Lynn, as well as many critics and commentators. To take one brief example, Linda Hogan, in two poems in her collection *Seeing through the Sun*, offers a series of images of personal and cultural identity and its boundaries. In "Wall Songs" she contrasts the wall created by the southern jungle, which grows over the roads and divisions created by men to "keep things separate" from the other walls that divide classes and peoples and "rise up like teeth out of the land / snapping Do Not Enter." In addition, there is the image of skin, which is boundary of the self but can also be a means of communication and connection, when "a lover / and I turn our flesh to bridges" (68). Her final conclusion here that "boundaries are all lies" is rather more positive and perhaps simplistic than her position in the poem "The Truth Is," which also deals with identity. Here she uses the idea of each of her hands representing a different aspect of her, a Chickasaw hand and a white hand. Don't worry, she tells us about the white hand in her pocket, "It's mine / and not some thief's." She dismisses an easy accommodation, or a positive view of hybridity that could be expressed as "a tree, grafted branches / bearing two kinds of fruit."

> The truth is
> we are crowded together
> and knock against each other at night
> We want amnesty
>
> Here I am, taped together
> like some old Civilian Conservation Corps
> passed by from the Great Depression
> and my pockets are empty.
> It's just as well since they are masks
> for the soul, and since coins and keys
> both have the sharp teeth of property. (4)

It may be "dangerous to be a woman of two countries" with "your hands in the dark of two empty pockets," but the property to be found in the pockets (keys and coins) represents a control of exchange and circulation (reminiscent of Cook-Lynn's gold standard) that she rejects. So do we see Hogan's poem as representing a defeatism consequent on personal introspection rather than the nationalist responsibility described by Cook-Lynn, or as an exploration of the freedoms of boundary crossing and free movement?

The terms here of hybridity and syncretism are, of course, the subject of extensive theoretical debate involving the general political and intellectual project of multiculturalism. Clearly any new openness to plurality, mixedness, and fluidity would seem to be something to be welcomed, and yet the very upbeatness of some of the celebrations of fluidity, and the easiness with which they fit with the positive values of multiculturalism, start to induce a sort of queasiness. Just as the poststructuralist stress on the circulation of signs, on meaning created by and within circulation and exchange, comes uncomfortably close to a capitalist apotheosis of exchange value, in obliterating concepts of use or labor as critical points of value that could offer some critical leverage on exchange value, so the idea of syncretic, invented, and re-created identity starts to sound uncomfortably congruent with the idea of the ultimate consumer, adaptable and, above all, ultimately interchangeable. This would be the universalism of the Enlightenment reduced to a universalism of common and homogenized needs.[3] As two recent commentators, Ella Shohat and Robert Stam, have put it: "As a descriptive catch-all term, 'hybridity' fails to discriminate between the diverse modalities of hybridity: colonial imposition, obligatory assimilation, political cooptation, cultural mimicry, and so forth. Elites have always made co-optive top-down raids on subaltern cultures, while the dominated have always 'signified' and parodied as well as emulated elite practice. Hybridity, in other words, is power-laden and asymmetrical.... Hybridity is also cooptable" (qtd. in McClaren 89). As well as undermining damaging boundaries of racism and chauvinism, the danger is that, as Peter McClaren has argued, "viewing identity as *mestizaje* . . . also opposes the challenge of some new forms of sociality based on cooperation, imagination, translocal cultural expressions" — and, we might add, some very old forms (88).

Seen in this light, Cook-Lynn's stubborn drawing of lines can be seen as an insistence on an irreducible difference, a point beyond which the circulation and exchange — and therefore co-optation, assimilation, and translation — will not go. Whether we want to call this strategic essentialism or whether this is to give the game away, to allow that in some sense all *is* convertible and reducible is another matter. Rather than just discuss this theme in general, though, I want to backtrack and look at one particular point that may help to throw into relief some of the issues surrounding cultural authenticity and authority, and in particular the difficulty involved in establishing boundaries and authority in a situation in which cultures are seen relationally rather than separately. Indian culture has been closely connected in Western thinking with ideas of authenticity and origins, and the ways in which elements of Indianness have been recirculated and denatured within white forms and systems have by now been fairly thoroughly documented. The use of Indian motifs or materials in various works of early American modernism, and their implicit relation to representations of African American culture, and, by contrast, uses of the same conjunction of Indian and African American elements in contemporary Indian literature are the basis of this examination.

Although Indians had been represented quite extensively in terms of the Romantic idealization of the natural and simple, both in Europe and America, the modernist interest in primitive art in Europe in the early years of the twentieth century influenced American painters and artists to reconceptualize the significance of Indian culture, but this new approach needs to be seen as a larger engagement with otherness. The modernist construction of a primitivist Other has recently been described by Barkan and Bush as "the defensive expression of a specific moment of crisis — the prehistory of a future whose unsettling shadow had just crossed the horizon" (2). From a contemporary postcolonial perspective, this sense of cultural transition and crisis within the West itself, with its accompanying sense of fragmentation and loss of community, could be seen as the result of not so much a loss as an implosion of empire, in which the racial Other eventually invades the metropolitan space itself, and therefore connects up very directly with debates of our own time.[4] There are ways in which the differing uses of African and Native American materials in Europe and America reflect a varying ability to see these groups as separate, primitive, and timeless, given the close involvement of African Americans with quintessentially modern cultural forms and the white mind's association of Indians with archaic ones.

In Europe one common strand of the interest in the primitive was an appropriation of objects and elements from other cultures in such a way as to elide and avoid the issue of the Europeans' historical and political relation to them. This happened in two ways. First, in positing primitive peoples as a totality as organic and static, Western artists were able to use any piece of work metonymically and see it as primal, universal, and original. Secondly, once any work was seen that way, it was possible to ignore the historical contingencies of colonialism. In fact, pure tribal objects, songs, and myths had histories and individual producers, but it is part of what Johannes Fabian has called the denial of coevalness to posit for them a place outside history.[5]

Nowhere is this more true than in the way that expressions of African American culture were treated in Europe as primitive and therefore unproblematically connected with Africa. The enthusiasm for Florence Mills, who sang and danced in a series of shows in London and Paris, including *Plantation Revue* and *Blackbirds*, and, especially in France, Josephine Baker, with her semi-naked *danse sauvage* in the *Revue négre*, as well as for a series of jazz bands, tended to be expressed in terms of their atavistic and primitive qualities. This appetite was then duly catered to in the presentation and selling of these shows.

Of course, there were those even at the time who could see this as an expression of the needs of the West rather than as any sort of expression of a primitive reality, and it is interesting to see the terms in which in France the conjunction of the ethnographic and the aesthetic is explored in perhaps its most informed and imaginative expression through the *Documents* group, whose members included Michel Leiris, Marcel Griaule, and Georges Bataille. Bataille referred to Lew Leslie's Negro revue *Blackbirds*, which performed in Paris in 1929, not as primal or primitive but as related to the needs of a febrile and ailing Western society. "The blacks who (in America or elsewhere) are civilized along with us and who, today, dance and cry out, are marshy emanations of the decomposition who are set aflame above this immense cemetery: so, in a vaguely lunar Negro night, we are witnessing an intoxicating dementia of dubious and charming will-o'-the-wisps, writing and yelling like bursts of laughter" (*Encyclopaedia Acephalica* 36–37).

On the whole, though, in Europe the need is to find a pure origin that can be linked in complex ways with the denial of the historical complicity with the realities of colonial exploitation. In moving from Europe to America, however, we find a complex set of similarities and differences. At one level it is easy to see the similarities, as America takes over European modernist concerns and styles, as famously through the Armory Show and the presence of African sculpture in Alfred Stieglitz's 1915 exhibition at the 291 Gallery. Interestingly, this was reported in a newspaper at the time under the heading "African Savages the First Futurists," reflecting the coalescence of the modern and the primitive, as well as the distinct ambivalence of the press reaction (Rubin 463). Where better than America, indeed, the quintessence of the modern, but also the source of many of the expressions of the primitive taken over by Europe, in the form of the Indian and the Negro, for modern and primitive to find a coalescence? But as soon as we introduce these elements of race, the differences between the American and European situations become crucial, and at this point it is useful to introduce a distinction made by Helen Carr between what she calls "the eclectic primitivism and exoticism of cosmopolitan, internationalist modernist artists and the emphasis of a particular heritage to form the basis of a cultural nationalism" (212). She is referring to a postcolonial use of native heritage as a way of decentering the Western assumptions of progress and superiority, which can range from Ireland to Latin America, but for my purposes here, the particular usefulness of the distinction is that it points to the complexity of the American situation, where we have side by side the cosmopolitan white modernists, influenced by Europe to use the materials of America eclectically, and the Indians and African Americans themselves, who are objects of this treatment, created as exotic primitives, but who are also potentially postcolonial re-creators of their image and their heritage for themselves.

A good example of the way Carr's category of white cosmopolitan modernist starts to change between Europe and America can be found in the work of the painter Marsden Hartley and his use of Indian motifs in his paintings and writings. Preceding any specific involvement with Indians in America on Hartley's part was his encounter with Indian artifacts in museums in Germany and France during his association with leading European modernists around 1914. As Gail Scott tells us, "Indian road shows, artifacts and culture were immensely popular in Europe during that pre-war period, and Marsden Hartley — along with many of his European artist colleagues — frequented Berlin's Ethnographical Museum and Paris's Trocadero Museum, where large collections of American Indian art had been gathered" (Hartley, *Collected* 328).[6] We might question whether these items, which included bead- and leatherwork from the Plains, pottery from the Southwest, and wood carving from the Northwest Coast, were being exhibited and seen as art, as Scott says, or as a part of the exciting conjunction of exotic and discontinuous elements that so excited the surrealists in their responses to collection.[7] In fact, it is interesting that unlike African sculpture, Indian materials were not exhibited specifically as art until the late 1930s.[8]

While in Europe Hartley painted a series of paintings, beginning in 1914, with names such as "Indian Compositions" and "Indian Fantasy," which incorporated traditional Indian images into a modernist assemblage of designs and abstract forms. He referred to this series as his "Amerika" paintings.[9] The effect of the spelling here suggests perhaps a German view of America, in which America is seen as itself primitive, and therefore representable by its primitives in European eyes, but in fact Hartley's own time in Europe had given him an outsider's view, too. The use of *k* also suggests a primitive dimension, and it is interesting that much later, the substitution of *k* for *c* in Black Power writings and slogans also signified a move from American to African orientation, a strategic political invocation of a primitive bogeyman of white America (and with echoes of the use of the letter by the Ku Klux Klan perhaps as well). Here, though, Hartley's titles reflect the way the Indian is exotic *within* America but also potentially representative *of* America itself, and it is this ambiguous status that I want to pursue.

A conceptual framework already existed in which the Indian was, at the same time, both a symbol of America, representing the original and natural, as opposed to Europe, and, under America's manifest destiny, a symbol of what had to be effaced and removed in order for America to exist as a historical, modern nation. This second aspect can be erased, though, in an ideological maneuver by which white artists can take on the spirit of the "vanishing American," and both Marsden Hartley and his fellow painter Max Weber wrote articles calling for a new American aesthetic based on Indian artistic values. During his trips back to America at this time, Hartley visited the Southwest and, like countless other artists and writers of the time, found what were apparently simple, natural cultures, imbued with aesthetic values inseparable from that natural life, which contrasted sharply with the materialism and shallowness of modern life. This view was reflected in his poem "The Festival of the Corn." This was the original and essential America that could be claimed as their own, not the modern America of cities, commerce, and mechanization. Primitivist modernism, then, sets itself against the threat of mass society. As Dilworth points out, "what these arguments about the Southwest's superior aesthetic value were also speaking about was class. . . . As much as artists were 'othering' themselves in their alliance with the region or with native Americans, they occupied an elite realm. They maintained strict boundaries between art and mass culture" (189). The artist was in a position to recognize this and therefore to take over from the tragically but inevitably vanishing Indians. In one of two articles he wrote on the subject, Hartley insists that "We are not nearly as original as we fool ourselves into thinking," but nevertheless, "We have the excellent encouragement of redman aesthetics to establish ourselves firmly with an aesthetic of our own" (14). It is worth considering what Hartley means here by "original": innovative, in the modern sense, or existing from the beginning, as in the primitivist sense? And is the move from "redman" to "our own" one of continuity or replacement? One of the conceits used in both essays is of the Indian as aristocratic guest and the whites as the inhospitable hosts. "Inasmuch as we have the evidence of a fine aristocracy among us still, it would seem as if it behooved us as a respectable host to let the redman entertain himself as he will" ("Red Man" 12). This rather breathtaking flight of fancy (in that it is, of course, diametrically opposed to the historical reality in which whites are the less-than-welcome intruders or guests) allows Hartley to present the Indian as temporary, about to leave, and the whites as permanent owners and inhabitors, so that his idealized view of these timeless and noble people is, as so often, only the flipside of an imperialist assumption of the manifest destiny of the whites to replace them, and the aesthetic aura is produced by the idea of their transience. At points he seems to argue for their preservation, but it is really their aesthetic that concerns him. "It would seem to me to be a sign of modernism in us to preserve the living esthetic splendors in our midst" (13).

Hartley contributed poems to Harriet Monroe's magazine *Poetry*, which in 1917 had a special issue on American Indian poetry, or Aboriginal poetry, as it called the poetry, offering "not translations but interpretations." The collection is a strange mixture, reflecting the same uneasiness as Hartley's about authenticity and originality, but one of the contributors, Mary Austin, develops some of these same ideas in her later volume of Indian poetry, *The American Rhythm*, in 1923 and then in an enlarged version in 1930. She offers "reexpressions" of American Indian song in which she finds a rhythm that is formed from an engagement with the land of America itself and is therefore potentially shareable by all the later Americans, "the very pulse of emerging American consciousness" (Chapman 11). In an earlier essay Austin had rejoiced that "Probably never before has it occurred that the intimate thought of a whole people should be made known through its most personal medium to another people whose unavoidable destiny it is to carry that thought to fulfillment and make of that medium a characteristic literary vehicle" (267). This gives the poetry a universal, transhistorical quality, which would be "the means by which men and their occasions are rewoven from time to time with their allness; and who is there to tell me that this, in art, is not the essence of modernity?" (57). This rather staggering non sequitur introducing modernity manages to cancel out historical differences, revealing in a usefully simplified and overt form the ideological work being done by the word *original* in the quotations from Hartley referred to above. This reweaving and unifying is crucial, as is the stress on the communal, in invoking an idea and an ideal of the original and primal America, but what is also intriguing is what needs to be carefully excluded.

Hartley points out that up to now the only recognizable Native expression was one with which Americans were less than delighted. "Other nations of the world have long since recognized Congo originality." For white Americans, though, it would be much more comfortable to claim kinship with the red, rather than the black, Native. "It is singular enough that the as yet remote black man contributes the only native representation of rhythm and melody we possess. As an intelligent race, we are not even sure we want to welcome him as completely as we might, if his color were just a shade warmer, a shade nearer our own" ("Red Man" 12–13). Why African Americans should be "as yet remote" in comparison with Indians or their color less "warm" than whites need not detain us, but we find in Mary Austin the same determination to privilege the Indian and exclude the African American. She defines the positive effects of rhythm in such a way as almost entirely to exclude what to most people of the time would be the most obvious instance of American rhythm, namely jazz. "The Amerind," she says, "admits none of the bond-loosening, soul-disintegrating, jazz-born movements of Mr. Sandburg's Man Hunt," which would lead to "spiritual disintegration." She is obviously bothered about how to cope with jazz and returns to it later in a long footnote. As jazz is "a reversion" to our earliest responses it could create disintegration, which would make "an excessive exclusive indulgence in jazz as dangerous as the moralists think it," whereas an intelligent use of it "might play an important part in that unharnessing of traditional inhibitions of response indispensable to the formation of a democratic society." So "original" must not be regressive or atavistic, and I think it is clear here that Austin is really skirting around race. The implication seems to be that jazz is acceptable when used intelligently (by whites of a certain class and education presumably), but when "indulged in" as by blacks, it is bad, whereas there are no such reservations expressed about Indian rhythms. In this she reflects the curious way in which jazz, when it was attacked, was said to be both mechanical and primitive, raising the specter of an inhuman and disintegrating modernity as well as a bestial savagery. Given this reactionary configuration, it is perhaps not surprising then to find Austin recycling the anti-Semitic characterization of the Jew to be found widely in modernist writing as the ultimate rootless cosmopolitan. Can the Jew, she asks, with his "short pendulum-swing between mystical orthodoxy and a sterile ethical culture . . . become the commentator, the arbiter, of American art and American thinking?" (qtd. in Dilworth 190).

If we return to Carr's distinction, then, we have a nationalist primitivism, but not one growing out of a particular heritage so much as latching on to a supposed heritage, claimed by means of a mystique of environmental kinship. Austin's privileging of Indian rather than African American as representative of America is characteristic of a larger maneuver that is later expressed as the concern for ethnicity as opposed to race.[10] If Europe could take two very different American products, Indian and African American cultural expressions, and subject them to the same decontextualizing and dehistoricizing operation in order to make them serve in their different ways as primitive, and primal, it was not so easy for white Americans. America could not so easily be turned into "Amerika," because the relation to these primitive others was not that of France or England to distant colonies, but a much closer and more ambiguous relation, stretching over centuries and deeply involved with the actual identity of Americans. The European use of both blacks and Indians to represent America, to stand metonymically for its primal and original energies, could not be so easily adapted by Americans. America, seen for so long by Europe as without culture, finally made an impact, but as Phyllis Rose, one of Josephine Baker's biographers, put it, "when it finally turned a face to Europe that face was black" (qtd. in Douglas 353). Clearly this was not a self-identification with which white Americans could be happy, given the unavoidable historical and political reality of racism and segregation. It is interesting to note that America's contribution to the 1931 International Colonial Exhibition in Paris included an Indian jazz band, known as the United States Jazz Band, in which Molly Spotted Elk played the tom tom and performed some Indian dances.[11]

Insofar as Indian was associated with purity and authenticity and African American with a meretricious modernity and hybridity, this affected not just white writers and artists like Austin and Hartley but any Indian writer whose work inevitably circulated in the same intellectual climate and was affected by the same patterns of production and distribution. I would suggest that this white-created cultural niche plus the real circumstances of cultural survival, which would inevitably involve a privileging of what was being destroyed rather than the valuing of the new forms and adaptations being created within the changing societies, resulted in a complex fusion of the aesthetic and sacred that focused on purity and origins rather than mixtures and inventions — or, to invoke Paul Gilroy's work on the Black Atlantic, on roots rather than routes. Those themes and forms of Indian literature that were therefore most widely acceptable were those most easily recognizable within the Western tradition as continuous with the concerns of Romantic nature poetry and a larger nostalgia for lost origins as expressed in early modernist fiction and poetry. (And a look in the New Age section of any bookshop would suggest that this is not just a thing of the past.) It is against this cultural background that we need to see the truly innovative work of recent Native American writers, in their refusal of traditional roles, or what had been assigned as traditional by the mainstream, as well as in the context of Cook-Lynn's nationalist demands. Looked at this way, the concern for mixedness, for impurities of all sorts, whether formal or racial, can be seen not so much as a refusal or betrayal of an Indian heritage or identity as a refusal of the limiting and simplified purities and archaisms of mainstream representations of Indians. In other words, it is an expression of those syncretizing and adaptive qualities that have been so crucial in cultural survival for Native Americans and that have not always been to the fore in Indian literature and especially in its reception and criticism. Clearly, recent critical works like Louis Owens's *Other Destinies*, which stresses the idea of the mixed-blood, not just racially but culturally, reflect a new emphasis in writers like Gerald Vizenor but also remind us of the existence of this theme in earlier writers, previously obscured by limiting assumptions about what Indian literature can or should be.[12]

Having dealt with some white representations of the differential role of Indians and African Americans, to typify what can be called the "purity-maneuver," I want to give a couple of eclectic and nonrepresentative instances of Indian representations. At the beginning of Sherman Alexie's *Reservation*

Blues, the legendary African American blues singer Robert Johnson arrives at the Spokane reservation. The novel is prefaced with the lyrics of one of Johnson's most famous songs ("I went down to the crossroad / fell down upon my knees"), around which the legend of Johnson's pact with the devil at the crossroads has developed, and with a quotation from the jazzman Charles Mingus, and this reflects the resolutely mixed and nontraditional tone of the book. While Johnson goes for help to a rather mysterious but spiritually powerful Indian woman, Big Mom, his guitar, with the power to inspire those who play it, triggers the success of a scratch group made up of Spokane Indians and two part-Flathead girls and calling itself Coyote Springs.

Their music is not traditional, as Alexie stresses, but is an "all-Indian rock and blues band."[13] When they appear in public, "A lot of New Agers showed up with their crystals, expecting to hear some ancient Indian wisdom and got a good dose of Sex Pistols covers instead" (40–41). They fail eventually, after being flown to New York to audition by white agents, whose names, Sheridan and Wright, suggest the U.S. Army generals of the last century. (Wright, in fact, seems to have been responsible for shooting the horses of the Spokane people, and the screams of these horses recur through the book.) Though rejecting the band, the producers latch on to the two white girl groupies and backup singers who are then packaged to offer all the acceptable aspects of Indianness for a mass market. Alexie gives us the lyrics of their song, which manage to invoke all the traditional Indian themes that have become clichés in popular representations.

> Can you hear the eagle crying?
> Can you hear the eagle crying?
> I look to the four directions
> And try to find some connection
> With Mother Earth, Mother Earth
> And my hair is blonde,
> But I'm Indian in my bones
> And my skin is white,
> But I'm Indian in my bones. (296)

There are echoes here of the strategy of Mary Austin, and Alexie is clearly critical of this sort of expropriative Indian essentialism, but he is also humorously critical of essentialism as it operates from within the Indian community. He gives us the text of an open letter in the local press criticizing the group's "ability to represent the Spokane tribe" given their association with white women and the Flathead identity of two of them. "Do we really want other people to think we are like this band? Do we really want people to think that the Spokanes are a crazy storyteller, a couple of irresponsible drunks, a pair of Flathead Indians and two white women? I don't think so" (175–76).

There is also, of course, some self-reflexive irony here about Alexie's own representativeness in his own project in this book, which as I understand it is to stress the irredeemably modern and mixed nature of Indian identity. In a very powerful passage that immediately precedes this letter, Thomas, the main character, hears Robert Johnson's voice. "Then the music stopped. The reservation exhaled. Those blues created memories for the Spokanes but they refused to claim them. Those blues lit up a new road, but the Spokanes pulled out their old maps. Those blues churned up generations of anger and pain: car wrecks, suicides, murders. Those blues were ancient, aboriginal, indigenous" (174). This is a complicated passage, and we can combine it with the ending of the book, if only because endings are so often revealing in locating some sort of ultimate value center in a book. Here we have Thomas and the two girls leaving the reservation for the city after the suicide of one of the band members. Robert Johnson stays with Big Mom, who sits in her rocking chair "measuring time with her back and forth, back and forth, back and forth there on the Spokane Indian Reservation. She sang a protection song, so none of the Indians, not one, would forget who they are" (306).

At one level then, there is a contrast of linear movement, expressing the new, with a timeless or cyclic movement that conserves, but in fact on the road to the city the three are accompanied by the shadow horses that have reappeared through the novel and whose slaughter in the last century represented white brutality. Big Mom seems to have re-created them, and the remaining members of the band in the car "sang together with the shadow horses: we are alive, we'll keep living. Songs were waiting for them up there in the dark. Songs were waiting for them in the city. Thomas drove the car through the dark. He drove. Checkers and Chess reached out of their windows and held tightly to the manes of the shadow horses running alongside the blue van" (306).

There is clearly an attempt here to blend together the traditional and the modern, to refuse the dichotomies within which Indians and Indian culture have been (mis)represented, but it is arguable whether this foregrounding of the mythic and traditional quite reflects the book as a whole, or indeed its particular strengths, or whether it is possible to rehabilitate or re-appropriate images that are already so heavily overdetermined. This raises the larger question of the extent to which traditional elements in works that use modern and traditional elements in apparently playful postmodern conjunctions are really still operating as, or can be received as, ultimately redemptive and traditional images.[14]

Where Alexie presents a playful conjunction of cultures, Leslie Silko's extensive and inclusive approach in her *Almanac of the Dead* is a much more serious affair, both aesthetically and politically. In the novel North American Indian history is placed in a larger narrative of global politics, and although the center of the novel is her native Southwest, it ultimately takes its place in a larger prophetic vision of the triumph of the Third World over America and the West, which involves a concern for cultural and political movements originating in South America and elsewhere, reflected in the titling of large sections of the book "Mexico" and "Africa." One of the prosecutors of the coming revolution, a black veteran of the Vietnam War makes radio broadcasts about the mixing of Indians and African slaves and the "first black Indian." The epic sweep of Silko's book draws a guarded approval from Cook-Lynn in that it adopts a nationalist and Third-World approach and creates a pan-Indian journey toward retribution rather than catering to a "nonindigenous mainstream readership," but its very inclusiveness also presents her with a problem. "While this is a heartening focus," writes Cook-Lynn, "it too fails in this nationalist approach, since it does not take into account the specific kind of tribal/nation status of the original occupants of this continent. There is no apparatus that allows the tribally specific treaty-status paradigm to be realized either in Silko's fiction or in the pan-Indian approaches to history" (*Why* 93).

This is the same reasoning that leads her to reject elsewhere the equating of Indian political aims with those related to civil rights, but here again we have the problematic equation of political and cultural sovereignty, which risks not doing justice to Silko's enterprise, by judging it in very circumscribed terms. She is much more directly critical of Alexie's *Reservation Blues*, quoting another reviewer's dismissal of him as the Indian Spike Lee and insisting that such books "reflect little or no defense of treaty-protected reservation land bases as homelands to the indigenes, nor do they suggest a responsibility of art as an ethical endeavor or the artist as responsible social critic" (Cook-Lynn, "American" 68).[15]

So far my overall approach in this essay has been to look at the role of white ideological investments in cultural essentialism in defining many of the prevailing literary terms and forms of Indian literature and to compare and contrast this with what might be seen as a more fundamental Indian openness to impurity and hybridity (though these words are themselves problematic). So the message could be that white attempts to elevate or preserve some sort of cultural purity in Indian literature are about as appropriate as Mabel Dodge Luhan's attempts to keep modern plumbing out of Taos, because it spoiled its timeless character, and that impurity and cross-cultural appropriation are themselves quite proper. But against this not only do we have to weigh Elizabeth Cook-Lynn's insistence on cultural specificity and the dangers of cosmopolitanism, but we also need to question whether all such appropriation is appropriate. Is there a different agenda in taking over other people's cultural products when you are already culturally dominant? Perhaps, but I am concerned that the terms in which this worry is expressed can just lead us back into another limiting essentialism.

A recent book by an Australian art critic, Deborah Root's *Cannibal Culture*, is an account of the many ways in which Western culture appropriates art objects and cultural properties from elsewhere (particularly the Third World). Her particular emphasis is the role played by ideas of beauty and art in that process. Root suggests that Western culture is cannibalistic. She borrows from Jack Forbes's use of the witiko or windigo figure and describes his use of the figure "not as a metaphor but as a technical medico-spiritual term." With the word "consumption," she makes a common but slippery transition. Our cannibal society is not just a metaphor, she says, because it does involve the consumption of real bodies (such as in exploitation of labor in world capitalism), but "it is also useful to extend the definition of cannibalism to forms of consumption that occur beyond the physical body of the individual or even the community. It is possible to consume somebody's spirit, somebody's past or history, or somebody's arts and to do so in such a way as that the act of consumption appears beautiful and heroic" (18). Underlying this passage is the idea that there is a difference between illegitimate appropriation amounting to expropriation and legitimate or "proper" use (and I am punning here on the idea of the proper, as relating to its Latin root, *proprius*, one's own). In a clearcut case such as the theft of a ritual object that is then exhibited, contextless, as art or the claiming of shamanic authority backed up by secondhand or fake ceremonial in New Age spirituality, we can see the point clearly enough. But is there really a securely established difference between use and exchange value that is at the heart of the distinction here? This is a larger theoretical question, beyond the scope of this essay, but at a more immediate level we can turn to a warning from Karoniaktatie/Alex A. Jacobs in a short piece entitled "The Politics of Primitivism":

Art means something to us, but when we seek to transfer values from the sacred to the profane ... we act just as they [whites] do in their blind assimilation of The Things That Are Ours into things that are now theirs. ... We must not act as cannibals to our own culture. We must not act as they do, we must not sell what is not ours to even give away. ... In Art, we must share our visions, we must investigate these values. The positive nature of acculturation is sharing, the negative is cannibalization or greed. (3)

But are the lines that clear? And is cultural property like other sorts of property? Can arguments for political sovereignty, for instance, be carried over intact into arguments over cultural sovereignty? And who has the power, the authority to represent, or to control representation, either from inside or outside? Cook-Lynn may be right to say that in the present climate "The role of Indians, themselves, in the storytelling of Indian America is as much a matter of 'jurisdiction' as is anything else in Indian Country: economics, the law, control of resources, property rights" ("American" 57). What seems altogether less clear is who has the authority to exercise this jurisdiction.

NOTES

1. See Eric Cheyfitz for an important discussion of the relation between ideas of the proper and cross-cultural power relations.

2. For a sense of the continuing relevance of the Marxism-modernism debate, see E. Bloch et al. Fredric Jameson's political orientation has meant that he has continued to offer a skeptical engagement with recent theoretical and artistic developments that could be said to keep alive some of the critical edges of reflection theory and realism.

3. For a fascinating personal meditation on the conflicting claims of Enlightenment universalism and ethnic particularism, or what he calls "ratio" and "natio," see Arnold Krupat (*Turn*).

4. The responses to the 1984 Museum of Modern Art exhibition of modern and primitive art, organized around the question-begging concept of the "Affinity of the Tribal and the Modern," have rumbled on, demonstrating the depth and complexity of the issues raised by the modernist engagement with primitive art. The relation of anthropological encounters and ethnographic writings to modernism has also been newly explored as part of a concern to textualize and contextualize ethnography itself. See William Rubin. See also James Clifford (*Predicament*) and Hal Foster (181–210) for influential discussions of the exhibition. See also Marc Manganaro.

5. For a discussion of this idea and an analysis of the use of the "ethnographic present tense," see Johannes Fabian.

6. See also Townsend Ludington.

7. See especially James Clifford's brilliant account of what he calls "ethnographic surrealism" in *Predicament of Culture*. The surrealists were more interested in Oceania and in the Northwest Coast of America and in general were more interested in the rich and random juxtapositions both within primitive art itself and within the Western museums that assembled it than in the abstraction and clean lines that Picasso found in African art. In the surrealist map of the world it is Oceania and Russia that dwarf both Europe and most of Africa. For a look at the conjunction of the modern and primitive in this context see Claude Levi-Strauss's account of shopping for primitive art in New York with Max Ernst in Claude Levi-Strauss.

8. See Aldon Jonaitis and Robert Fay Schrader.

9. For a brief account of Hartley in the context of the American use of the primitive, see Gail Levin, "American Art," in Rubin, 453–74.

10. See David Murray ("Racial").

11. I have not been able to discover if there were any black performers or contributors to the America exhibit, but it would support my general argument if, as it seems, there were not. See Bunny McBride, 158. McBride's account is one of a resourceful woman, secure in her sense of her own Indian identity and heritage but willing to perform largely within the forms and roles in which Indians were presented to the general public. Her interest in what various sorts of "primitive" materials had in common was not just at the level of the popular portrayal in entertainments, as McBride tells of her attending lectures by Marcel Mauss and assisting anthropologists with the mounting of exhibitions at the Trocadero. Where then do we put the emphasis? At one level her whole career can be seen as cooptation by a white entertainment industry, with a tragic collapse, but at another we have a woman making her way and creating a remarkable life.

12. Indian poetry has perhaps shown the different strands in operation most clearly. This question might be approachable through a Bakhtinian distinction between the dialogical possibilities of each form, but I think there are other ideological assumptions at play here as well, which go beyond the scope of this particular essay. It is noticeable how many Native American writers use both forms either separately or within the same work, in comparison with white writers. This is presumably to use and move between the disjunctions between lyric and realist, but it would be interesting to develop this further. The idea of the fragment and the whole and their roles in the literary creation of the effect of the sublime in Romanticism as opposed to the use of the fragment in modernism and differently again in postmodernism does have ideological connotations when applied to cultural loss and reconstitution. One way of going on from here would be to invoke the normal distinction between modern and postmodern as nostalgia for the whole via the fragment, or free play with, and acceptance of, fragments. This could have the consequence of making most Indian writing Romantic and modernist, with a few postmodernists (Vizenor, King). By the same token, we might want to distinguish between the so-called white shamans. Gary Snyder would then be Romantic and purity oriented, but Jerome Rothenberg would be a more experimental modernist, aware of the importance and role of juxtaposition and fragmentation without wanting to reconstitute the whole.

13. For a discussion of the overlapping of blues and recent Indian poetry and song, see Rebecca Tsosie.

14. In Thomas King's *Green Grass, Running Water*, for instance, the fact that we have Indian characters with names like Lone Ranger, Ishmael, Robinson Crusoe, and Hawkeye, plus a huge array of literary references and jokes, is perhaps not as fundamental as the fact that the creation stories they tell ultimately circumscribe the historical narra-

tive of the hydroelectrical dam and the personal lives of the other characters, in the same way as Silko's Grandmother Spider Woman does in her nonprose sections in *Ceremony*. (The question has also arisen over Vizenor's conjunction of trickster and postmodern strategies.)

15. Craig Womack voices similar misgivings in his essay in W. S. Penn's collection of essays dedicated to this issue. "What bothers me is making mixedblood identity the primary focus of one's identification or one's writing. I'm wondering if identifying as mixedblood, rather than as a part of a tribal nation, diminishes sovereignty" (32).

... whoever controls your definition controls your sense of self. And so the more writers we have and the more readers we have and the more audience we have, the more Native American people are going to be able to claim themselves, and take it back from Hollywood, take it back from the anthropologists.

Paula Gunn Allen [Laguna/Sioux/Lebanese],
in *Winged Words: American Indian Writers Speak*

Tricksters of the Trade

"Remagining" the Filmic Image of Native Americans

JOHN PURDY

So much criticism has been devoted to the ways makers of movies and books have misrepresented American Indians that it has become almost clichéd to call attention to the fact, at least in academic circles. However, all too often, challenges to the representations simply focus upon their inaccuracy: the stereotypical images they impose. These challenges ignore the fact that accuracy and "authenticity" have become heated, contentious issues only recently and that they are of interest to a relatively small audience: Native communities and artists, of course, but also scholars and academics for whom the economic, sociological, and political ramifications that misrepresentation carries with it are intolerable.

Even a few years ago, realism in portrayals of American Indians had very few proponents and even fewer practitioners. Portraying complex human beings negotiating their lives and doing it well did not generate box-office revenue. Portraying helpless victims made money, as did images of essentialized Indians; beaded and buckskinned braves and squaws, fierce warriors, and politically correct, often dead or dying, practitioners of lost mysticism filled the seats in movies. And all of it has been criticized time and time again.

However, today, despite the highly significant contributions of critics, or "opinion leaders" as Steven Leuthold terms them, to contemporary social discourse, the inaccurate images and false impressions perpetuated by the entertainment industry persist, and this perniciousness has become a formative force for a few prominent Native authors and filmmakers who have made this issue a central element of their books and movies. They have met with limited success in challenging popular representations, for it is a complex and difficult task, and in order to be effective, one must have an intimate understanding of both the attraction the images possess and, more importantly, the psychology of their initial inscription. It is this primal dynamic, this act of enculturation, that must be engaged, and the texts that do so must also reach a wide audience. They must be "popular."

In the late 1990s, Walt Disney Productions released an animated movie based loosely upon the historical characters Pocahontas and John Smith, and it is a fit text to use to reengage this discussion of representation. Aimed at an audience of young people, the next generation, this movie came at a time when the debate about accuracy and authenticity — refueled by the immense popularity of the movie *Dances with Wolves* a few years earlier — had reached a fevered pitch. *Pocahontas* was released despite the controversy. It is also well situated for this discussion because Disney — first the individual and now the corporation — has become one of the most influential forces in inscribing and perpetuating inaccurate, stereotypical images through three generations.[1] Since financial resurrection in the 1980s and the subsequent acquisition of numerous other entertainment enterprises, including its move into cable television, the Internet, and expanded production of films, Disney has once again spearheaded the revival of the conventions of depiction that have been challenged time and time again. In other words, the conventions, with a little marketing, still work; they maintain a hold upon the imagination of society, despite decades of critical challenges. Why?

This hold is understandable; it may be problematized, possibly even shaken, but not dislodged by critical studies. One reason is very simple: such studies are not a part of the popular literary canon. Although academics involve themselves in continuous debate about the conventions of misrepresentation, this debate has not surfaced in any appreciable degree in the popular consciousness of people around the world.[2] In those instances where it has, such as immediately after the release of *Dances with Wolves*, it has been presented as documentary; in other words, this debate has engaged the general public on the same level as editorials on the politics of identity, whether an author is "Indian enough," or whether team mascots, such as the Atlanta Braves or Florida Seminoles, are appropriate. Put even more simply, the sign "Indian" carries with it popular, easily evoked, and dismissive reactions to issues of sovereignty, of nations owning their own cultures and futures.

Objections to depiction may bring a degree of attention and rational thought to bear upon anthropological details presented in printed or film texts, but they do not address or reenact the drama of the texts' original impression, and therefore they do not seriously challenge the interpretative mechanisms that have evolved over long periods of time in relation to shifting matrices of social interactions. In simple language, the criticism does not work on the same psychological level as Disney. To do so, it has to consider, and react to, the social, political, and economic forces that provide the context out of which the impressions are created and thereby must contend with the relational politics that emerge whenever an image is produced for our consumption.

To complicate matters, these forces are not static, but fluid, coming together at moments in time in profoundly powerful configurations that have a direct effect upon the impressions we form. It is important to understand that not only the original texts but also critical challenges to them work within this human reality; thus, both the challenged text and its opponents must be considered in light of their agenda and their views of their intended audiences. For example, the audience that comprises the locus of power in the United States today and for the last thirty years or more is certainly one that has unique roots that need careful, critical attention. It is also the first generation raised on and by television.[3]

I am a baby boomer. This means that I was born not long after World War II and therefore am one of a large wave of young produced following a time of global conflict and violence, as well as at a time when there was a realignment in economics and politics on a global scale. It is only recently that I have begun to consider the significance of this fact and to wonder about its possible connections to the evolution of both Hollywood fantasies and Native American literatures. (After all, *House Made of Dawn* by the Kiowa novelist N. Scott Momaday won the Pulitzer Prize as my generation was in college, and many of the other artists whose works ushered in the "Renaissance" of contemporary Native literature are themselves boomers.) Demographers and social scientists have charted the obvious effects such a dramatic population increase had on society, and one immediately apparent consequence of it was felt in our schools as enrollments rose. Another was in the entertainment industry, which was quick to capitalize on the vast financial potential to be exploited by the sudden appearance of such a vast pool of potential consumers. The two — school and cinema — are closely connected.

For instance, the baby boom launched the career of Walt Disney. Although it is true that Disney was a popular cartoonist long before the war, it is equally true that the advent of television and its proponents' reactions to this new, burgeoning youth market made him a national icon; it also placed him in a position of immense power to affect my generation's perspective, through his camera lens.[4] During the 1950s, Disney's career as a moviemaker was established; more importantly, the television programs marked by his distinctive style became central to the boomer generation's culture. His subject matter for both movies and television shows in the 1950s is quite revealing: he used popular fairy tales (and thus all the cultural baggage and potential they carry with them) and the equally appealing historical fictions of the colonial past in America, such as tales of Daniel Boone and Davy Crockett.

Disney's "texts" were aimed directly at the boomer generation, who thus functioned as test group for his pedagogy of imagination management, what he continuously and ironically referred to as "make-believe." It is interesting to consider this common phrase; it is usually translated as play, as creative acts of the imagination, and this is certainly true for Disney, but in this context it could also mean to make believers out of us all.

Interestingly, his movies and television programs were also accompanied by the means for dramatic reenactment of their scripts in the "real," the material world of their audience, through play: one of the most formative elements of the human psyche because of its absorption of the imagination. The material stage props — replicas of coonskin caps and flintlock rifles — were the 1950s and 1960s precursors of the lucrative marketing campaigns that, today, precede the release of movies with figurines of the characters and other toys related to the stories they present, often distributed through another corporate icon from the 1950s, McDonalds. This melding of the abstract and material, the illusory and the physical, by way of connecting imagination and behavior is intriguing. In fact, the same terms are often used to describe ceremonies and rituals, the very core of cultures. The impetus behind the Disney model, though, is for immediacy and gratification — fast food and playful diversions. It is not unique to this generation, of course, but the ways it came to shape American society and the entertainment industry during the last half of the twentieth century are directly relevant to the reception of images of "Indian" and of Native texts.

Equally significant is the fact that concurrent with these entertainment industry innovations Disney was actively engaged in the education market with animated course films for educators (a postwar extension of the training films he made for the army). One ubiquitous example is *Donald Duck in Mathmagic Land*, and these pedagogical "tools" — some of which focused upon American history — are still in use in some schools today. It is in the conjoining of the two industries that the subliminal effects upon this generation can be understood; when the physical spaces of classroom and theater (and home, if one considers the immense popularity of television in society in the 1950s) are no longer clearly demarcated, the line between entertainment and education, between playground recess and class pedagogy, is similarly blurred. Since the Aristotelian ideal is to delight *and* instruct, the melding of the two realms in the (baby) booming postwar economy of the 1950s makes a certain sense. Moreover, for both Aristotle and Disney, history — in other words, looking back — was a foundation out of which a philosophy of the present emerged, but where is the line between reality and fantasy in our imaginative reconstruction of the past? This is, of course, the postmodern dilemma, and Disney nicely avoided its quagmire through a strategic retreat into an *imagined, reenvisioned* past. As contemporary critics have pointed out, Disney's canon "not only 'cleans up' history and political struggles, nature and culture, gender and sex/uality, but elevates sanitization to pedagogy. The ways in which Disney instructs audiences in what Henry Giroux calls a 'politics of innocence' are lessons that locate Disney film at the center of cultural ideology and its pedagogical urge" (Bell, Hass, and Sells 8).

I have a vivid, not-so-innocent memory from one American history class dating from the original Disney era. Even now, so many years later, I can visualize one distinct image from our history "textbook"; the cover design of that book, the part of it I saw most often, was forgotten long, long ago, further testament to the power of the remembered image. It was one of the myriad visual representations of the myth of Pocahontas. In this illustration, the young woman is shown throwing herself between the bound and kneeling John Smith and the angry Powhatan, who holds a huge, pointed stone above Smith's head, prepared to execute the colonist. This was an impressive image for a young person. But why? It would be easy to dismiss its attraction by simply saying that it has "everything" that a person going through the hormonal hell of puberty needs for gratification — implicit sex and overt violence — and it is true that these two motifs are very real and present in the illustration *and* the myth. Its appeal may be more complicated than that, though.

As I look back at it, I realize that the depiction had an inherent power. The artist, probably from the seventeenth century, was obviously talented, but he also drew upon shared, culturally defined behavioral and imagistic conventions to engage his audience.[5] The method of execution, beheading, was a commonplace European tradition, and the characters in the scene reflect the aesthetic of the time: they are derivative of the human forms one can find rendered in other paintings of the era. The details had only been adopted and adapted to fit the new subject matter and locale. The Renaissance physiques had been draped in animal skins and feathers, the stone had replaced the ax. Thus the "primitive" was, and still is, constructed.[6]

But I did not know this nor had I consciously investigated the image's aesthetics at the time. The *impression* the image created can only be explained in terms of my production of the imaginative *drama* the image itself suggests and the context in which it originated. Drama is, of course, what drew my generation to the Disney images on television and in the movies, and its fundamental conventions — for both the entertainment and history industries of the time — hinged upon conflict and its self-gratifying resolution. This convention possesses some interesting implications.

First, the hero — John Smith, the colonizer and thus the harbinger of the future on the North American continent, the forebear of American society in the 1950s — seems to have lost and is about to pay the price. The method of execution holds its own intrinsic shock value as well; the idea of dying in such a manner provides the initial hook for the viewer, at least when viewed in the 1950s by a young person. The image provides a brief and safe thrill of danger that is simultaneously mitigated by the selfless, loving sacrifice of the young and desirable Pocahontas.

I believe there are several subtexts at work here, and that they have always existed when this image was viewed over the last two hundred years by Euro-Americans, and that these subtexts speak directly to Disney's own representations of colonial history. One of the subtexts centers on the apparent success of the "primitive." In this imaginative drama, our social Darwinist concept of progress and its analog, modernity, seem to have lost. This obvious visual fact is, however, mitigated on two levels: the first is the immediate dramatic effect of the intervention of Pocahontas, and the other level is the situation of the viewer. In other words, this image resided in a history book — a location, ostensibly, of "fact" — that chronicled the triumph of the colonists. I knew that Smith and "his side" (read: my side) had won, that his story did not end on that day, and, at least subconsciously, that his story would culminate in the very existence of the history class in which I was sitting and his story and image were central. "Progress," then — economic, political, and sociological — had prevailed. The "best" of the "primitive" had been subsumed (anything serving to help forward the current social order) and the worst rendered invalid and impotent (anything resisting).

Another subtext can be found in the nature of the hero, who is saved from an untimely and undignified death and apparently by his sex appeal. The angry father is shown to be in error, for Smith's rescue signifies that his sentence was an unjust one. He was the innocent victim. The impression the scene creates is intricately tied to, but extends, the emotions generated by the conflict inherent in the conjoining of sex and violence; the emotions emerging are compounded by an equally powerful sense of self-validation and gratification based in the political correctness of the colonial paradigm the scene enacts. In other words, Pocahontas's attraction to the modern man is presented as inevitable as the colonization of the Americas. Thus, the image and its drama validated the society into which I was born and the gendered politics and history I was learning.

This version of Smith's narrative is identical to those of famed Indian fighters Daniel Boone and Davy Crockett, revolutionary patriot Johnny Tremain, or any of the clones Disney created; weekly, the televised images of the colonist persevering against seemingly insurmountable odds, the patriot rising victorious from apparent defeat, were pervasive. These inspirational testimonies were then reinforced in the classroom. In each venue, the Other was simply costumed to fit historical circumstances and thus provide the subtext's rhetoric: the furs and leggings of "Indian" were replaced by the uniform of a Mexican soldier at the Alamo, and so on. It was, after all, the cold war, and this burgeoning sense of oppositional nationalism was pervasive. But what marks it as significant for this discussion is that it came at a formative time for the boomers. Aristotle's dictum had assumed an interesting, albeit schizophrenic, dimension, and it is small wonder that with such repetitive imaging — where the threat of communism, or simply "the Other," seemed pervasive — the images should become so indelibly inscribed. From Disney's point of view, the popular heroes and stereotypical images of the Other were needed to provide comfort in a time of potential chaos, for they provided simple binary structures and a sanitized social validation.

In his study of Hollywood's westerns, Leuthold synthesizes the various theories surrounding an audience's reactions to inaccurate images, and I quote his summary at length since it raises some of the issues of this discussion:

Some theories of communication posit that [Native American] opinion leaders help guide the opinions of broader publics. For example, a "two-step flow" model of communication argues that media representations affect viewers only indirectly, filtered through the influence of interpersonal relations and opinion leaders. In this model, the ideas of opinion leaders may affect the diffusion of information in important ways; they help viewers frame the information that they receive from mass-mediated sources. Some theories shift the agency of interpretation more heavily to communities of viewers, regarding audience members as active processors of information. For example, uses and gratifications, reader-response, and reception theories argue for the existence of diverse communities that interpret media representations according to their own needs. ("Native" 157)

In an endnote, he further grounds his own "limited effects" model: "Diffusion theory builds on the idea that interpersonal networks lead people to filter media messages. Thus, the relation of an individual to groups of interacting individuals affects the individual's interpretation and evaluation of media. Effects of the media are limited by social variables such as stratification or centralization, which will affect the flow of media influence" (186). The problem with these models is that "opinion leaders" may in fact have been supplanted by the image producers; in other words, what happens if Disney or his descendants become the opinion leaders? Or what happens if there is not a great enough disjuncture between an audience's perception, ingrained over generations, and the misrepresentation given in a recognizable package?

I have two simple questions at this point by way of summary of the first part of this discussion. First, how could the history book image persist in my memory, long after the historical accuracy of the event has been challenged and its narrative rewritten? In other words, what is there inherent in the imaginative drama that makes the image so evocative? The answer given above — that the original inscription engaged the greatest power of humanity, the imagination — is only partially correct, for here the imagination could be employed only within very limited constraints. In other words, I was free to situate myself voyeuristically in relation to Pocahontas and Smith, as long as my "reading" of the scene operated within the bounds of the "history" represented in the image and book before me. It is a safe voyeurism, requiring little reflection since the outcome of the drama is, literally, history.

Yet another element of the answer is that the drama operated through some interesting extremes and hinged on sudden reversals and thus became memorable: that is, it became worthy of retention due to a gratifying sense of hopefulness. Since the outcome of the drama is understood, one's imagination can align with only two characters: the couple. For a young male, this means an alignment with the suitor: Smith. One minute, he is about to lose his head, and the next he is part of the family, the favorite of chief and daughter. John Rolfe, Pocahontas's English husband, was conveniently excised, and the picture matched, much like the recent Disney remake, the ages of Smith and Pocahontas. All is forgiven, colonist and indigenous are "married," and out of this coupling a nation is born. The history lesson is compelling. Given human nature, and in this case the gendered nature of Pocahontas, it was all inevitable. The conflict is resolved and no one is hurt; much as in Disney's *Peter Pan*, the indigenous threat was not real, after all.[7] The potential for tragedy has been diffused by a *comic* resolution.

My other question is perhaps obvious: can one reinscribe the image? It is, after all, an elemental part of my memory, but its mythic drama is communal as well. It has been etched deeply, and Disney's remake of it continues the conditioning into the next generation. But there are some contemporary analogs that may be useful to consider since they reinforce similar nostalgic revisions of the past, particularly for the dramatic play that inscribed some of the fundamental Disney canon in the first place. Consider today's "Mountainmen Rendezvous," where boomers put on the clothes and technology of the popular cult heroes who lived the earliest form of Manifest Disney: Boone, Crockett, Bridger, Meeks, and others. There are, as well, Civil War and medieval reenactments. At such gatherings, childhood's artificial weapons and outward trappings — plastic rifles and coonskin caps — are displaced by the adult boomers' zealous adherence to the material accuracy of a way of life long dead. Nonetheless, it is still an attempt *to imagine*, through dramatic play, how life was in the past. Ironically, it is in the attractive intersection of authenticity and imaginative reenactment that the legacy of Disney may find its greatest challenge, for that is exactly how the legacy was born: in imaginative and dramatic activity.

It is on this level that a few contemporary Native artists have attempted to engage the popular power of Hollywood's conventions of reinventing the American Indian. Rather than simply constructing their own binaries — creating alternative characters, for instance, who provide a "Native perspective" — these artists appropriate the conventional images and employ the "tricks of the trade" to recontextualize them in situations that dislocate their audience's earlier, imaginative experiences with these images. The artifice of the drama is co-opted, and it thus becomes revelatory through an audience's imaginative reenactment of history. In a way, they may have anticipated a recent psychological study in which people successfully removed their recurrent nightmares through "imagery rehearsal": the imagining, while "awake," of revised variants of the dreams that haunt them.

I want to examine three artists and how they attempt to "remagine" the images, for their texts evoke both memory and imagination with the hope of reinscribing the meta-images of Hollywood. In all three, sudden comic reversals figure prominently. To keep the print and visual media connection alive, I examine a work in film, a script and the film produced from it, and a novel that employs very deliberate connections to film. In the case of Gerald Vizenor (Anishinaabe) and Thomas King (Cherokee), methodology hinges on humor; in the case of Victor Masayesva (Hopi), there is humor as well, but it is heavily ironic and inhabits the dramatic frame around a documentary that directly confronts the inaccurate representations found in film, matching "fact" with fact, film footage with film footage. His work is therefore a fit bridge between the usual critical challenges to representation and the more imaginative approach of the other two artists. Although the media may vary and the approach each artist takes as well, one can discern a shared theoretical stance in each artist's work, and more than a bit of the trickster.

Masayesva's recent movie, *Imagining Indians*, covers eighty years of Hollywood's Indians, from the silent movie *The Battle of Elderbush Gulch* to *The Dark Wind*. However, the core of the film consists of long sections focused upon the commodification and appropriation of Native materials and lifeways in general, including sacred objects but also contemporary art. Thus, Masayesva's eye is far-reaching, and his narrative makes no distinction between these issues and those provoked by other analyses of Hollywood's canon.

Throughout the documentary portions of the film, Masayesva juxtaposes Hollywood footage — its images and history — with interviews of Native people who were in some way concerned with or involved in movie productions. Given the fact that for many people Hollywood provides their initial, sometimes sole, images of Indians, which by the way is Masayesva's thesis, this use of film footage, with a new context surrounding it, is well considered. At times, he juxtaposes newspaper clippings (and thus "real-world" controversy) with the spoken words of the people he interviews, and in one section he presents the words of promoters of Hollywood movies in a comic-book format; thus, he destabilizes "truth" and "fact." The packaged images the public has been fed clash sharply with the "truth" of events behind and beyond the camera. The image and thus its mystique are shown to be false: the elaborate construction of romantic, self-serving imaginations employing the artifice of film.

Given the bulk of his examples, then, and the numerous interviews, the pervasive nature of the appropriation and misrepresentation he sees at work in society are revealed. The evidence should be compelling, but his hope to dislodge that propensity in society may not be accomplished through this element of the film alone. Pointing a finger at the myth and calling forth reality may not effect significant change; contemporary political campaigns suggest as much, wherein the "image" is everything and reality only at times tangentially interesting. In other words, by calling forth and documenting the inadequacies of the apparatus through which he is working, Masayesva leaves a convenient escape route for his audience. The documentary element of his movie, despite its innovative use of techniques of the trade, does not result in a dramatic reenactment that evokes conflict or resolution. Viewers are removed and remain at a comfortable distance from the issues.

The central, metaphoric drama that interweaves throughout, providing a frame for the film, is promising, however. It dramatizes the attitudes explored "objectively" in the documentary. Interestingly, Masayesva makes use of the gendered-contest convention so prominent in Hollywood's imagination, pairing a white male dentist with a female Indian patient. Significantly, their interaction takes place within a dental clinic room that has a collection of movie posters covering its walls. One of them, in fact, is for a movie from the 1930s: *Captain John Smith and Pocahontas*. There are two Hollywood film genres that are pervasive in this section of the film and also represented in the posters on the walls: the "captivity" and thus cross-racial romance narrative, and the war narrative.[8] The motif of dentist/authority, patient/subject, replicates the personal and painful implications of the two genres, as well as the Pocahontas myth.

Despite the fact that he tries to "anesthetize" the woman, the dentist — dressed in medical garb but also wearing a bone choker — is oblivious to her growing discomfort; tellingly, she is silent throughout as he articulates his own agenda, thus revealing his beliefs. To do so, he evokes *Dances with Wolves* and his hero, Kevin Costner, with whom he identifies. (The blurring of actor/en-actor is telling.) The dentist is impressed by how easily "he learned your language, and you picked up on his"; how "you took him into your hearts"; and how he could relate to "the spiritual lifestyle you people had." The lack of distance between romantic fiction and personal reality is an obvious subtext to the monologue throughout the scene, as is the emphasis on and indictment of the verbs' past tense: the implied loss of all the dentist deems valuable and therefore worthy of appropriation. John Smith lives again, but his is now a safe, privileged tradition.

The dentist has a plan to bring the historical lessons from the movie into being. He has made contacts with "some New Age people who are into real estate and travel, down in Phoenix," and together they intend to build a "Higher Consciousness Resort" where — for a price — people can come for a weekend of "intense Indian Spiritual Seminars." This is merely another variation on a theme of the Disney model — the blurring of education and play — and the seminars would be dramatic play through imaginative, revisionist enactments. Masayesva is being satirical, of course, but the satire is closely aligned with New Age reality. His portrayal of it is comic in context but hinges upon attitudes inherent in a long-standing colonial paradigm, the mystique of colonialism itself, which is to derive profit through the promotion of one's revised image of the Other. The desire for a quick reversal of fortune — here both spiritual and financial fortune — in favor of our hero, the dentist, is a compelling tradition. John Smith was, after all, a seventeenth-century realtor.

The fact that Masayesva's interrogation takes place through a gendered contest is important, especially when one considers the conclusion of the film. Here, the patient rises up in revolt, attacks the dentist, and takes away his drill. With this, she attacks the lens, the camera, slowly and deliberately etching it with the colonist's own instrument: a reinscription with a vengeance. Once the image the camera records is completely obscured, she pushes the camera over. The screen goes black, and a dialogue begins in an indigenous language. This Hopi filmmaker has made his statement, using conventional tricks of the film trade to topple the apparatus and thus call attention to our reliance upon it.

There are tricks, and then there are *tricks*. In fact, the most common word used to discuss Gerald Vizenor's art is "trickster." This is understandable, given his consistent wordplay and his construction of characters very obviously patterned after trickster characters to be found in indigenous literatures. However, it is in his own employment of dramatic, comic reversals — the elemental business of the trickster — that Vizenor uses to "remagine" popular representations of history and Native peoples. At once humorous and poignant, these scenes truly delight and instruct, and thus impress new perceptions on old conventions.

The central character of Vizenor's movie *Harold of Orange* is Harold Sinseer, de facto leader of the Warriors of Orange, "tricksters in the new school of socio-acupuncture," who "talk about mythic revolutions on the reservation" (55). In other words, from the opening scene one is aware that a "new school" is derivative of the old, that it employs a pedagogy based in language ("talk"), and that it is founded upon the idea that applying pressure to sociological points can have a curative effect for the body politic. As in acupuncture, the point where one must apply pressure is not necessarily in close proximity to the pain or ill being treated — not, in other words, on the economic or political reality of Native Americans but upon the often stereotypical images of them that feed, if not create, that reality. This, in other words, is not a documentary, and it does not reveal symptoms; instead, it displays their underlying orientations, through imaginative interaction. Subjecting the popular myths to the pressure of his reversals thereby forces his audience to reassess them on a level beyond reason and logic, beyond the easily dismissed opinions found on editorial pages in newspapers; this is the playground of the trickster where drama carries the message. This approach is indeed a "mythic revolution" through the "remagining" of the myths of representation so ingrained in the social psyche as to be comprehended as "fact" and therefore functionally invisible; Vizenor makes them visible. As Harold says as they depart for their meeting with an Anglo board of directors of a charitable foundation, once they have had their way "that foundation pack won't remember nothin we tell them but the truth" (58). There are numerous examples in the movie in which "truth" emerges from the sudden, abrupt, comic reversal of popular untruths. I focus on two that are representative: one dealing with a popular myth of history and one with the dynamic of cultural interaction as espoused by Hollywood through the genres of romance and war movies.[9]

As the Warriors of Orange escort the board of directors to various points around the city, one finds several scenes in which Indian and Anglo are paired as they travel on the Warriors' "school" bus. This pairing generates dialogue — a dialogic interaction — that has misunderstanding at its basis, healing as its goal. For instance, in one scene an older trustee raises an old and pervasive theory that attempts to explain the presence of Native Americans in the western hemisphere, a long-standing dilemma dating from first European colonial contact.

ANDREW: I have considered the origin theories of the American Indians. . . . Some are *quite* interesting. I find the Bering Strait migration theory to be most credible. . . . How about you then, what are your thoughts on the subject?

NEW CROWS: Which way?

ANDREW: Which *way*? Why, what do you mean?

NEW CROWS: Which way across the Bering Strait, *then*?

ANDREW: Yes, I see. . . . Well, I hadn't really thought about it that way. Which way do *you* think?

NEW CROWS: From here to there, we emerged from the flood here, we are the first people, unless you think we are related to the panda bear. (66)[10]

When Andrew counters with the observation that there is "so little evidence to support your idea," a rebuttal made feeble by the equal truth that there is no material evidence to support the Bering Strait theory as well, New Crows responds in a way to bring into relief, reverse, and thereby shake the fundamental beliefs of his audience: "Jesus Christ was an American Indian" (66).

In very short order, Vizenor has dramatized images, popularly ingrained in his audience, that are an attempt to explain phenomena under the guise of scientific (and therefore objectively verifiable) fact, history. By reversing those images — by problematicizing the directional framework inherent in the paradigm — he imaginatively demonstrates the ideological and thus ethnocentric foundations upon which they are based. Simultaneously, he valorizes indigenous origin stories — the elemental narratives of who Native peoples are and how they came to be where they are — and challenges written "history" with myth, including that of Christ. He has forced a "remagining" of orientations, frames of reference, and thus representations with which we are all familiar. He has made us laugh, then reorient. In other words, Vizenor is the Anti-Disney.

Later in the movie, the Warriors take the board of directors to a park where, as they step down from the bus to play a game of softball, Vizenor once again reverses our orientation. The wholly Anglo board is dressed in red T-shirts that bear the word "Indians" in white letters, and the Warriors wear white T-shirts with "Anglos" in red lettering. In preparation for the game, the conflict, Harold moves between the two teams as they huddle, changing shirts accordingly to match those of his audience, first the Warriors and then the board members. His admonition to the former is "we are the 'Anglos' and we're here to win and win big. . . . Play by the rules if you must, but rape and plunder to win the game" (76). Violence, sex, and colonialism again, but here the war genre — the racial conflict — is mitigated by the comic nature of the game itself. To the "Indians," he makes a call for them to remember "what the missionaries said our elders said around the fires" and tells them that they "are made in dreams and the white man is the one who must win. . . . When we help him win we are free and soon the white man will want to be like us" (77). This appropriates the Disney model while undermining the myth of the inevitability of colonial domination, so prominent in the history book illustration of Smith and Pocahontas; it is not only called into question but also made absurd. When Vizenor's audience laughs, it subtly shifts its orientation.

It is difficult not to equate this exchange also with the history implied in the illustration of Smith and Pocahontas; it is she who will "help them win," and he who wants to appropriate or co-opt the Native. However, here the straightforward articulation of the colonial agenda is complicated by the humorous image of Indians labeled as Anglos; the rearticulation of the Pocahontas agenda — to aid the colonist — is undermined by the cutting irony of the "translators": the missionaries who possess the words of the elders, the ethnographers who write down Native history and thus control attitudes and therefore the future. The inevitability of colonial domination, so prominent in the history book and illustration of Smith and Pocahontas, is called to question, and the true agents of the conquest are made apparent. Vizenor's audience laughs at the absurdity of it all.

Thus socioacupuncture works. The movie abounds with similar examples, and at the center of them, one finds the dynamic, gendered contest between Fannie and Harold. Interestingly, in the screenplay's opening scenes there is a reenactment of a woman/man configuration reminiscent of the Pocahontas/Smith binary, with an interesting twist.

As Harold walks into the coffee house, the "screen is filled with a large photographic silhouette of Harold and Fannie posed like the statue of Hiawatha and Minnehaha" (55). The statue represents two other popular literary constructions dating from colonial literatures: the Anglo imaginative mating of two romantic figures.[11] This is, of course, analogous to the Smith/Pocahontas myth, but since Fannie is not a Native American, it aligns Fannie (Anglo student of Native lifeways) and Harold (Indian) in a comic reversal of the Smith/Pocahontas paradigm. The Indian, here, owes the Anglo; Harold borrowed $1000 from Fannie in college, and now she wants to be paid back. Also, Harold wants her help to secure a large grant from the foundation, which will help his warriors live well from the "tax-free bonds" in which they will invest the monies that are supposed to fund the growing of coffee "pinch beans" on the reservation. In this instance, Harold has become the seeker of financial ease — the colonial agenda of John Smith — and the Anglo board the possessor; Harold's methodology humorously reverses their respective situations. Harold tricks Fannie, though, so that the debt is absolved without costing him anything. With her passive assistance, they manage to get the grant, using one board member's stereotypical, racist ideas about Indians as the final selling point. The "grant" will thus fund the revolution.[12] The colonial agenda has been called forth, reversed, and situated in a comical, rather than deadly, narrative.

Thomas King's novel, *Green Grass, Running Water*, very clearly locates the fundamental basis of the Pocahontas/Smith configuration in a culturally defined mythology and in humorous vignettes juxtaposes it with its means of dissemination in contemporary times. Here, the action centers on the confrontation of stories and mythologies, and unlike my school history book, the outcome is anything but certain.

For instance, throughout the novel short episodes pit an indigenous creatrix — Sky Woman, Changing Woman, and so on — with male deities and characters from Christian mythology: G O D, Christ, Noah, and so on. In the scenes in which King places them, the latter do not fare well in the drama; they are ineffectual, self-absorbed, and ultimately impotent. Unlike the Smith story, wherein the colonist's impotence is short-lived, here there is no sudden reprieve offered. The characters' absurdity derives from the tension between their self-constructed and oft-articulated images of self and sense of power and their inability to see their actual ineffectiveness: a tension the audience easily witnesses through King's dramatization. Their inability to adapt to their surroundings, preferring instead to confront their environment and thus try to impose their own sense of order and hierarchy upon it, sometimes violently, aligns them with the Disney model. In the history books, these attitudes prevailed, they "had their way," but here they are unsuccessful. The creatrix, however, flows smoothly from world to world, from story to story, unfettered by attempts to dominate her. At no point does she beg to save the life of a colonist. She is no Pocahontas in the gendered contests with the masculine deities of Euro-American mythology.

These vignettes are interspersed throughout, as are the narratives of characters whose lives are equally interwoven with the images of Native peoples perpetuated through the popular media of literature and film. The four central characters — four old Indians of indeterminate tribal affiliation and gender — move about through these stories, ostensibly on a mission to set the world (perhaps the reader) aright. Their names are telling: Hawkeye, Lone Ranger, Ishmael, and Robinson Crusoe. (At times they have a companion, Coyote.) This co-opting of popular, fictional Anglo characters who all had an indigenous "sidekick" or partner foregrounds the motif, so prevalent in Disney's model, and comically reverses it. Like the Smith and Pocahontas myth, these popular pairings seem at first innocuous enough, apparently calling for a personal interaction where an intercultural, interracial binary is insignificant; but in Cooper's, Defoe's, and Melville's novels (as well as the film versions of them) and in the popular 1950s television program *The Lone Ranger*, the boomer audience never doubted who the hero, the star, the master is, nor whose culture will survive and prevail.[13] King inverts these roles and thus subverts the convention of representation. Moreover, in his "remagining" of the conventions, racial binaries are blurred by the more important concerns of attitudes: colonist *and* Native.

These four ubiquitous Indians come into the narrative of the Blackfeet characters Charlie and Lionel, who are competing for the love of Alberta. She, however, wants to have a child without the complications of dealing with its father. Such a self-determination makes the love triangle humorous, made so by Alberta's rejection of the assumptions upon which the Pocahontas myth rests. King very cleverly engages the myth at another level, moving from its mythic basis to its myriad manifestations in contemporary life and popular culture. This also implies the ways that the myth has been internalized, by Native and non-Native alike. At one point, all the characters are in separate "locations," yet all are watching the same John Wayne movie on television, or else reading its book-bound equivalent. The ubiquitous influence is obvious, and although — much like Masayesva — King conflates the specifics of individual movies to capture the essential details of their formulae, Hollywood stories do not fare any better in his novel than biblical stories. He co-opts the heroes and images, and their dramatic reenactment leads the audience's imagination into a dramatic, comic reversal of the very tenets upon which inaccurate images of Native Americans rest.

Charlie is an attorney whose father, Portland, is a movie actor, a perpetual extra in westerns. However, although Native, he does not look enough like the popular Hollywood image of the indigenous, so he has to wear a fake nose to make him recognizable as "Indian" and thus marketable. In his later career, even this will not work, so he goes "on stage" at the Four Corners, a burlesque theater. At one point Charlie visits the club, and King's point about "burlesque" — here defined as the Hollywood representation of Indians — is quite clear. The announcer comes on stage: "And now, straight from engagements in Germany, Italy, Paris, and Toronto, that fiery savage, Pocahontas! Put your hands together for the sexiest squaw west of the Mississippi" (238). What ensues is a variation of the female/male configuration of the myth, with Charlie's father springing on stage "in costume" and threatening the defenseless Pocahontas. He strips her, but before he can commit the obvious conclusion to the act, he is confronted by a cowboy who defeats him and makes him crawl "off the stage in defeat." The cowboy then "began dancing with Pocahontas, their groins pressed together tightly, the cowboy's hands clutching the woman's buttocks" (239). The myth has been revised and popularized, and the fundamental conclusion — white man gets Indian woman — is comically re-dramatized. Portland then summarizes the tradition succinctly: "It's a dumb routine.... But that's acting" (239). That's acting, indeed.

This cross-cultural, sexual melodrama — the basis of the romance genre — is brought forth in other variations in the novel, including a continual allusion to captivity narratives, from the appearance of Mary Rowlandson in the first pages to the filmic versions found in such movies as *The Mystic Warrior* (equated here to *Hanta Yo*) and *Dances with Wolves*. Concurrently, the western war genre (and thus violence) is ever-present. The romance and war genres are conflated into the quintessential *The Mysterious Warrior*, the favorite movie of Lionel's boss, Bill Bursum, who owns an appliance store in which he constructs a huge display from television sets configured to resemble the continental United States: he calls it The Map.[14] Here, while playing the old black-and-white John Wayne movie that has come to symbolize the popularized representation King works into other elements of his novel, Bill is shocked to watch as — in direct opposition to the script and all his previous viewings of the drama — the cavalry coming to Wayne's rescue disappear, and the Cheyennes kill him and all his men, as the four old Indians watch in the background, one dressed in a colorful Hawaiian shirt. The convention, so abruptly reversed, becomes immediately visible, and the ideals conveyed through the Smith/Pocahontas image are dislocated using the implement of their original inscription: imaginative drama. Trick the trade, trade and trick.

In brief conclusion, then, *Imagining Indians* ends with the violent overthrow of the apparatus through which representations and images have been created and perpetuated; though, of course, this is all accomplished by means of that apparatus: Masayesva's camera and direction, which dramatize events for us. In *Harold of Orange* and *Green Grass, Running Water* the violence may be deferred, but Vizenor and King also manipulate the apparatus itself — the evocative power of film and novel, respectively — to turn the stage upon which images of Indians have been imprinted into an imaginative quagmire, a humorous destabilizing that ultimately has as its goal a "remaining" of images and the theoretical foundations upon which attitudes of the Other rest. Unlike the Disney pedagogy, here we cannot imaginatively identify with the colonial hero, for to do so would require us to conceive of ourselves as absurd, our agenda flawed, and our "sidekick" our equal, if not our superior. When boomers laugh at these works, we laugh at ourselves and thus at the Disney tradition of resurrecting and perpetuating the myth of colonial correctness and its portrayal. This is perhaps the most powerful tool that can be employed: an imaginative and dramatic self-reenactment through self-doubt, the angst of our generation and the genesis of postmodernism. Methodologies aside, each artist has a finely tuned awareness of the pervasive nature of the myths that have driven much of America's history, and a "sinseer" desire to reinscribe them.

NOTES

1. The popular myth that the individual is supposedly cryogenically preserved somewhere under his Disneyland speaks volumes to his centrality in the psyche of this country as it developed in the twentieth century.

2. In fact, awareness of critical studies seems not to have surfaced in the industry's consciousness either. Ted Turner — former spouse of activist Jane Fonda and one of the most influential (and richest) people in the U.S. entertainment industry — is a self-proclaimed champion of Indian causes, yet when meeting with representatives of the Native American Journalists Association to promote one of his television specials about Native Americans, he was asked about the mascot of his baseball team, the Atlanta Braves. He reportedly responded, "For the most part, I haven't heard that any one really has a problem with the name Braves" ("Medium Rare"). Often, supportive discourse is extremely focused and of short duration; in a word from the industry's lexicon, it is merely "hype." As Leuthold rightly surmises, opinion leaders have a profound effect upon the ways society, that is, the audience, responds and interprets images on screen, but what of the background of the leaders themselves? Like us all, they, too, are bound by sociological forces that have shaped their orientations; when these orientations are challenged, they are equally defensive.

3. In fact, within the last few years, corporate America has made increasing use of this generation's popular culture, with commercials employing popular musical hits from the 1950s and 1960s and popular figures from that era as well. Also, Hollywood has recently remade numerous movies from the era, including family movies made popular by Disney.

4. One obvious example is the way that, during his program, Disney spoke directly to his audience while also carrying on conversations with animated characters such as Mickey Mouse. This blurring between electronic transmission and live performance — the dramatizing of prerecorded, highly manipulated text — and between lived experience and fantasy is immensely provocative.

5. Given the era of its production, I am making an assumption of gender here.

6. Perhaps one irony of the early pictorial representations can be found in the ways the Other was so closely aligned, physically, with the colonists themselves. Despite su-

perficial physical differences, the humanity of the subject was very obvious; what differed was material — technology, clothing — or cosmological. This is an odd mixed message, given the binaries of the era, the conflict. In this way, the representation may come close to works found in the 1950s. For instance, Daniel Boone's sidekick in the popular television series was Native born but educated (read: civilized) in England.

7. This is yet another movie from the 1950s.

8. The war genre includes a scene in which Gary Cooper and his cavalry troops withstand an attack by the Cheyennes, who charge their position down a shallow river; this is almost identical to the charge found in several places in King's novel.

9. I should note here that I am drawing material from two sources: the screenplay and the movie. There are distinct variations in the two, which I note when necessary.

10. This scene is from the screenplay and is slightly different from the film, in which New Crows' first response is simply "Which way?" This opens the possibility for the board member to question the answering question, which could mean "Which way do you want me to think?"

11. It is attractive to paraphrase Vizenor's words during the softball game: "Remember what American writers said our ancestors did."

12. In a comic exchange between two board members, the nature of this revolution is once more outlined:

ANDREW: Kingsley, tell me, is he serious?

KINGSLEY: Harold insists that he is a trickster . . .

ANDREW: A confidence man?

KINGSLEY: No, a tribal trickster is not the same. . . . He is rather sincere, even innocent, artless at times. . . . He believes that he can stop time and change the world through the imagination.

Andrew is nonplused; he pulls his ear and frowns.

ANDREW: With a foundation grant of course . . .

KINGSLEY: Of course. . . . Who could change the world without a foundation grant?

The primacy of the imagination, coupled with wordplay focused on "foundation grants," carries much of Vizenor's humor forward.

13. For a survey of "master" discourse in film, see Prats.

14. It is interesting to consider the critical work of Louis Owens here, particularly his discussion of "the map of the mind" from D'Arcy McNickle.

Our own experiences and our own lives don't fit the stereotypes . . . our experience is denied us.

Linda Hogan [Chickasaw], in
Winged Words: American Indian Writers Speak

Telling Stories for Readers

The Interplay of Orality and Literacy in
Clara Pearson's Nehalem Tillamook Tales

JAROLD RAMSEY

Anyone hoping to engage a body of traditional Native American narratives as literature would do well to reflect on Melville Jacobs's challenge in 1962, based on his long, often frustrating, and unrecognized work with Native repertories in the state of Oregon: "Are Oregon's Indian literatures so shabbily represented, in such deteriorated versions, or so bleakly unaccompanied by backgrounds of the sociocultural systems which had maintained them, that annotative commentary on their features of expressive content and style is not possible?" ("Fate of Indian Oral Literatures" 96–97). Perhaps here and elsewhere in his writings, Jacobs, like some of our contemporary theoreticians, does paint too dark (and proprietary) a picture of the difficulties in such study, and in particular it might be objected that he seriously underestimates the possibility that informed and sympathetic Euro-American readers can grasp the imaginative substance of Native texts and at least something of their formal strategies. But the obstacles before us in doing so are considerable, not just in terms of the loss of ethnological and linguistic information that Jacobs emphasizes but also in terms of the cultural and literary biases that we tend to bring to any textualized oral-traditional material.

Consider the texts that Melville and Elizabeth Jacobs presented in *Nehalem Tillamook Tales*: typical of their kind, they come to us from three radical removes. First, they have been transcribed from one verbal mode of representation into another — that is, from oral performance within an anonymous, nonliterate tradition into print. Second, they have undergone translation from the matrix of their Native language into English — in the present instance, Clara Pearson actually told her stories to Elizabeth Jacobs in English but apparently did so through a process of rapid self-translation. Third, these narratives come to us as expressive embodiments of a culture radically different from our own, so that in reading such narratives, we must somehow manage to "intertextualize" them — that is, view them simultaneously in the dim light of what we can know about the Tillamook cultural way and in the glaring light of our own way.

Pursuing such material in one of these lights without the other is certain to yield either of two forms of interpretive distortion all too common in intercultural study. If we engage these texts exclusively as Tillamook Salish materials, then we tend to restrict them to the status of artifacts, museum relics of a vanished people, and neglect or ignore altogether their value as verbal art; if, on the other hand, we engage them uncritically as "stories" in our terms, without the benefit of ethnographic understanding, then we inevitably misappropriate and co-opt them ethnocentrically according to our preconceptions about literature and its ends and means.

The latter distortion is, of course, the more common and apparent, disfiguring most attempts to "claim" Indian traditional literature wholesale as "American literature" from Hiawatha on, as Arnold Krupat, David Murray, William Clements, and others have shown. But the imposition of a strictly anthropological or linguistic perspective on the Native repertories has had, I think, its own pernicious consequences over a century of scholarship, in severely retarding the recognition of the rich verbal artistry of these repertories and of those who performed them—an artistry that Native Americans have clearly cherished (what else made these stories persistently memorable to them?), and that can and should speak to us, over the dislocations of literary mode, language, and culture.

In the ongoing work of ethnopoetics, embracing anthropology, ethnology, folklore, linguistics, and literary theory, these two perspectives are held to be ideally complementary, each essential to the aim of fully revealing the literary achievements of tribal peoples. In Dell Hymes's judicious observation, the pioneer linguists and ethnographers who recorded American Indian stories and songs "preserved more than they knew: authentic monuments, to be sure, but something more. We must work to make visible and audible again that something more—the literary form in which the native words had their being—so that they can move again at a pace that is surer, more open to the voice, more nearly their own" ("*In Vain*" 384).

Now we should turn to the particular case of Mrs. Clara Pearson's stories in *Nehalem Tillamook Tales*. In terms of the kinds of interpretive difficulties I have been outlining, it is surely one of the most accessible scholarly collections of Native texts now available, and one of the most readable, most "open to the voice" in Hymes's terms. The fact that Pearson told her stories to Elizabeth Jacobs in English might raise serious questions of verbal authenticity (as it does in many popular collections), except for two countervailing facts. First, Pearson (who was literate in English) was fluent in Tillamook Salish (specifically in the Nehalem dialect) and had learned her repertory of stories in that language from her father.

Second, the research of May Mandelbaum Edel on variability in Tillamook storytelling reveals a remarkable degree of stability and continuity in the literature. Edel made a systematic comparison of Pearson's Tillamook-language dictations to her in 1931 and Pearson's dictations in English to Jacobs in 1934. She then examined the same stories in Franz Boas's 1890 transcription from informants of an earlier generation and found very little difference between the three sets of stories on the level of plot. She concluded that "the duplicated stories are virtually identical in both accounts. There is no major reworking of materials to distinct literary ends. There are a few characteristic differences in style — particularly a greater expansiveness in the English version — but for most of the tales the abstracts are interchangeable" (Edel, "Stability," 116). Evidently, then, unlike other Native communities, where considerable innovation and improvisation by storytellers is acceptable by convention, among the Tillamooks a convention of literary conservatism prevailed. Pearson's memory that she and other children were made to learn the stories "line-by-line" in special winter sessions readily explains how this convention was maintained, even in latter-day Tillamook times (Jacobs and Jacobs, *Nehhalem* vii; subsequently cited as NTT).

So in Clara Pearson's fluent, energetic English texts we are presumably close to the narrative substance and order of her traditional Tillamook models. But the dynamics of her tellings were far from traditional. Elizabeth Jacobs remarks that "early in our work I suspected that Mrs. Pearson, while telling the stories in English, was doing so by means of a rapid and close translation from [Tillamook] into English" — a hunch that she subsequently confirmed with her collaborator (NTT, viii). The image of this accomplished storyteller thinking her stories in Tillamook and rapidly translating them into English is appealing, and expressive, I think, of the vital persistence and adaptability of Indian oral-traditional literature and of the literary skill of tradition-based Indian storytellers. Some years ago I heard a Wasco Chinookan matron, an old acquaintance whose considerable storytelling prowess I had never guessed at, perform a well-known Wasco story ("The Deserted Boy") in English "with all the trimmings," breaking into the Wasco language (*kiksht*) for the story's dramatic songs and then, catching her breath, telling her audience of Euro-American schoolteachers with good-humored exasperation, "I wish I could be giving you this in 'Indian' — it's hard to get it right in English!" — and then going on, for her own delight, it seemed clear, as well as for ours, in what appeared to be a very swift and agile process of translation, not only from the one language system to the other, but also from the one culture to the other. Pearson —

who had acquired a certain popularity in her community for telling her stories in English before her work with May Edel and Elizabeth Jacobs — would no doubt have sympathized with my friend's exasperation and applauded her efforts at a very complex intercultural translation (Edel, "Stability" 117).

Overall, without doubting their essential authenticity relative to Tillamook tradition, I find in Pearson's English-language narratives extensive evidence of her accommodation to Euro-American audiences or, to be more precise, to the prospect of such a readership. Perhaps she was encouraged in this by the Jacobses, who appear to have aimed at a balance of scholarly standards and general readability in their book. (At an early stage of their work they were thinking of preparing a "popular edition" of it.)[1] But the main accommodations are clearly Pearson's own — and they almost certainly have something to do with her practice of translating her stories from Tillamook into English as she told them. What I mean is that the continuous process of translating the words of the stories must have prompted her to adjust the style of her tellings as well, seeking not just semantic but also literary intelligibility in the new language and in print. On this point, at least, it seems necessary to challenge Edel's assertion that the stories in *Nehalem Tillamook Texts* show "no major reworking to distinct literary ends."

For example, there are her numerous, carefully setoff and generally very helpful asides and explanations. Such "editorial" commentary is not a feature of her Tillamook-language tellings to May Edel, suggesting that in her English performances, she was consciously adjusting her repertory to non-Native listeners and readers (Edel, "Stability" 124–25).[2] Some of the explanations in *Nehalem Tillamook Tales* are specific to particular episodes, as with her careful summary interpretation of story #14, "Wild Woman," a tale of incest between a brother and sister, focusing on their son: "This story shows how a young person who is born in disgraceful circumstances through no fault of his own will obtain a strong [spirit] power" (*NTT* 58).

Explanatory material of a different sort frequently appears, as Edel notes, at the conclusions of Pearson's English tellings: namely, etiological interpretations of the stories as origin-myths ("Stability" 125). For example, after the Elk brothers have killed a murderous Beaver, it is mythically decreed that "No more will any Beaver kill people. He will live in a cave in the wintertime, and in the summer he will travel in the water. He will be just a beaver then" (*NTT* 108–9). Such mythic "codas" are, of course, common in the recorded texts of many Western Indian repertories, but Edel observes that, except for Pearson's "Transformer-cycle" stories, they are lacking in her Tillamook-language tellings ("Stability" 124). Why then did she tend to add them to her English performances? Perhaps because whereas they were once implied as part of the context of such stories for Tillamook listeners, and thus optional in performance, they would not be to Euro-Americans, and so she spelled them out in her English texts.

Elsewhere, Pearson offers commentary on characters in her stories, helpfully noting in passing how the behavior of a character in some episode typifies his or her role in the whole Tillamook mythology. Thus her typological summary of Ice as an actor in the adventures of his nemesis, the trickster-transformer South Wind: "Ice was a bad old man but he was comical too. He just could not leave anything alone, he had to have his nose in everything" (NTT 146). In general, such commentary by recitalists is as rare as it is valuable, helping us to appreciate how a particular character or story is aligned with what the Nez Perce scholar Archie Phinney called the tribal "mythbody": "Any substantial appreciation of [Indian] tales must come not from the simple elements of drama unfolded in them but from vivid feelings within oneself, feeling as a moving current all the figures and the relationships that belong to the whole mythbody" (Phinney ix).

Likewise, in telling her stories Clara Pearson usually seems to strategically defer to our Euro-American impatience with the formal repetition of actions according to tribal cult-numbers that is so prominent a structural feature of American Indian oral tradition. (The Tillamooks were unusual in following a dual, gendered cult-number system — five for males, four for females. See M. Jacobs, *Content* 226, and Hymes, "In Need" 158 ff.) Instead of drawing episodes out to their full five (or four) verbatim reenactments, in her English retellings she typically notes the fact of the repetition and then jumps from the first to the last (and climactic) event in the series: "The next two brothers went the same way. Everything was just the same except for the fifth one, the youngest brother. Why do none of my brothers come home? I must go and look for them" (NTT, #35, 115). After a similar abridgment in another story, Jacobs asked her why she had departed from convention, and she replied, "There is no use telling it over and over. . . . those old people would always tell the same thing over and over for each of those brothers. There is no sense in that because it is only the last one, the youngest, the fifth brother, who does differently. So I tell about the first and then jump to the last" (NTT 33). The emphasis here in phrases like "no use" and "no sense" would appear to be on the circumstances at hand: telling her stories in English for transcription, with the prospect of their being published and read by non-Native readers.

Again, May Edel's transcriptions of Pearson's performances of these stories in Tillamook remain mostly unpublished and untranslated, but the evidence available now indicates that Pearson did not take such liberties when she was telling them to Edel in their original language — which is exactly what we might expect ("Stability" 117, 125; "Tillamook" 52–53). In any event, in her English tellings she seems to be impatient with the traditional narrative patternings, dutifully noting what she is synopsizing but then getting on with the main line of the story in Euro-American fashion. To explain her technique in terms of acculturation per se is too simple, surely: on this point as on others she seems to be following a conscious strategy of adjusting old stories to new contexts and conventions of understanding, new literary needs.

Such structural alterations on Clara Pearson's part do not change the outlines of her stories, as Edel has noted, but they are the more striking for being departures from the Tillamook convention of nonvariation in storytelling, and as such they seem to underscore the idea that in her performances for Elizabeth Jacobs, she was skillfully recomposing her Tillamook repertory for specific intercultural reasons. But it is in the distinctive texture of Clara Pearson's narrations that we find, I think, the most salient evidence of her self-conscious adjustment of the Tillamook repertory toward the Eurocentric print-based literary mode. Edel does glance at this difference of texture between her Tillamook and English versions, speaking of it as "a greater expansiveness" and "a greater richness in detail" in the English texts, but she does so, it seems, only to provide "exceptions to prove the general rule" of her thesis about the consistency between the two sets of texts ("Stability" 125–26).

Compared to most Native American narrative texts — Melville Jacobs's presentation of Clackamas Chinook myths, for example, or Franz Boas's 1890 versions of some of these same Nehalem stories — Pearson's storytelling style is persistently rich (beyond her interpolated glosses and explanations) in overt descriptive, motivational, and behavioral detail and, as regards the narrative itself, in expository and transitional material. In contrast, Melville Jacobs (speaking of the great Clackamas storyteller Victoria Howard) observes that "[the] recitalist never once verbalized a motivation, feeling, or mood of the actors in a myth or tale" (*People* x). This to-us-disconcerting sparseness and abruptness in most Native texts is, of course, expressive of a style of storytelling that is premised on the mediative advantages of oral performance and on a Native audience already familiar with the elements of what is being told; in Pearson's texts, it is replaced by a style that appears to be largely independent of both advantages, although eminently "listenable" in the mind's ear (like all good prose).

Consider the expressive fullness and accessibility of the following, which opens the tale of a man's weird sojourn with Thunder Bird:

A man lived at Tillamook. In the wintertime he went far up small streams to spear steelhead. When he went fishing he wore a water-proof cape. It was fastened at the waist with a belt. He wore a spruce-root rain hat. It was held on tightly by an inner cedar-bark band. One day he put on his cape and his rain hat and started out. It was a bad day, hailing, and there was lightning. When the hail stopped he would go along and look for fish. He did not get any. Soon again there was thunder and lightning. He became angry, he said, "Confound it! That Thunder!" He cursed him. "I cannot get any fish," he said. "You [Thunder] might as well come along and take me with you!" Then how it hailed! He stood under a tree for shelter. Now he saw a man, a huge man. The big man said, "You wanted me to come. I have come to take you home with me." (NTT #51, 167)

Pearson goes on from this masterful beginning to develop a wonder tale of an ordinary mortal living with giants (Thunder Bird and his wife); her management of imaginative scale is worthy of Swift's in *Gulliver's Travels* and is quite as rich in evocative details, both of the physical disproportion between the man and his huge but good-hearted hosts and of their reactions to each other's size. Thunder Bird's wife, for example, is enchanted with the man's skill in making his own spears and knives, which she can barely see — "Oh, you are so cute! How can you manage to make things so tiny? My goodness! You who are so little know so much about building things!" And the man's own Gulliveresque curiosity about the giants leads him to wonder about their sexual practices — which old woman Thunder obligingly describes with gusto: "Yes, yes, grandchild!" she said. "We are very large indeed. When we copulate, when grandpa lies on me, we reach quite high. We must have big, wide covers to cover ourselves." Then he was ashamed. "After this," he promised himself, "I will not think any such foolish things" (169–70).

Both in the explicit physical detailing of scenes in such passages and in their direct rendering of emotions, then, Pearson diverges considerably from the characteristic dramatic terseness of Native American oral narratives, at least as we usually get them in text form — approximating, I think quite self-consciously, the texture of Euro-American prose narrative. Again, I am dwelling on this feature of *Nehalem Tillamook Tales* not to denigrate its contents as somehow less than authentic but, on the contrary, to suggest that these stories may well represent an important but neglected evolutionary stage between oral-traditional and print-based, authored Native literary art. Was Clara Pearson, one might ask, an avid reader? What kinds of fiction did she like and perhaps take as models? Did she actively help Elizabeth Jacobs in getting her dictations "right" on the page? Did she ever go to the next step of "self-dictation" and actually write out her own stories, as many of our best modern storytellers — Jay O'Callahan, Donald Davis, Jackie Torrence, Diane Wolkstein, Rafe Martin, to name a few — are doing? These are, alas, questions without answers, but I want to propose that one of the fascinations of these stories is that in their readability, according to Eurocentric conventions, they anticipate the work of latter-day Indian writers like Leslie Silko and James Welch, in whose novels and stories Native oral traditions are radically transfigured in modern English, asserting their vitality anew despite the radical change of medium.

When I undertook preparation of *Nehalem Tillamook Tales* for re-publication in 1990, I invited Dell Hymes to contribute commentary on the Pearson/Jacobs texts according to his concept of "measured verse" in Chinookan and other Western Indian literatures. His tentative analysis and verse re-presentation of one story, "Split-His-Own-Head" (#37), appeared in the new edition, and since then Hymes has continued to work on his thesis that Clara Pearson's English tellings display her competence in the conventions of the traditional Tillamook repertory by following a strict system of measure, on the level of parts, scenes, stanzas, and lines of verse as the organizing units of the text.

How does this argument square with my claims here that Pearson was self-consciously adjusting her Tillamook originals to circumstances of translation, transcription, publication, and reading, and that the texture of her stories in English is that of very readable prose? If the two arguments are at odds, it is clear that (as Hymes remarks about study of the Tillamook repertory in general) resolutions and last words will have to wait until May Edel's Tillamook texts and translations become generally available and a long-awaited dictionary of the language appears (Hymes, "In Need" 157–58). But for now, it ought to be said that his position and mine on *Nehalem Tillamook Tales* are not as mutually exclusive as it might seem. I am persuaded by his general argument that English texts like "Split-His-Own-Head" are, in fact, organized as narratives by the same patternings of events, scenes, and stanzas that presumably "measured" their Tillamook originals. For Pearson to endeavor to follow these traditional narrative patternings even while she was self-consciously accommodating the stories to Euro-American literary understandings in the ways I have been discussing certainly seems possible and would testify all the more to her intercultural literary competence.

But the texture of the narratives in *Nehalem Tillamook Tales* does look, sound, and feel like the texture of good prose to me: meaning that they seem to grow freely out of sentences rather than out of a system of lines; that narrative discursiveness and generously amplified detail are the rule, rather than "poetic" selection and compression; and that the moment-by-moment unfolding of the stories seems in the main to proceed linearly (helped out by the serial elisions noted above), rather than by the incremental repetitions of a priori patterns.

Where a Hymesian measured-verse retranslation of, say, a Clackamas Chinookan text first read as prose is generally a revelation of rediscovered expressive form, the recast verse text of "Split-His-Own-Head" seems somewhat artificial to me, alongside the supple prose sentences and paragraphs of Elizabeth Jacobs's text. And I suspect that my resistance would be even stronger to measured-verse representations of Clara Pearson's most fully elaborated and compelling stories, like "Thunder Bird" (#51, discussed above) and her unforgettable horror-tale of sibling incest, "Wild Woman" (#15).[3] Maybe, once all the Tillamook-language material now in manuscript is available, masterful stories like these can serve as "test cases" for the issue at hand, allowing us to sort out the virtues and the limits of measured-verses analysis as applied to the Tillamook repertory. But, for the time being, I continue to hold that, given the texture of the stories and what seem to have been the special circumstances of Clara Pearson's work on them with Elizabeth Jacobs, they have come to us rightly in the form of prose. Not the slipshod, more rough than ready prose of most published textualizations of Native oral-traditional narrative, but rather a collaborative medium, involving both transcriber and teller.[4]

I am aware that these are propositions bristling with theoretical implications, but for reasons of space I cannot do more here than note a few of them. The process I have identified in Pearson's "storytelling for reading" obviously has considerable bearing on the subject of Father Walter Ong's *Orality and Literacy*—but between Ong's theoretical formulations and the particulars of the case at hand, I find very little to connect. What Pearson is doing with oral tradition does not fit his category of "secondary orality" (136–37), and his elaborate checklist of the formal and psychodynamic differences between orality and literacy seems mostly irrelevant to her accommodations to reading (ch. 3). Perhaps it is not unfair to say that in this we touch on a major shortcoming of Ong's pioneering study: that in its severely dichotomized scheme it neglects situations—as with Indian writers for over a century now—where orality and literacy are not polar opposites but rather modalities of discourse and representation that can "speak to" and energize each other, even when the circumstances are intercultural.

Ong declares more than once that, contrary to the speaker's sense of his auditors, "the writer's audience is always a fiction. The fictionality of readers is what makes writing so difficult" (102, 177). We might well theorize in these terms about Pearson's "audience," or rather her apparent shift from tribal audience per se toward readership—and a non-Tillamook, Euro-American readership at that. What would this mean? The evidence is clear, I think, that for Pearson it entailed a kind of intercultural solicitude—leading her to re-imagine and re-present her Tillamook originals in performance so that at least some of their cultural nuances, which tribal auditors once registered without help, could be understood by outsiders like us, beginning with her scribe/editor/first reader, Elizabeth Jacobs. Likewise, it entailed anticipating intercultural misunderstandings over narrative conventions, on the score of repetition of actions, for example (as we have seen) and adjusting her tellings accordingly.

Pearson's "reader-solicitous" practices are not unique in the domain of transcribed Indian texts. When Gilbert Minthorne performed the Cayuse/Nez Perce hero-story of Fish-Hawk's raid against the Sioux for Morris Swadesh, his concluding words poignantly expressed his satisfaction in completing an intercultural collaboration whose literary product would have a kind of validity and permanence as a text, whoever might read it. "Thus they told the story, and all the people know it. This is a true story; now then, we have made it, and it will always be a true story" (Ramsey, *Coyote* 10).

And all through Harry Robinson's work with Wendy Wickwire to record his Okanagan repertory, his literary interest in collaborating to provide "an opportunity for readers to experience storytelling straight from the source" (as Wickwire puts it) is explicit, resulting in story-texts that, like Pearson's, are rich in descriptive and explanatory details, clearly anticipating the needs of readers to come. In his own words to Wickwire: "The stories are worked on by [b]oth of us you and I" (14, 10).

Such texts amount to exact and instructive opposites to the all-too-familiar case of Native traditional stories being utterly transmogrified by Eurocentric writers and editors so as to read like fairy tales, just-so stories, or adventure tales. For their part, Clara Pearson and Harry Robinson were doing something very different, in making their accommodations to the creation of texts — something expressive of their belief in the continuing vitality and significance of the old stories in spite of change, and expressive, too, of their integrity as keepers and conveyers of Native tradition. In these terms, again, they are worthy forerunners of Indian writers to come.

Considering Clara Pearson, we would do her and her stories a great disservice if we see her only as "the informant," only a faceless, passive vehicle or conduit of oral tradition. It seems to me that Pearson's artistry is tangible on every page of the texts she made with Elizabeth Jacobs: in her adjustments from hearing the stories in Tillamook to reading them in English; in her sure-handed refabulation of old narrative formulas into scenes of great dramatic vividness and power; in her loving evocations of the distinctive weather and landmarks of the Tillamook homeland; in her exploitations, both broad and subtle, of the Tillamook taste in humor; in her gift for enriching the texture of her stories by devising startling images and figures that are all her own, as when brave little Muskrat returns sunlight to the people after its theft by Beaver: "He carried that sun just as if it were a clock!" (*NTT* 84).

Thinking of Clara Pearson and her work alongside two other Northwest Indian storytellers who were also providentially discovered and recorded as "the last of their kind" — Victoria Howard of the Clackamas and Charles Cultee of the Cathlamets — some would no doubt counsel skepticism about claims for artistic value in such material. After all, so the argument runs, it is all too easy in our appropriative culture to guiltily valorize last survivors and their sad artifacts just for being last. But maybe this position is backward. The literary legacy of Clara Pearson, like that of Victoria Howard and Charles Cultee, suggests that over the years she may have come to be the last surviving and definitive keeper of her people's literary art precisely — tragically — because she was a gifted and dedicated artist.

NOTES

An abbreviated version of this essay was first presented at "A Symposium on American Indian Literatures" at Cornell University, April 3, 1998; parts of it are adapted from my introduction to Elizabeth and Melville Jacobs, *Nehalem Tillamook Tales* — hereafter cited as *NTT*. Elizabeth Jacobs's Tillamook Field Notebooks and Research Notes are used by permission of the trustees of the Whatcom Museum of History and Art, Bellingham, Washington.

1. In Packet 106 of Elizabeth Jacobs's Tillamook Field Notebooks and Research Notes (in the Melville Jacobs Collection of the University of Washington Archives), there is a draft of a brief introduction (dated 1941) to what she describes as a "popular edition" of Clara Pearson's stories, as suggested by the director of the University of Oregon Press, George Belknap. The Jacobs's persistence in getting *NTT* into print was heroic: the collection was originally accepted for publication in the *Memoirs of the American Folklore Society* in 1935–36, returned in 1940 "for lack of funds," then accepted by the University of Oregon Press in 1941 — but not published until 1959, well after Pearson's death in 1948. I am grateful to the Whatcom County Museum of History and Art for permission to use manuscripts in the Melville Jacobs Collection.

2. In the only Tillamook-language/interlinear translation text published by Edel, a story about the trickster Gatc'elau, or "Ice," and corresponding in some details to story #1, "The Round Trip of Ice," in *NTT*, Clara Pearson offers no explanations or editorial comments. See Edel, "The Tillamook Language," 52–53.

3. I examine the "Wild Woman" story (under the title "Wild Woman and the Brother and Sister Who Marry") from a narratological perspective in "Uncursing the Misbegotten in a Tillamook Incest Story" in Ramsey, *Reading the Fire*, 96–120.

4. Although Elizabeth Jacobs was on the whole a careful transcriber and editor of Clara Pearson's dictations, she acknowledges that she did rephrase some of her collaborator's colloquialisms — "I have frequently substituted a better known English syn-

onym where I felt that the unique flavor or accurate meaning of the original would be undisturbed by that exchange" (*NTT* viii). In fact, as such "minor" emendations accumulate, they can change the texture of Pearson's telling, as is seen in the following comparison of a passage from a text in *NTT* and its unedited original in Elizabeth Jacobs's Tillamook Field Notebooks. Each passage tells of the distress of the Tillamook trickster South Wind, who has gotten himself pregnant. Jacobs's edited text reads: "Now something became wrong with South Wind. He did not know who did it or how he had become that way, but he was pregnant. He did not know how it could have happened but he knew what it was that was wrong with him. Soon, all by himself, he began to have labor pains. Oh, he suffered, suffered, suffered, he felt as if he were dying because, as you know, there was no place for the child to come out" (*NTT* #38, 141). The unedited original text reads: "Something got the matter with him. Don't know who did it or how he got that way. But he got in the family way. He don't know how it happened. But he knew what was wrong and he began to have labor pains all by himself. Oh, he suffer, suffer, suffer, he like to die, because, you know, there's no place for it to come out" (Field Notebook #111, 61). To what extent such rephrasings and emendations would limit the validity of close verse-analysis of the texts in *NTT* remains to be seen.

. . . many of the photographers wanted to photograph Indians to appear to be traditional. They wanted the perfect Indian, before he vanished. They dressed Indians from a trunk, pastiche junk, and in fact there are photographs of Indians who are wearing feather headdresses — feather dusters, because that's all the photographer could find to decorate them with . . . if you're a tribal person and you want to confront or get a piece of all of that or step into the shadow of that photographic image of power, you dress up like the photograph. You'll be instantly recognized.

Gerald Vizenor [Chippewa],
in *Winged Words: American Indian Writers Speak*

Cooperation and Resistance

Native American Collaborative Personal Narrative

KATHLEEN M. SANDS

Twenty-three years ago, driving the two-lane highway from Tucson to Sells, Arizona, site of the tribal headquarters of the Tonoho O'odham Indian nation, I hummed with anticipation, eager to begin my first fieldwork project.[1] The road cutting across the Papagueria Desert was lonesome. Only lavender ironwood blossoms and splashes of yellow paloverde flowers and blue lupine colored the grey-green monotone of boulders, cacti, and jagged peaks. The air was soft, the desert familiar and promising. And I was ready — so I thought — to solicit a comprehensive personal narrative from a Tonoho O'odham man. With his agreement, the project would culminate in a book-length collaborative autobiography. And I had reason to believe he would agree, if for no other reason than that he was trapped in a full body cast as a result of being hit by a car. I knew from a friend of his, one of my professors, that he was thoroughly bored with the routine of the tribal hospital and would welcome a diversion, especially if it gave him an opportunity to tell his life story.

Though we had never met, Theodore Rios was not a stranger. I had read a series of transcripts of interviews with him, collected by an anthropologist and archived at the University of Arizona, where I was completing my doctoral work.[2] I knew a version of Ted's life story; I carried his distinctive voice in my head. I knew he could tell a story — "a good one" — as he often later characterized the incidents and events he narrated. I had been studying Papago language and culture, and I had nearly memorized the Maria Chona/Ruth Underhill *Papago Woman* collaborative autobiography text that had generated my interest in Papago culture and that has been the focus of a great deal of critical scholarship since the 1970s.

As I rumbled across the cattle guard at the entrance to the tribal hospital, the vibration it generated in my beat-up Rambler station wagon was indistinguishable from the flutter my nerves produced. The confidence of the open road gave way to a sense of panic. In a rumbling, clattering instant, I realized I

134

was crazy to assume that I could mediate the telling of a Native life. I recognized that I did not begin to know enough to even make a proper beginning, let alone see the project through to publication. I was right on both counts. That cattle guard shook some sense into me, but, of course, I had gone too far to turn back. I parked and walked into the shade of the hospital and into the responsibility of inscribing a life that both haunts and drives my work even today.

Ted agreed to the project, and we started working together, neither of us initially negotiating how the project would work. We simply signed a letter of intent regarding publication rights — coauthorship — and began a conversation that went on regularly for months and intermittently for years. Inexperienced and nervous, I started out asking far too many questions, hardly allowing him a chance to answer. He forced me to slow down, often ignoring my questions and telling his life his way. When he was released from the hospital, we continued to meet regularly at his home, a short walk from the mission at San Xavier. He slowly recovered, we made a film together,[3] I finished my degree and moved to Phoenix, he ended up in a rest home not far from where I was living, I published an article on his sense of multiple audience,[4] he went back to San Xavier, and the stories stopped when he died. He gained a little local fame from the work and film and article, but the book — it didn't happen, not in time for Ted. The failure is entirely mine. Ted told "a good one." I just didn't know how to get it from tape to print, and I'm not sure I do even now, after twenty years of study and scholarly writing about Native American collaborative autobiography. When I began, I knew too little; now, perhaps I know too much. Both conditions are paralyzing.[5] But I am beginning to see Ted's story as a way to examine the process of collaborative personal narrative. The unfinished work we did together, taken in the context of the history of critical work on ethnographic and literary personal narratives, may offer a way to open up to critical scrutiny the process of the transformation of narrated life to inscribed text. Ted's story may be "a good one" for initiating a more useful and honest way to think about, talk about, and write about the negotiation of two separate individuals from two separate cultures who have separately conceived ideas about the intention and the value of the encounter they work to transform into cross-cultural inscription.

What I have just done is the oldest trick going for establishing the credibility and "authority" of the collector/editor of Native American collaborative autobiography. It is a convention of the "genre,"[6] one of its worst, since through modesty and expressions of care and concern and a heavy dose of personal background, it usurps the power of the Native narrator and places the credentials of collector/editor as the singular criteria for the "authenticity" and value of the inscribed narrative.[7] The twist — at least I certainly hope this rather

painful self-revelation is not simply another example of conventional strategies — is that the project I've just introduced is a twenty-three-year failure —
my failure. The credentials are honest, but the claim to authority is false. If I
had felt authoritative — a false and hegemonic concept to begin with — about
completing this work, it would have been in print years ago. Instead, I have
packed the transcripts of the sessions with Ted from Phoenix to Oregon and
back, to Greece and Portugal. The burden has not grown lighter with time.

However, the last two decades have not been entirely wasted where the Rios
narrative is concerned. I have studied ethnographic autobiographies, literary
autobiographies, theory of autobiography and ethnography, postmodern theory, oral tradition ethnopoetics, and the new ethnography; I know much more
today than I did when I crossed that cattle guard at Sells. Despite becoming
more educated on the subject, essentially what I have accumulated in two decades — besides quite a case of guilt — is a lot of questions, a vocabulary that is
still inadequate to the task, a high level of discomforting self-consciousness,
and a growing recognition that failure is, indeed, a tough teacher. But maybe it
is also a beginning point for attempting a new way of inscribing a collaborative
autobiography project, one that acknowledges degrees and impacts of cultural
difference and reveals the complexities of the field experience and the transformation of that sometimes cooperative, sometimes resistant, process into a
written text. Am I ready to finish the Rios project? I think so. But that's another story.[8]

What I want to do here is use my experience of failure with the Rios narrative as a point of departure from which to examine some of the techniques,
strategies, terminology, conventions, theories, and critical assumptions that
act as impediments to comprehension of the process of Native American collaborative personal narrative. My intention is not to denigrate the work that
has been done in this field; great breakthroughs have been made in the century
since Native American life stories began to be inscribed, especially in the 1990s.
But as I read new published texts and critical works on this topic, my concern
grows that Native American collaborative narratives are being misinterpreted,
that reductive theoretical paradigms are being applied to extremely complex
literary productions. Maybe because I have been in the field, I am not satisfied
with purely textual analysis. Maybe because I have been there, I believe Native
American personal narratives are not, as they have been characterized recently,
examples of colonialism.[9] I believe, in fact, that they are acts of narrative resistance.

I use the term *resistance* in a very specific sense. I do not want to suggest that
Native narrators who speak of their lives resist the collaborative relationship or
that they use the narrative process as a deliberately subversive venue. Though I

can certainly cite examples of what I think are subversive texts — Geronimo's, for instance — I believe Native American collaborative autobiographies are not usually so overtly politically charged. Rather, I see narrative resistance as an inevitable but rarely examined outcome of the personal cross-cultural exchange. As David Moore points out, "A dialogic system generates interactions, *oppositions*, and alliances" ("Decolonializing" 19; emphasis added). Thus I introduce the term *resistance* in order to name what I see as an inherent part of the dialogic that occurs between collector/editor and narrator in Native American collaborative autobiography. Further, I see resistance in the collaborative process as most clearly articulated and available in the areas of Native linguistics and cultural aesthetics. Native narrators resist the conventions and language of Euro-American autobiography. Their Indian voices persist even in the most oppressive collaborative works.

That is not to say that I do not recognize colonialism as a significant factor in the collection and publication of Native American personal narratives.[10] Collaborative autobiographies are never ahistorical; they are the product of their times, the Native narrator's experience and memory, and the conventions of the collector/editor's discipline at a particular moment. Many, even those recently published, are clearly situated in what James Clifford calls the salvage mode ("On Ethnographic" 113). They are intended to provide "self-narrated" records of representative individual lives in what were assumed to be vanishing tribes. These collaborative narratives clearly fall within the perimeters of the larger U.S. policy of dominance over Native peoples. In effect, they objectify Native narrators by inscribing them as representatives of dying cultures or aspects of traditional cultures. In them, the dynamics of culture change and survival, both pre-encounter and that affected by tribal encounters with Euro-American culture, are often ignored in favor of narratives that focus exclusively on traditional lifeways. They are, despite the conventional use of present tense in their presentation, framed in the elegaic mode.

Addressing salvage ethnography as it impacts the processes and products of collaborative inscriptions is important and useful. For example, Helen Carr's recent analysis of *Papago Woman* — to remain temporarily consistent in terms of looking at O'odham literary production — historicizes the relationship of Ruth Underhill and Maria Chona by demonstrating the dominance of Underhill's salvage agenda in the text originally published in the 1930s. She notes that this "text embodies the period's primitivist critique of modern life," pointing out that the text "stresses the Papago's sensitivity to natural rhythms, and the calm peaceful tempo of their lives." She states, "Underhill has chosen to emphasize the rituals and harmonies of Chona's life. Relations with government officials, references to the support the Papago gave to the U.S. against the

Apache, the eventual establishment of the reservation — all which must have been part of Chona's experience — never appear" (245–46). In sum, Carr notes, "the central oppressive power in Chona's life," Euro-Americans, is absent in the text (249). Carr demonstrates that postcolonial theory allows the critic to uncover the allegory of salvage inscription. By foregrounding colonial relations between Underhill and Chona, Carr emphasizes cultural difference, an important element of collaborative personal narratives, but the analysis of difference is lopsided. Focus on the collector/editor, as is the case with most criticism of collaborative autobiography, presumes that the collector, as participant in a dominant culture's ideology, controls the text. Thus critics often miss the power of Native American narrators to use the collaborative process to express difference, to use the narrative events to their own ends, and, in some cases, to actively resist the collector's cultural and ideological agenda.

Until recently I, like Carr, have focused on omissions in collaborative Native American narratives — and in their methodological introductions — believing them critical to uncovering the collection and editorial processes that shape inscription. What is not addressed in texts has seemed to me at least as valuable as what appears in print. The unspoken, or at least uninscribed, ideologies and attitudes that mold written texts have offered evidence for editorial manipulation. I have been reading Native American autobiographies as what James Clifford calls "fictions" (introduction, Clifford and Marcus 5–7), not in the sense of false, but as made things, in this case monologues made from dialogues, *partial* representations of lived encounters and piecemeal narratives that are "multi-subjective" and "power-laden" (15). I have wanted to know all the parts — and still do. I long ago lost faith in the verifiability and reliability of any personal narrative and shifted my critical strategy to the postmodern focus on subjectivity. Like most scholars in the field, I began analyzing both ideological and disciplinary biases imbedded in the editorial decisions and statements of collectors as a means of opening up subject position in the narrated text.

The advantage of that strategy has become embarrassingly clear to me as I consider both my own work and the work of such critics as Arnold Krupat, David Brumble, Hertha Wong, Helen Carr, and others in light of my role as a non-Native scholar. Consciously or unconsciously, I think we have all assumed that the collector/editor is the key to unlocking these cross-cultural autobiographical texts because we assume he or she possesses the exclusive power to control the narrative presentation. The new ethnography has made it very clear to literary critics that how what goes on in the field is inscribed by the fieldworker is not only fair game but appropriate game for the scholar. As critics, empowering ourselves to interpret collaborative personal narratives, we also identify with collectors/editors even when we are most critical of their techniques in presenting orally narrated lives. We are most comfortable analyzing text produced by scholars like ourselves. We know our academic disciplines and the changing theoretical models that influence the collection and publication of such texts. We understand the monologic — monolithic — nature of the published autobiographical text.[11]

And if we are dissatisfied with the absence of full reports of field methodology, of editorial practices, and of dialogic representation, we can excuse our limited critical insight on the basis of inadequate information by citing Clifford's statements about the partial nature of cross-cultural representations (introduction, Clifford and Marcus 7). We fall back on the "classical dichotomies of Self and Other, Subject and Object, the West and the Rest," but as Ruth Behar points out, these oppositional paradigms "have become hopelessly inadequate in the face of feminist and minority cultural critiques, the growing strength of various forms of 'native' anthropology, and the increasing borderization of our world" (165).

Notwithstanding the above criticism, we have done good work — recovered and brought important narrative texts into the critical arena, developed useful techniques for penetrating certain elements of collaborative texts, analyzed the history of the genre in its disciplinary and political contexts, and succeeded in moving some Native American collaborative autobiographies into the literary curriculum. But what our emphasis on the collector/editor has not done is adequately focus on the negotiation of text by two people in a collaborative partnership. We do not really comprehend Native poetics and politics. We have placed so much of our attention on the published text and the history of the disciplines that have produced them and so little on ethnographic and historical data, on tribal oral traditions and their performance aesthetics, on tribal language systems, and on actually doing the kind of fieldwork that leads to personal narrative inscription, that we have limited ourselves to reading Native American collaborative autobiography almost exclusively in terms of Euro-American political and literary theories.[12] We privilege the power of the collector/editor because it is our own power. We presume that because collectors/editors are members of the dominant culture, the power relationship in the collaborative process is unidirectional. What we do not recognize, or at least do not write about, is Native power because it is Other. We are ill-equipped to critically examine the evidence of difference in Native narration. It resists us.

The one critic thus far who looks directly at collaborative personal narrative as culturally resistant text writes, I think significantly, from a Native American perspective and himself resists the didactic deadpan of scholarly text. Greg Sarris, in his analysis of Elizabeth Colson's *Autobiographies of Three Pomo Women*, is in a unique position as a mixed-blood Pomo to recognize the resistance strategies at work in this text. He knows Pomo storytelling firsthand and proves it by narrating several stories in the course of his critical essay. He begins his essay with a personal narrative, quoting tribal women elders' admonitions about talking to outsiders: "Careful what you tell." "Don't talk much with outside people" (82). Then he explains, "When the professors visited each summer, Nettie became silent. Eleanor gave short flat answers and told stories no one in the house had ever heard" (82).[13] Given this personal evidence, he suspects that the three Pomo women from whom Colson solicited narratives edited their stories as they told them — they resisted in the very act of cooperating. He speculates that they responded within the context of attitudes toward outsiders — "Rejection. Distrust. Anger. Hatred" (93) — that he has been taught characterize Pomo-white relations. But he is cautious. Early in the essay he admits that in addressing the three autobiographies, his "impulse as a critic was to say what was truly Pomo" so that he "could show what Colson missed, how ignorant she was as an outsider to Pomo culture." But he checks himself and asks, "But who am I to speak for and define the central Pomo or any Pomo?" (83). This questions points to the collaborative nature of all Native texts. Each is in some measure communal in origin and ongoing performance; each expresses cultural and individual sensibilities in varying degrees over time, and no single voice can claim authority to speak for some essential tribal way of experiencing and articulating culture.

Later in his essay, after examining Colson's statements of methodology, Sarris speaks as a scholar of collaborative Native American autobiography and asks, "How do I deal with those fundamental questions, specifically those I raised about Colson and her biases? About the Indian women's biases and how the Indian women may have edited their spoken narratives for Colson. . . . And what are my own biases, my position as a reader?" (87). The latter question directs his analysis of the Pomo women's texts toward linguistic patterns that would have influenced narrative style but that elude the non-Pomo reader. He notes that although Pomo English speakers of the late nineteenth century could not have replicated Pomo syntax in English, they likely would have adapted salient features of the language to their English narrations, such as "copious use of verbs" as a thematizing agency in English, which, he emphasizes, is a subject-oriented language (97–98). He illustrates his point by carefully examining the narratives, arguing that they retain linguistic features of the Pomo language in spite of Colson's clear admission of occasionally inverting and knocking into more "English shape" the sentences the women spoke (95). For instance, Sarris quotes Colson's lines: "Those boys made that thing. They were singing, singing, singing: and they were making some kind of feather basket with red feathers" (qtd. in Sarris 95). He then juxtaposes this with what, on the basis of his linguistic study, he speculates would have been typical of unedited verb thematizing: "Singing, singing, singing, making thing, them boys. Singing and same time putting red feathers on. Singing and putting red feathers. Making thing with fish tail on, them boys" (95). Knowledge of—I would qualify that by saying about—the Native language is, he argues, essential for recognizing Native narrative resistance.

He also points to nonchronological narration as characteristic of the Pomo storytelling aesthetic. This feature, which is common to many tribal narrative styles, is almost always "corrected" by collectors/editors.[14] However, in the field encounter, it is part of the narrator's literary control by means of which the relational character of both Native American literatures and cultures is affirmed. Sarris's point, and mine too, is that cultural and linguistic contexts inform the reading of even a highly edited text. His analysis of the Pomo narratives, while giving substantial attention to Colson's role in the collection and editing processes, places equal if not greater weight on Pomo culture and aesthetics. It emphasizes a balance of power in the collaborative production process and argues for much closer attention to the stylistic details of the body of the narrated text as it appears in print.

In making the point at the beginning of my discussion of the Sarris essay that his critical work in reclaiming the Colson text for the Native narrators is facilitated, perhaps initiated, by his membership in the Pomo community, I do not mean to suggest that non-Natives are not capable of effectively compiling Native American texts or writing criticism about them. Rather, I want to make the point that effective partnership in the production of these texts and in insightful scholarly writing about them requires more than literary and theoretical know-how. It demands intensive study of oral traditions and linguistics, which will aid the collector/editor in respecting and inscribing the tribal stylistics of the narration and enable the scholar to penetrate the printed text and examine the narrative in relation to specific tribal oral styles.[15]

The other important insight that the Sarris essay offers is attention to the positioning of the reader in relation to the text, overtly acknowledging the influence of the intentions and the knowledge the critic brings to interpreting a collaborative text. Though Sarris's self-reflexivity is not revolutionary, it demonstrates what I hope is a growing recognition that the text the critic inscribes is every bit as unstable as the autobiography under examination and that the tools and critical strategies we have brought to these texts over the past two decades are inadequate for examining Native narrative voices.

Although resistance in a collaborative text may be elusive and require specialized knowledge or circumstances, as in the Pomo autobiographies, it is often overt, even under the most repressive circumstances. The oral traditions narrated in the autobiographical text may provide the means of comprehending the form and level of Native resistance, if we are sufficiently schooled in the tribal traditions to recognize their intention.

Geronimo's Story of His Life, recorded, edited, and published in 1906 by S. M. Barrett, is a case in point. I have been puzzled for years that this text has not received critical attention except for one chapter in Arnold Krupat's study of Native American autobiography, *For Those Who Come After*. I suspect that most critics see this as such a "corrupt" text that they have avoided it. As Krupat sees the text, Barrett, by presenting Geronimo's life history in terms of the emergence of social science objectivism and salvage anthropology, refuses Geronimo "the context of heroism" or even "individuality." Barrett, he notes, describes Geronimo as "no different from 'any captive,' any 'prisoner of war,' no world historical figure, but just another 'vanishing type'"(63). I do not argue with Krupat's evaluation of Barrett's agenda; however, I believe it is a mistake to read this narrative exclusively in terms of Geronimo as a colonized victim of U.S. policy and the recorder/editor's social science theorizing. Again, emphasis on the collector/editor prevents a balanced reading. First, it ignores that under the most repressive circumstances, Geronimo articulates clearly his terms for narrating — he refuses to answer questions or be interrupted in any way during his telling. Further, it ignores the narrator's adaptation of Apache traditional literary conventions to his own experiences. Even cursory reading of the narrative reveals that Geronimo frames his life in relation to his tribe's oral tradition, implicitly relating himself to the mythic heroes of his people. Given the circumstances of his imprisonment and Barrett's social science approach to the project, Geronimo's narrative strategy is not only cleverly resistant, it's subversive, one suspects even tricksterish, a way of ensuring that his life story will be incorporated into an enduring form of tribal oral storytelling. Geronimo thwarts Barrett's imposition of demeaning "tragic" stereotype and employs what Gerald Vizenor calls a comic holotrope. If you pay attention to what Geronimo actually says in his narrative, you will recognize that he is using a tribally affirming way of talking back to the dominant culture.

When traditional storytelling incorporated into collaborative text is recognized as a means of creating subjectivity, not just as a way of establishing tribal identity and narrative authenticity, the reader can begin to appreciate the control the narrator retains even in a highly edited, highly suspect text.

In the examples I cite above, Sarris brings a great deal of specialized knowledge of Pomo culture and language to the text in order to uncover the resistance exerted by the narrator. Thus I see his work as a breakthrough contrasting markedly with more conventional literary and theoretical scholarship that imposes theoretical models but does not examine how the narrator uses tribal language and aesthetics to resist being overpowered by Euro-American forms and intentions.

I would like to turn now to what I see as another kind of breakthrough, one that offers a new model for the presentation of Native personal narrative and for the scholarly analysis of the collaborative process in a single volume that resists both autobiography and disciplinary conventions. In what I see as the best example of recent work in the genre, the partners in the collaboration deliberately incorporate multivocal self-reflections on the project into the volume they produce, allowing the reader a great deal more knowledge of the collaborative process than has heretofore been offered in published autobiography. In this volume, not only is the collector/editor self-reflexive, but the Native collaborators articulate their perceptions of the process of narration and inscription. This book makes our work as critics nearly obsolete, except for pointing out the strategies used by the partners in the project.

Life Lived Like a Story: Life Stories of Three Yukon Native Elders, narrated by Angela Sidney, Kitty Smith, and Annie Ned and edited by Julie Cruikshank, is a remarkable example of shared power and balanced collaboration achieved by the active resistance of the narrators to the totalizing conventions the editor initially brings to the project. Oral tradition dominates this book, not just in the incorporation of traditional stories into the individual women's stories, but because the women's personal stories are told and presented in terms of the conventions, not of Euro-American literary autobiography, but of oral tradition in content and style. Since I have written at length on this book elsewhere (Sands, "Collaboration") I won't repeat extensive examples. Instead, let me innumerate the ways in which this volume resists Euro-American literary expectations. First, the narrators resist chronological narration; their stories move almost seamlessly back and forth in time, interpreting historical and individual memory by means of tribal memory, demonstrating sophisticated integration of multiple tribal literary forms rarely seen in a published text.

Second, in these narratives, place is not allowed to function as symbolic setting, as it does in many Native personal narratives; it is an immediate catalyst for contextualizing contemporary story in clan and tribal mythology; it is not simply the site of traditional life but the locus of contemporary experience. The collaborators literally take the collector/editor to the places that are both personally and tribally significant and teach her place-names and stories by which to understand their personal experiences and narrations. Thus their tribal methodology is critical to the narrative process, as it has been and is in Native communities. Native cultural aesthetics and literary conventions shape the telling of personal experience in a way not common to Euro-American text.

Third, the narrators insist — and I use the term deliberately because Cruikshank resisted their resistance at first — upon being presented as other than individually autonomous. They narrate themselves as shaped by and shaping their communities and oral traditions. For instance, Smith incorporates lengthy remembered (read reconstructed) conversations into her narration, thereby situating herself in community interactions and even as the topic of community conversation. Dialogue emphasizes kinship and relationality in terms of placement within the community social structure. This, of course, is directly antithetical to the privileging of individuality, of uniqueness, at the core of Euro-American autobiography; it suggests that subjectivity, like inscription of identity, is provisional. For these Native women subjectivity is not singular but inextricably connected to tribal myth, history, and contemporary experience.

Fourth, the juxtapositioning of traditional speeches and song and stories with personal narration is a technique calling attention to the interaction of texts. These narrated lives are inherently heteroglossic. Contemporary narrative speaks to and is resonant with oral tradition and historical narrative. Further, it is dialogic; voices of the past, dialogue from both past and present, and self-reflexive interpretation all share narrative space. Thus narrative in this volume is multiply resistant to monologic inscription, the conventional mode of Euro-American autobiography.

Combined with Cruikshank's very comprehensive methodological discussion, the inclusion of raw text in the volume, and the voices of the narrators directly discussing their intentions for the project, these collaborative autobiographies offer perhaps the most overtly resistant inscription of Native American lives to date. Not only the narrators but also the collector/editor are resistant to the usual conventions of this Indian autobiography. She consults with and negotiates the presentation of the narratives every step of the way. Tutored by her collaborators to understand that for them narrative is an analytical mode, she follows their lead by narrating her experiences with these three women and thus incorporating her interpretation of the narratives into her own text. At one point, she notes, "by imbuing place with meaning through story," the narrators "seemed to be using locations in physical space to talk about events in chronological time" (347). Her recognition of cultural difference at the most basic levels of phenomenological conceptualization leads the reader toward a recognition of the Native character of the narratives in the volume. Cruikshank is ultimately the best critic of the collaborative process that produced this volume. Between the narrators and Cruikshank, all the intertextuality that usually has to be provided by the scholarly critic is already present.

Cultural and aesthetic resistance in all the narratives that I have discussed and in many more that could be addressed needs attention. If we ignore it, opting to see Native American personal narrators as powerless victims of institutional collectors and inscribers, we simply perpetuate the colonial process. It may ease our collective guilt about the texts we study and the careers we have based on Native cultures to read and write about collectors/editors as colonial agents, but it does not advance the discipline. It is a ready-made paradigm that requires little more than picking out the right incidents and examples to prove an already obvious point. I simply do not think Native American narrators are victims. I think they have used and still use this form of storytelling to their own purposes. Far more often than not, those purposes have been obscured by editors, but even in the worst of examples, we should not assume that Native voice and intention have been obliterated.

As I outline above, collaborative inscription of a Native American life depends on a unique relationship developed between two or more individuals from different cultures that takes place in a particular setting and time. As Ruth Behar notes, the "conversations and interactions in the field can never again be exactly reproduced. They are unique, irrecoverable, gone before they happen, always in the past, even when written up in the present tense" (7). Further, the collector never "hears an account identical with that which the same narrator would give to another person" (6). Given the impossibility of transforming the field encounter into a text that comes close to evoking the performance of personal narrative, it is very easy to become discouraged about preparing a collaborative autobiography for publication. But ultimately, the partnership of Native narrator and collector/editor, once undertaken, demands inscription. The question is not whether to inscribe, but how. As Shaobo Xie notes, "In a world burdened by a few centuries of coloniality, it is impossible to construct identities and forms of knowledge uncontaminated by universalist or Eurocentric concepts and images" (17). It is naive to believe that Native personal narratives can be published without colonial contamination, but it is possible to re-envision collaborative personal narrative as neither indigenous nor colonial, but inscription that inhabits "an intervening space," what Xie terms "the Third Space of enunciation, the hybrid, ambivalent, in-between space of signification" (17).

If Ted Rios's story seems to have gotten lost in my discussion of Native American collaborative personal narrative, it has not, not really. The work we did together is in one sense irrecoverable, as ephemeral as a memory, but it is also accessible, recorded on tape and in transcriptions, and is potentially transformable into a genuinely collaborative text. For the present, it is the foundation of all the views I have expressed. It is his narrative and his active partnership in the project we began together that has shaped how I read the texts I have discussed here. Ted was the victim of a hit-and-run driver when I first met him, and certainly he was the victim of U.S. Indian policies that went into effect long before he was even born, but he was not a narrative victim.

Now that I have said what I have had to say, I need to say one more thing — a kind of epilogue and caveat. To one degree or another, every collector/editor of a Native American collaborative autobiography has wrestled with the issues I have put forth — at a pace presumably faster than I have — and simply found it impossible to solve the problems inherent in transforming narration to inscription. She or he has accepted to one degree or another a level of responsibility most literary endeavors neither recognize nor accommodate and has gone ahead and published the work in the best possible form available at the time.[16] Maybe there comes a time to stop carting the transcripts around and get down to inscription, even though I distrust my capacity to represent, let alone evoke, the complex interactions that produced the raw text of Ted's narrative. Maybe this is just my long apology for all the mistakes and inadequacies the Rios autobiography will reveal when it comes into print. Memory fails, words fail. Being a culture broker, Native or non-Native, is risky. The shudder I felt crossing that cattle guard at Sells over two decades ago resonates in my mind and bones. But now, as then, it is too late to turn back. Ted and I made a deal. He took the risk and narrated his life. You will be the judges of how well I hold my end of our bargain.

NOTES

I would like to thank the members of the Native American Literatures seminar at Chateau de la Bretesche, Brittany, France, June 23–25, 1997, for their comments and suggestions for revision of this essay, which was first presented at the seminar. Of particular value were questions, observations, comments, and terminology offered by David L. Moore, Paula Gunn Allen, Kathryn Shanley, Hartwig Isernhagen, David Murray, and Kimberly Blaeser. A version of this essay appeared in *Studies in American Indian Literature* 10.1 (1998): 1–19.

1. Formerly called Papago, the tribe officially changed its name to Tonoho O'odham, meaning desert people, in the late 1980s. Anthropological documents that predate the change use the name Papago, and many tribal members use the two terms interchangeably; however, contemporary ethnography and official documents use O'odham. The tribe resides on the second largest reservation in the state of Arizona; it abuts the Mexican border and extends westward to the Gulf of Cortez; a small part of the reservation is just ten miles from Tucson and is the site of one of the Kino missions, San Xavier del Bac.

2. The Doris Duke collection at the University of Arizona houses a number of tran-

scripts of interviews with O'odham men and women. The one with Theodore Rios was collected by Timothy Dunnigan. This transcript is particularly useful in analyzing topics Rios chose to discuss or avoid, depending on the gender of the collector.

3. The film, in which Rios narrated several stories to me and two students from the University of Arizona, was later aired, in part, on a show called "Rocky Mountain Mix" broadcast from Denver, Colorado. But the actual purpose of the filming was as a pilot for *Words and Place*, a series focused on Southwest Native American writers and traditional storytellers developed and produced by Larry Evers.

4. See Rios. This article demonstrates the control Rios exerted on the telling of his life in relationship to his sense of multiple audiences and supports the argument in this essay.

5. In the introduction to her book *The Life and Times of Grandfather Alonso*, ethnographer Blanca Muratorio makes a comment I empathize with regarding the difficulty of moving from collecting to publishing. She says that her editing decisions "involved substantial risks of accurate representation, as the recent general literature on oral narratives specifies in considerable detail." She claims, "If all those guidelines are followed to the letter the ethnographer could be easily paralyzed into not publishing at all, a decision that in my case would have betrayed an explicit request of the subject" (16). I find my situation somewhat different but parallel to Muratorio's.

6. Discussing Native American collaborative personal narrative as a genre has been going on for several decades, but the term itself is a Euro-American imposition of a literary category onto a form that is neither Western nor accommodating to the conventions referred to by the terms *genre* and *autobiography*. Process, rather than genre, seems a more useful way of discussing this hybrid Native/Euro-American collaborative form of narration and inscription. Abandoning genre classification and the use of the term *autobiography* might also redirect critical focus away from the collector/editor toward more careful examination of the Native American narration.

7. Both the terms *authority* and *authenticity* are counterproductive in the discussion of Native American cultures and literary production; they perpetuate the hegemonic relationship of Western to Native cultures. More useful is David L. Moore's term *fallibility* as he uses it his discussion of cultural property in this volume.

8. See Rios, "Telling a Good One."

9. Nor do I believe *postcolonial* is a useful term in discussing Native American collaborative autobiographies if this term is seen as "a counterdiscourse of the formerly colonized Others against the cultural hegemony of the modern West with all its imperial structures of feeling and knowledge" (Xie 9). Tribal discourse from oral tradition to contemporary written literature cannot be reduced to merely responses to hegemonic systems; it exists independently in relation to local communities and literary criteria, not only in relation to Western political structures and forms of discourse.

10. Colonialism as a "disembodied world system, or capitalism in the abstract"

(Muratorio 14) is not very useful. Only when we examine it at work at the local level, which is the case in collaborative Native American autobiography, can it become a tool for analysis; however, that analysis tends to be historical, not literary, in its intent. Applied specifically, as T. J. Jackson Lears notes, "by clarifying the political functions of cultural symbols, the concept of cultural hegemony can aid intellectual historians trying to understand how ideas reinforce or undermine existing social structures and social historians seeking to reconcile the apparent contradiction between the power wielded by dominant groups and the relative cultural autonomy of subordinate groups whom they victimize" (568). As applied to literary texts, colonialism tends to move the critic away from elements of the narrative to speculation on the social relationship of the dominant to the dominated.

11. For a critical reassessment of the issue of the monologic in Native texts, see David L. Moore's "Decolonializing Criticism." This essay addresses the problem of simply viewing the interactions between collectors and Native narrators as colonialist in a broader and more theoretical sense than is approached in this essay.

12. Throughout this essay I have used the term *collaborative* in referring to Native American personal narratives because I genuinely believe that whatever the outcome, the process is a dialogic collaboration. Though my stance on this issue may be debatable, I will stand by the term until something more precise appears. What gives me more difficulty in discussing the topic is the term *autobiography*. The term has been the focus of a good deal of rumination in this field, and in the past two decades a number of critics have come up with adjectives to make it more appropriate to discussion of Native American personal narratives — as-told-to autobiography, bi-autobiography, composite autobiography, ethnographic autobiography, mediated autobiography, etc. None seems very satisfactory because these narratives do not conform to the conventions of Euro-American autobiography, which is the source of the genre terminology. Further, the inclusion of the term *autobiography* in critical scholarship of Native American personal narratives may actually contribute to missing the elements of resistance. We read what we expect to find in the genre as it is defined in non-Native studies, instead of what is actually in the text. I often use *personal narrative* as a synonym for autobiography, but that is not satisfactory either because there are many kinds of personal narrations that do not incorporate the characteristics of this hybrid form of literary expression we usually call American Indian or Native American autobiography. I think we need to become much more sophisticated in our categorization of these narratives. For instance, might collaborative biography better suit some works usually listed as Native American autobiographies? The next question, of course, has to be, which ones? But even answering that will not solve the problem because it simply substitutes another Euro-American term to describe a form of literary inscription that is shaped by two separate literary systems. Whether debating such terms is ultimately a productive endeavor is problematic, but recognizing the difficulties that imprecise language imposes on the

accuracy of scholarly criticism seems to me imperative to accurate reading of collaborative texts.

13. The issue of narrative silence as a strategy for protecting cultural knowledge is a topic that deserves full discussion but is beyond the scope of this essay. It is addressed in detail in this volume in David L. Moore's essay on cultural property.

14. Sarris is not the first to point out that collectors/editors regularly restructure narrative sequence to establish chronology in Native American collaborative narrative and that in doing so they usually eliminate repetition as well. David Brumble, for instance, takes up this issue in his 1988 book on the genre. In that discussion, however, as in Sarris's, the demands of publishers who market primarily to mainstream American audiences who expect chronology in a life story are not broached. Nor does either critic address what I think is a more interesting issue: Muratorio points out that "in a single narrative such as a life story often there is more than one sense of time expressed by the subject, including that of the editor who, by the way, does not necessarily need to have only one sense of time" (16). So while I am sympathetic to the importance of an inscribed text revealing multiple concepts of time, and to the critic analyzing whatever form of time is inscribed, I would not posit that merely an absence of chronology is a solution to the tension between Native and Euro-American narrative conventions of time.

15. Hertha Wong's attention to traditional narrative styles and expressive categories in *Sending My Heart Back across the Years* offers an example of the value of reading published collaborative narratives in the context of traditional forms of self and communal expression.

16. Perhaps my own collaborative experience and other instances of fieldwork on this topic have made me more sympathetic to collectors/editors and Native narrators than some of my colleagues are.

My acquaintance with native Americans starts at an early age. It's the period of Sunday afternoons spent in front of the then black and white Portuguese TV broadcasts watching what was the usual choice of either middle class family dramas or good old westerns.

Paula Mota Santos, in
Native American Women in Literature and Culture

Western Literary Models and Their Native American Revisiting

The Hybrid Aesthetics of
Owens's The Sharpest Sight

BERNADETTE RIGAL-CELLARD

Non-Native literary genres and myths have been integrated into contemporary Native American fiction to represent Native American concerns. *The Sharpest Sight* (1992), in which the author, Louis Owens, has explored several nontraditional Native systems of representation, provides a clear example of how a text negotiates the intricate identity quest of the protagonists, who all stand between several histories and mixed ethnic roots in one of the spaces and times that have achieved the largest hybridization of cultures, "contemporary California."

The Sharpest Sight stages various themes that surface in many contemporary Native novels: the quest for identity of young mixed-bloods (Choctaw-Irish and Mexican) traumatized by their having to bear the brunt of white American violence that leads to the destruction of the intimate union between two brothers; salvation thanks to spiritual guides; importance of the proper rituals, particularly toward the dead and their bones; and humor and warmth of the Native community. What gives its originality to the novel, then, is that Owens decided to weave with these quintessential contemporary Native preoccupations certain Euro-American literary strategies, little used by other Native authors, notably one of the foundations of Western thought, Greek mythology, and one subversive genre of the twentieth century, the *roman noir*, a particularly stark and dark form of the mystery novel.

The detective story had already been somewhat used by several Native authors—James Welch in the *Indian Lawyer*; Linda Hogan in *Mean Spirit*, in which FBI agent Stace Red Hawk finally found his identity through his unraveling of the Osage murders—but the police investigation had then remained marginal. Owens, on the contrary, successfully maneuvers a *roman noir* from beginning to end to build the structure of identity of his characters. Furthermore, by blending the ingredients of the *roman noir* (sex, murders, and power) and its specific aesthetics of violence with the Greek myths of healing through

152

love and violence, Owens throws a different light on the evil woman, the aggressive male, and contemporary society.

The ingredients of the *roman noir* buttress *The Sharpest Sight*, and the part played by the avatars of Greek mythological characters force the Choctaws to come to grips with their fundamental nature. The function of violence, while significant, does not remain within the limits of the one traditionally found in the *roman noir*, because it is subverted by the recourse to magical realism.[1] Additionally, the relevance of the issue of cultural appropriation will be discussed: By borrowing a foreign system of representation, does Owens fulfill his own postcolonial agenda in this particular novel?

The *roman noir* is different from the simple detective or mystery story, which originated in Europe. The *roman noir* is characterized by its terse style, its causticity, its detachment. It is not so much interested in solving an enigma as in exploring the reasons for the problem and the consequences. The investigator is not simply an astute brain but a full-fledged protagonist willing to die for the sake of the truth, because he is disgusted with the corruption of the powerful elites and wants to cleanse society at whatever cost. Alain Lacombe has shown that the *roman noir* is the pointer of the specificity of American society. Its authors underlined the ambiguity of a country unable to gather behind the star-spangled banner of the American Dream, and they succeeded in rendering in a frightening way the malaise hampering the most powerful nation in the world (Lacombe 9–11). Lacombe analyzes the genre as the mediator from the original American myth of space to the myth of survival through power, thanks to a sudden realization of the power of evil and to an initiatory journey for the protagonists (20). Because the struggle for power implies the struggle for space, the setting of the *roman noir* includes necessarily a city, of any size, which condenses all the ambitions of a community. The mythical and geometrical representation of the fractured American dream, the city stands for the instrument of racial injustice, something that is particularly well exploited by Chester Himes, and the clash between the newcomer, the stranger, and American violence is the ideal pretext to reveal unsolvable antagonisms (Lacombe 103–4).

The Sharpest Sight corresponds to all these characteristics. The setting is in California, and though it is not in one of Raymond Chandler's or Dashiel Hammett's urban sprawls, it is, however, connected to their evil influence since it lies on Highway 101, which links the two metropolitan areas. The city of Amarga is in north San Luis Obispo County, which falls under the jurisdiction of deputy-sheriff Mundo Morales, and which was Chumash territory. A quotation toward the end, "la mar amarga" (235), underlines the "bitterness" of this particular space. It is a medium-sized city with its share of crimes and murders.

The tragedy in three movements (ambition, transgression, death), which follows the rules of Greek drama and those of the *roman noir*, can then unfold. The book first exposes the fatal error, the *harmatia*, which is the transgression and the double murder. Then, it stages the investigation, which is threefold: Where is the body? Who has done it? Who are we? At last, the resolution and catharsis: violence to purge violence, one's real identity discovered and accepted. The three unities are also respected: time — during one fall and a winter, "there was only a single time" (156); place — California and Mississippi, which can be seen as the magical double of California; action — the metaphorical police investigation.

In a *roman noir*, the thirst for power throws those who have it against those who do not. Often the mayor fights against the sheriff, who in turn sides with the powerful citizens to fight against the losers. Women fight against men. In small towns the sheriff is the heir of divine power (Lacombe 94). In Amarga the part of the mayor is played by Dan Nemi, the county supervisor. We find no judge here, but many officials want to protect the social *status quo* and despise the righter of wrongs, Mundo Morales, who, as required by the genre, belongs to the losers. Furthermore, in a Native American context, the nonwhite law enforcer is under the orders of white officers who do not trust him (something that Tony Hillerman has effectively exploited in his novels), and Mundo is rapidly threatened by the federal investigator: "You're a suspect, Mundo. You ought to know that. It's logical. The missing man's last visitor, best friend, maybe the ex-boyfriend of the girl he killed, father of her unborn child perhaps" (84).

The Sharpest Sight functions as a discourse on power and on the myth of space. Since it is written from a Native stance, it must be read as a dramatically parodic discourse on this myth. By appropriating the strategy of the *roman noir*, Owens appropriates the one Euro-American genre whose basic function was to denounce, from within, the evils of American society. Thus, one understands better why he chose it to represent his tragedy: he could then subvert, from within and from without, the very social system that led to it.

Owens invents a double murder that finds its explanation only in American territorial expansionism, achieved first through the conquest of the continent, then through the worldwide imperialism that led the nation into Vietnam. The novel starts with Mundo's half-hallucinatory vision of the corpse of Attis McCurtain in the furious waters of the Salinas. One learns later that Attis had stabbed his girlfriend to death, and, like his friends, the reader understands that his death avenges the murder he committed. According to Georges Bataille, "authentic literature" is Promethean, and its goal, the communication between people, can be achieved only through a recourse to evil, to the violation of the interdict. One could then accept the transgression of Attis and of Owens, who has imagined so much violence, as the expression of their Promethean task, of their surpassing their human limitations. But such a feat is forbidden to them, precisely because of the Promethean task that the white Americans have set for themselves in their boundless conquest of space. Attis is bound but is no Prometheus. He killed because he accepted to fight in Vietnam and came back mentally impaired (a plot line found in most Vietnam novels). His uncle says, "They put a terrible medicine in (him). . . . There is something loose in the world now" (97). Violence comes from the American political power, which is condemned in the novel.

In a particularly important scene, Attis's father, Hoey McCurtain, asks his other son, Cole, what he plans to do about the draft. It is significant that the father should then remember how President Jackson betrayed Pushmataha's Choctaws, whom he removed to Oklahoma in spite of their support during the Battle of New Orleans: "that's what you owe those bastards" (20). Ironically this talk takes place while the two men put up a fence in the middle of the hills over Morro Bay, the only job we see them perform. We don't know the purpose of these fences, unless they are meant to express the author's derision toward such a need to fence in a territory. The words of the two men are punctuated by the blows on the posts to force them into the ground, a ludicrous and violent rape of the earth, and a sterile one since the posts will not turn into trees.

As we have seen, in the *roman noir*, the archetypal motive for the murders is the thirst for territorial and financial expansion, and it is logical that the genre should have appeared during the Great Depression, when the gap between the haves and the have-nots grew abysmal. Owens wants to show how American society today is still eaten away by the same greed, and how the dispossessed are always the Natives. Yet, he also stages other people who undergo the same violence: the Chicanos, through Morales, the village idiots, the hoboes, shot at on the train. All these are characters straight out of Steinbeck, who was writing at the same time as the major authors of *roman noir*. Incidentally, Owens, who wrote two books on Steinbeck, pays him homage by choosing the Salinas, along which he lived, as the river of *The Sharpest Sight*.

Mundo Morales, the other dispossessed, the spiritual twin of Attis, now embodies the law, but it is again rather ironic since those who granted him the favor consider him more like the sheriff of the film *Blazing Saddles* than as a real law enforcer.[2] The tanned brother of Marlowe, he is most of the time alone in his office, which he calls "a hole" (27), attempting to fit together the pieces of the puzzle. Trying to swallow his "grapes of wrath," he keeps repeating that his family used to possess the land the Nemis now own (14, 22). Dan Nemi, "Pillar of the community. Man without a stain on his record, unless you call diddling the coach's wife a stain" (85), stands for the handsome rancher suspected by all, but against whom the officials will attempt nothing. He would be a caricatured J. R. if Owens had not made him the father of the murdered girl, Jenna, so he is a man who is hurt and loving, a plain human being.

Owens also mitigates the dispossession leitmotiv of Mundo by pointing out that the land the Morales once possessed had previously belonged to the Chumash, whereas Mundo innocently says, "But I thought Indians never really *owned* land" (14). However, he later questions his own naivety and confesses: "And it belonged to the Indians and we sold it for a quart of whiskey" (42, taken up again 181–82). It is also said that he does not like maps, for "the first thing they did when they wanted to take something away from you was draw a map; that's what the viejo had said" (39). All these remarks on the property of the land structure the novel and, because of their phantasmagoric repetitions, remind us of the obsession of Faulkner with its misappropriation, particularly in *Go Down, Moses*.

If we pursue our analysis of violence in *The Sharpest Sight*, why does Attis kill Jenna if he loves her? The PTS (post traumatic shock) invoked by the doctors can explain a certain form of violence, but not necessarily the violence against the loved one. Such a murder does not really belong to the *roman noir* either. We must perhaps move out of the genre and look at other Native texts, in particular those of James Welch, to whom Owens is very close. In *Winter in the Blood* and *The Death of Jim Loney*, men are extremely violent toward their lovers, usually white, in particular during intercourse. Owens has explained that this violence derived from the infantilization imposed on minority males by the conquest or slavery and segregation. It is said in *The Sharpest Sight* that American culture in general infantilizes everyone: "that's what people wanted to do to us. . . . to turn us into kids so we couldn't know who we really was" (109). The men are thus unable to establish a proper relationship with their women. Attis clearly suffers, like Welch's narrator and Jim Loney, from psychological immaturity. In a dream, which in a Native context must be seen as a formative vision, Cole sees Attis cry like a baby (68), and it is said further that Hoey found him after the war in a fetal position, "laying on the ground all curled up, and he was crying" (142). Stabbing a knife into his girlfriend's heart could express his inability to accept the love she offers him in a disinterested gesture of "color blindness."

The name *Attis* finds its justification in such an act. In ancient times Attis was the Adonis of the Phrygians, who, according to the legend made famous by Catullus, became mad when he entered the forest of Cybele, the Aphrodite of the Phrygians.[3] She did not like men, and he emasculated himself to please her. He then asked his companions who had undergone the same fate to sing the glory of the goddess. The next day, when he realized what he had done, he lamented for his lost motherland, wondering where to look for it. When Cybele understood he was not going to serve her, she sent her lion to bring him back. As soon as Attis saw the lion, he fled toward the wilderness and remained a slave for the rest of his life (Catulle 52–53).

Attis in *The Sharpest Sight* could then embody the Native males psychologically castrated by the whites, not knowing anymore where to look for their motherland and being obliged to remain the slaves of the fierce goddess. Furthermore, we must note that Cybele does not castrate her males herself but induces them to self-castration: the ancient Attis does so because he is in a trance, as is true for the modern one also. He stabs his lover in a pitiful parody of the sexual act, which he has been made incapable of performing, and goes into a mental prison where he remains in the trance inherited from the war.

What about Attis's family name *McCurtain*? Like the African Americans who bear the names of the slave masters, the Natives here bear a white name, an Irish one, "Irish my ass" (15), one that is very meaningful since it implies a curtain, reminiscent of the veil that trapped little W. E. B. Dubois when he understood that he was different from the other pupils, a veil that he spent his whole life trying to dispel: "I remember when the shadow swept over me. . . . I was shut out from their world by a vast veil. . . . Why did God make me an outcast and a stranger in my own house?" (214). When Hoey goes back home with Cole after putting up the fence in the middle of nowhere, they are caught in the fog, a very symbolic one at that: "The fog curled up the cliff and over the berm of the highway so that they breasted it like a flood" (60). They have to dispel the veil hiding their true nature. The fact that McCurtain is the actual name of Owens's relatives is also highly significant since we can then clearly see the autobiographical exploration here at work.

In certain versions of the legend, Attis dies at an early age at the foot of a pine tree in the forest of Cybele. In the novel, we can see the reenactment of such a premature death in the murder that sends Attis floating down the river, all the more so when we learn that the one who puts an end to his suffering is called Diana, who is constantly associated with pine trees in the novel.[4] The daughter of Dan Nemi and the sister of Jenna, Diana is the central female character of the book and embodies many of the characteristics of the femme fatale typically found in the *roman noir*.

From Mundo's standpoint, Diana can only attract men sexually and dangerously, for he feels that the Nemi women "radiated it, a kind of dangerous-feeling sex. Smart sex" (78). The first time he sees her, which is the night he has the vision of Attis's body, he can make out her provocative silhouette "seeing the slim arch of back and breasts and the shadow of long hair" (4). The second time she clearly evokes Diana the fatal hunter and her prey, here a possible leopard, for she wears a "black leotard top." The forest in which Attis was lost is found on her long skirt: "On the skirt was a pattern of pine trees" (49). In her bedroom she has set up a small altar with candles, and "The aroma of sweet grass laced the room from the incense holder." Trying to seduce Mundo, she offers him a strange herb tea "of earth and grasses, with a faint suggestion of pine" (222), which makes him vomit, and it is precisely this purgative, a catharsis in the original sense of the word, which leads him to understand she is guilty of the murder of Attis. For in fact, in agreement with the attributes of the goddess, she has revenged her innocent sister but also protected the miserable men around her. By killing Attis she has mercifully restored the harmony he was demanding (134).

Yet, in spite of her appearing in control, Diana belongs to the group of characters searching for their identity. She is waiting to go to college (she has given her tuition money to the orderly who helped Attis escape from the hospital and meet his death) and lives between two worlds, teenage and adulthood. Her long sessions in front of her mirror can be interpreted as her attempts to go beyond the *mirror stage*. The violence she has to bear during her rape, supposedly intended by her rapist to teach her a lesson, reproduces the violence that renders women victims. Constantly called "bruja," the witch through whom evil operates (it is said that Attis slept with her thinking she was Jenna, an act in the tradition of Thomas Kyd's and Cyril Tourneur's macabre tragedies), she finally denounces the spinelessness of the males who want women to bear the responsibility for their own mistakes: "That's what all men want to think. . . . That we're witches, and you're all poor innocent boys" (222).

In the *roman noir*, women belong to three complementary groups: the woman as obstacle, the woman as refuge, the woman as object — that is, as the instrument of the mystique of damnation (Lacombe 145). In half the novels of the genre, the women are not inferior to the men but equal to them, and in six out of seven of Chandler's novels, the woman is the murderer. If Diana Nemi looks like these women because she plays the part of the "bruja," the mythological perspective in which Owens places her elevates her above the women of the *roman noir* to perform a cathartic function for herself and the male characters. It is precisely her murder of Attis that launches the plot and authorizes the quest of identity, because the body must be found for Mundo to impose himself as genuine "deputy sheriff" and for Cole to take care of his brother's bones and become the true Choctaw he yearns to be. It is also for Diana's benefit that Attis's father prepares a ritual sweat bath to purify her after her rape. Through his sharing it with her, he cleanses himself of his thirst for revenge, and even though he does not know yet she is the murderer of his son, he seals hereby the recovered harmony between the two clans, in a Shakespearian fashion, since in many ways the family feud acted out here reenacts that of *Romeo and Juliet*.

Owens has thus embarked on a forceful strategy to represent American violence that goes beyond the two murders of the original plot. It reaches its climax at the end. When Dan Nemi goes to revenge the rape of his daughter, the rapist, Jessard Deal, slits his throat open and then starts stabbing Mundo Morales before being shot by Hoey. "Two women in a ranch house near the river were a denouement" (262), the narrator remarks in the typically terse statement of a detective story. The end of the novel is so apparently gratuitously brutal that one may wonder about Owens's purpose. He has explained that violence characterizes American society and that he wanted to expose it in order to denounce it, which is fundamentally the goal of the *roman noir*.

We may then consider that *The Sharpest Sight*, and the *roman noir* in general, perform a ritual of evacuation of evil through evil. Such an interpretation supposes that one accepts as a premise the instinctive aggressiveness of the human being. Violence in America is no longer channeled as it previously was, and as it still is in more organized societies. It is completely wild as it bears on the very members of that particular society, not just on foreign enemies as it logically should, unless one considers American society as a crazy quilt of antagonistic urban tribes.

In *La violence et le sacré*, René Girard explains how in organized societies the process of rejection of an evil object, *katharma* in Greek, operates through rituals, *katharsis*, the taking of specific drugs: "an overdose of evil that leads the crisis to its paroxysm and provokes the expulsion of pathogenic elements along with one's own" (430).[5] In order to survive, a given society must perform rites that, like in a homeopathic treatment or in vaccinations, serve to "inject" a little "violence in the social body to make it more capable of resisting violence" (Girard 433).

The starting point of *The Sharpest Sight* implies a vendetta since Attis killed the white girl to make her atone for what the whites had forced him to undergo. Her sister kills him to revenge her. The rapist is killed. The father of the girls is killed since he is a rich land owner and embodies the white power elites. Mundo is ready to prevent these crimes through the recourse to more violence if need be. Now Girard tells us that a sacrifice exists as an obstacle to violence.[6] A single victim carefully chosen and groomed, a human or a symbolical scapegoat, should have been enough to put an end to this murderous vendetta, and Owens, in the same line of thought, narrates how in the Choctaw tradition there existed a specific rite to protect the group from its own murderous impulses, the Choctaw duel. It implied that the surviving duelist was then killed by his second, which meant that those willing to kill were also willing to be killed likewise and thought twice about it: "That kind of dueling kept a town pretty peaceful" (96, 141).

The Vietnam War, constantly present in the book since many characters are veterans and speak about it a lot, is emblematic of our times deprived of meaningful ceremonies, for it was perceived as a senseless butchery, and there were no cathartic homecoming ceremonies, which caused a disproportionate number of postwar traumas. Attis's father has understood it all when he comments on the behavior of his son in these terms: "What came back was just part of him, but the only part we still had. I read that there used to be ceremonies for warriors coming back home, ceremonies that would take the evil out. Maybe something like that would have put him back together again. But we don't know those ceremonies anymore" (142).

If each society is in search of a scapegoat, we can perhaps read *The Sharpest Sight* as the quest for several scapegoats that would each accept bearing the brunt of the violence of the protagonists. One would take on the violence between the whites, one the violence against women, and one the violence against the Natives. The scapegoat must be foreign to the group it is supposed to purge, and we can see how in the course of American history, African Americans and the Natives have always functioned as the sacrificial victims of the violence of the whites, which found itself safely channeled outside the white community. This might explain why, not having been able to turn the whites into their scapegoats, the African Americans cannot deflect violence and keep turning it against themselves.[7]

Owens may then be trying to turn the tables, like many "ethnic" writers. Attis embodies the perfect scapegoat for the mainstream. A stranger to them, he was trained, like traditional victims, before being sacrificed on the altar of Vietnam. One knows that this war was cruel for the soldiers, in particular for the Natives, who were supposed to be able to see at night and to crawl noiselessly (20, 168) and who were sent on dangerous reconnaissance missions more often than they should have. Furthermore, the territory was so foreign that the war had to be made into a metaphor and Vietnam made into a national scapegoat to channel collective impulses. The psychological importance of the number of casualties on the American side, historically and proportionally very inferior to that of the French earlier and, of course, to that of the Vietnamese themselves, suffices to demonstrate the ritualization orchestrated here.

However, we must go further in our analysis. Mundo also went to Vietnam and came back, shocked but psychologically "normal." Moreover, several episodes show that Attis had always been violent, to the point of threatening his own brother. Violence seemed to have inhabited him from the beginning, and since he could not expel it ritually in an acceptable way, it was transformed into a murderous transgression. This, in turn, could be digested by society only after a new act of violence, ritualized through the catharsis operated by Diana, which allows afterward a new departure for the cleansed group.

Girard's theory seems to me the only one able to explain the strange character of Jessard Deal, an "outsider" both to the two clans and to the major plot, a character that Owens seems to have created only to endow him with all the attributes of the scapegoat. One could see him as the satanic double of the wise uncle in Mississippi, as the Evil Gambler of the Chippewa pantheon, whom Gerald Vizenor often stages in his fiction. Like this supernatural Gambler, Jessard Deal pulls the strings of life and death, since he introduces himself in these terms: "The moral world comes to deal" (79). He uses this phrase again when he is on the point of killing the sheriff: "This is death. The real thing, Mundo, that for which the moral world must always deal" (250). This red-bearded giant is always crouching behind a mirror, like a spider, a habit that provokes a scene typically out of a *film noir* in the end, when Mundo shoots at what he takes to be Jessard only to shatter a mirror, while the murderer catches him from behind.

Jessard's bar, very famous all around the county, functions as a parodic sacred space, the only one left to men today, where people go to purchase their own little ritual of violence, staged every week by Jessard, who sharpens the aggressivity of his customers: "Jessard rehearsed the room like an orchestra, drawing out the extra desperation from desperate men, whetting the cutting edge of his customers. And when the wild edge had been honed to a killing point, Jessard Deal would come out from behind the bar and start to take all the meanness into himself. . . . [He] had wished it and brought it all to an exact pitch with care and precision" (80).

He is accomplishing here the rites meant to groom the victim, who must be robust (hence well fed), purified, and aware of his or her role: "All of them, any of them, friends or strangers. Jessard groomed them, fed them fine pretzels and stout beer, honed their dull-edged violences until collectively their violence met his own, and then he flung himself against them. And they always came back, nervous, drinking hard and fast because any night might be the night, drawn toward Jessard Deal as if he represented some dimly sensed ritual, frightened almost to death of their host." (80)

Either Owens has read Girard, or the descriptions of such rituals, or he has had a clever intuition. Girard rightly said that literature is far more perceptive than all the other human sciences. Jessard ambiguously stands for both the priest who prepares his victim and the victim himself, since he receives the blows into his own body. Ironically, he slits open the throat of Dan Nemi on an archetypally American altar, mockingly sacralized here, a pool table. He is then sacrificed by the Choctaw father and dies in a river of purifying blood. In a gory ending of the textual circle, this river echoes the Salinas in which the purified and almost innocent body of Attis was floating in the very beginning.

Jessard shares with the high priests of ancient times an impressive erudition and recommends to Mundo the reading of Robert Frost, Jonathan Edwards, and Tennyson. He states: "I believe we are all essentially and fundamentally evil. But we are born innocent of our full potential. We must grow into our evil" (212). When he rapes Diana he teaches her that "Loneliness is the essential human condition. Connection is made through pain" (234). And just before reaching his evil climax, this former prisoner destroys his own house in a typical Day of the Locust apocalypse, salvaging only his books. This intellectually refined and instinctively primitive character is perhaps the only true scapegoat of the novel, since he is, as we saw, an outsider yet an Anglo-Saxon; he can thus at the same time channel the violence of the whites and the nonwhites alike and can atone for the sins of the whites. The fact that his horse is called Bucephalus confirms such an interpretation since such a name sends us back again to ancient times, to the horse of Alexander the Great, the archetypal white conqueror.[8]

Owens has written a subversive Native version of "regeneration through violence," an American tradition to which the *roman noir* also belongs. The struggle that originally was conducted by the white settlers against the Other, the Indians on the frontier, is now reversed on the last Californian frontier. The Natives can in their turn confront their previous aggressor and reconquer their territory. This is why Hoey and his son Cole travel back east through the great expanses of Arizona, New Mexico, Texas, and Oklahoma in the last chapter. This counter-epic has already begun on the second page of the novel with the cat that confronts the readers with a fantasy universe to make them perceive another level of reality, that of Choctaw culture. Intertwined with the Greek metaphor of the search for truth and the punishment of hubris, it superimposes another level of reference on the aesthetics of the *roman noir* to operate the reintegration of the cleansed protagonists into their intimate community.

Literature can be interpreted in terms of sacrificial substitution, and the *roman noir* offers a perfectly ritualistic catharsis to its readers who accept such a strategy the moment they choose the book from a special section in their bookshops. Often classified as "mystery," the works of Owens will not disappoint those readers who do not expect an identity quest novel. Since *The Sharpest Sight* tries to heal evil, not only through more evil (which is allowed by the aesthetics of the *roman noir*), but also through a spiritual initiation into the good (which is allowed by the aesthetics of magic realism), we must see it as an incantatory work in itself, as a ceremony of purification and rejuvenation.

Thanks to his clever use of culturally diverse characters, to his playing with intertextuality and above all with intermythology, Owens seeks to expel from himself (because of the many autobiographical overtones) and from his readers vengeful urges, which are certainly legitimate ones but which, if left unchecked, could only perpetuate the morbid circularity of profane violence. To paraphrase the conclusion of Girard (481), after having made plainly obvious, in a perfectly rational light, the role of violence in our society that has emerged from the sacred, Owens invites us in a perfectly irrational, magical light to reimmerse ourselves into the spiritual realm, the only one that will allow us to reinvent a ritual violence, partly literary, to save us from our self-destructive impulses. This can be achieved for Diana Nemi only when she accepts growing into a mature woman and for Hoey, Cole, and Mundo when they accept their irrational Choctaw or Mexican roots.

If Owens has written here from a Choctaw stance, could we consider that he has "appropriated" Greek mythology — much as Hillerman has been accused of doing with Navajo culture — all the more so since his European roots are mostly Irish, not Greek? Could we also say, along with someone like Elizabeth Cook-Lynn, that Owens and other university writers who are labeled "Native authors" should not be considered as authentic Native intellectuals since they move too much out of the reservation and hop on any kind of fashionable trend (foreign mythology and literary genres)? These lines of reasoning, which are often heard and not just in intra–Native American circles, are damaging for the freedom of the artist, whatever his or her medium and ethnic background, and they send us back to the quarrels of the nineteenth century that led Henry James to counterattack with *The Art of Fiction*. Those who criticize writers such as Owens who are at ease in a cosmopolitan culture hold that fiction for the socially disadvantaged, whether Native, African American, or other, should be understandable by the semi-literate members of such social groups and should have a didactic and revolutionary social function. Yet, "intellectual fiction" can fulfill the same function, and in the case of *The Sharpest Sight*, even if all the mythological references are not grasped, the overall meaning and message of the book can be understood by most non-erudite readers, and it can operate at a subliminal level. Moreover, if it were more basically "reservation Native" in its symbolic system of representation, would it be better read on the reservation? We must grant to Owens the liberty to give an aesthetic representation not contained in Native lore to the quest of his Native characters if he finds it is thus staged more forcefully.

Yet, there is a trap Owens might have fallen into here, and it is one of his own doing. In his work of criticism and in *Other Destinies* in particular, he adopts the analysis found in *The Empire Writes Back* about the inclusion in postcolonial fiction of ethnic material not graspable by the mainstream readers. This postcolonial revenge implies that these readers, not able to pierce this hermeneutic code, will feel excluded from a community they have conquered physically but never fully spiritually. In *The Sharpest Sight*, it is true that the non-Choctaw will have a problem with the Choctaw expressions and mythological references, but what about the Choctaw readers who are not versed in Greek mythology? The strategy is blatantly double-edged, since those who have access to Greek mythology will also manage to have access to Choctaw material, thanks to books in particular, which is also the plight of most postcolonial writers in search of ethnic data. It would then seem that in *The Sharpest Sight* postcolonial rhetoric joins colonial rhetoric and its reliance on the European canon, best represented by the recourse to Greek mythology to buttress a plot.

Ironically, Owens did not feel guilty appropriating non-Native material when he chose Greek myths, and European readers do not feel he is guilty either. Those structuring stories are there for anyone to use if they can help to understand one's origins and social relationships. Most of us will feel that, whatever the origins of authors, they are perfectly entitled to select the systems of representation that they judge to be the most appropriate (in the other sense of the word) to express their concerns. It is clear that if one does not know the intricacies of Greek mythology, the text of *The Sharpest Sight* will never reveal its subtle meaning; nor will the meaning be clear if readers do not know anything about Choctaw traditions. But this is true of all literatures, and has always been so, which is a point the postcolonial discourse seems to forget.

Owens's literary message might well be that today's Natives, many of them mixed-bloods like himself, can survive spiritually only if they try to grasp and come to terms with the complexities of their multicultural legacies. Interestingly, if before and after *The Sharpest Sight* Owens has played with intertextuality to prove his point, it seems that he has had less recourse to the intermythology that has here connected an impressive network of symbols. Also, even though he has remained within the mystery or detective genre, he has not written, so far, such a brilliant *roman noir* as *The Sharpest Sight*, with all the rich developments about corruption and violence for which the genre allows. As in *Wolfsong* (before *The Sharpest Sight*), the hybridization at work in *Bone Games* and *Nightland* appears to be more focused on Native belief systems, which in itself sends a specific message about the search for identity at which Owens is aiming, clearly a recentering toward the Native half of his self.

NOTES

1. Owens's special brand of magical realism — that is, everything connected with the water metaphor, Mississippi, the wise relatives, and the various animals charged with a particular Choctaw symbolism — is not analyzed in this essay.

2. The twin motif is paramount here and complex: Attis and Cole, Attis and Mundo, Mundo and Cole, Jenna and Diana. It is often found in literature and also in various Native origin stories. Twins embody duality and complementarity but also, Girard tells us, strangeness since two beings appear when only one was expected. Because of that, in some cultures one of the two children was ritually killed, if not both. That Attis was killed may be the reenactment of such a practice. Yet it more probably symbolizes the destruction of wholeness perpetrated by colonization. Without his other half, Cole cannot feel whole. Mundo, the Chicano, is the half brother of Indians. Jenna and Diana are the two sides of the female coin, victim and avenger.

3. Interestingly, Cybele, a Phrygian goddess, was often identified with Rhea, the queen of the universe sent by Zeus as messenger to Demeter, and in *The Death of Jim Loney*, Jim's white lover is called Rhea. Though she fails, she could appear as a messenger, or a new Diana.

4. Attis's floating body looks somehow like that of Chandler's *Lady in the Lake* and also that of Ophelia, a Shakespearian echo to be found later in the *Romeo and Juliet* motif of *The Sharpest Sight*.

5. My translation of Girard's lines. Here the original text reads: "un supplément de mal qui pousse la crise au paroxysme et provoque l'expulsion des agents pathogènes avec la sienne propre" (430).

6. In *House Made of Dawn*, Scott Momaday tells us the same thing when he shows the sickness from which Abel suffers after killing the albino instead of trusting the runners who ritually expel evil from the community.

7. Such an interpretation allows us to understand the otherwise irrational anti-Jewish campaign of the Black Muslims, who cleverly share this scapegoat with many whites and hence limit the possibility of retaliation from the part of the too powerful American majority.

8. Here again the reference is polysemous, for the noble Bucephalus has turned into an old nag who tries to help Mundo look for the corpse in the end. The fact that its master calls it a "fart-bag" sends us back to the horse in *Winter in the Blood* whose fart revealed his origins to the narrator, a reference all the more obvious since the complete insult of Jessard is: "One must have a mind of fucking winter, you old fart-bag" (150).

Everybody in this country thinks they know what Indian is, when mostly they know what the media thinks it is. And that goes for the Indian people as well as for the non-Indian people. The first thing that happens to an immigrant who comes over here is she's sitting up watching late-night TV and she learns all about Indians in John Wayne movies.

Paula Gunn Allen [Laguna/Sioux/Lebanese],
in *Winged Words: American Indian Writers Speak*

Identity and Exchange

*The Representation of "The Indian"
in the Federal Writers Project
and in Contemporary Native
American Literature*

HARTWIG ISERNHAGEN

The following discussion rests on the observation that Native American literature originates where other Anglophone indigenous literatures originate as
well: in an intercultural space given and defined by their "Anglophony." This
does not mean that such literatures "are" intercultural in any sense beyond the
fact that their place of origin constitutes a "situation" or *scene* (in the Burkean
sense) to which they cannot *not* respond.[1] They may do so by affirming their
interculturality and stressing their communicative intent; they may also reject
their situation of origin as a debilitating and paralyzing one and constitute
themselves predominantly in separatist gestures — all of this will take place
within and with regard to the intercultural scene.

If one accepts that premise, one will also have to accept as probable what
may anyway be intuitively acceptable: that the discourses employed by Native
American literature today are in part indebted for their strategies and traits to
discursive changes and developments in the overall repertoire of Anglophone
literature and (if only for reasons of cultural-geographical proximity) above
all of American literature in English. For the past, indeed, we have little difficulty in embedding Native American literary patterns in this context; we will,
for instance, admit without hesitation that Simon Pokagon and Tekahionwake
are "Victorian." Even in discussing these earlier authors, however, there will
frequently creep into the critic's voice a tone of (at best) apology or (at worst)
subtle accusation — as if such contextualization were in some manner illicit,
and as if these authors could have, unlike any other authors any time in world
history, spontaneously emancipated themselves from their cultural environ-
ments and the discursive constraints operative in them. In discussing contemporary authors, contextualization in the larger repertoire, which is routinely
designated as "white," even more automatically (and unthinkingly) results in
implicit or explicit charges of "inauthenticity," which may be why it is, on the
other hand, so often avoided altogether. There *is*, indeed, some positive recog-

nition of isolated "influences," such as Hemingway's on the terse sentence structure of this or that novel or Faulkner's on the multivocally internal narratives of, let us say, Momaday or Erdrich — but the coupling of two so widely disparate authors in the second example indicates already how little such influence hunting really elucidates. Its problem is precisely that it does not place the authors in a complex discursive field, that it does not attempt to define what sort of discursive scene their writing reacts to and comments on. To identify a "source" is too precise, in a sense, to answer the purpose.

The following attempt at a general placing of contemporary Native American writing in a general twentieth-century scene may very well be at the other extreme: too "general," too imprecise. But that remains to be seen.

The problem that "minoritarian" writers encounter as they negotiate the discursive scene or scenes in which they are writing is history, as a product of historiography. Even where it is not openly or even programmatically apologetic, historiography will have an implicit tendency toward the affirmative. This is generally implied in its being an attempt at sense-making — as is any form of narrative. The problem is also a more specific result of the way in which traditional historiography tries to make sense: in terms of the motivation and purpose (avowed or unavowed, known or unknown) of the actors, or at the very least in terms of some motivational or causal direction, some "line" that will make the narrative consecutive and "rational" by telling how *this* came from *that* and led to a third thing. We all know that, and we all know the resulting tendency of historiographic texts to slip into the perspective of the winners even where they had just sympathized with the losers. It is not only that — in terms of the vulgar truth — history is written by the victors; it is also much more insidiously and invidiously written (even by much later generations, by writers from other cultural systems and with different intellectual and ideological allegiances) in such a way that the motivations and purposes of the victors, and the results that obviously favored them, will provide the dominant terms in which the line of the narrative is constructed. In this way, historiography only mirrors one of the less endearing aspects of historical societies themselves: that they very quickly come to terms with power, however illegitimate originally, by legitimizing it. That it would be one of the more interesting tasks of historiography itself to describe and analyze this process does not generally seem to be recognized.

As an apologetic enterprise, historiography has little room for the minority, for difference. Its narrative generally seems to make less sense — that is, it seems to contribute less to the ongoing communal process of historiographic sense-making — the more it questions the legitimacy of power, of the dominant.

(There are obvious limits to the truth of this statement: historical accounts will be said to lack depth or complexity or some such value if they become altogether too apologetic; but at this point, I am interested in the other limit.) It is in this sense entirely comprehensible not only that it has been difficult to write a *useful*[2] representation of Native Americans, as a group and frequently as individuals, into U.S. history as a whole — which could still be understood in terms of the victors not wishing to acknowledge how they won — but also that the historical representation of Native Americans in general has been problematic: not only their representation in historical texts, which has been hotly contested for ages, but also their representation as "historical" in narratives of other kinds, above all literary.

The implication here is that the many histories of destruction that we do have (or of degeneration, or whatever the uncomplimentary term may be) do not give a good account of what exists today as social structure, cultural network, and the like. At best they will only give a good account of what does not (any longer) exist. And that, in a sense, is not history: that, for those living today, is the text of being outside history. This essay neither attempts to write a better history nor indicates how it could be written — among other things because I am not a historian. I am also not going to entangle myself in an argument about the ethnocentrism of my own view of history, about what it begs and obscures, and about the fact (readily admitted) that the worldviews of many Native American groups will imply or presuppose or suggest different notions of historical existence: ones that are usually referred to as being cyclical or associated with myth and ritual. Nor do I attempt to deny the obvious: that many texts in the ample body of Native American literature that have come into existence during the last quarter century operate precisely in terms of such a model of history, by advocating it or by structuring themselves in its terms.

What I would, however, like to point out is that in so doing, and by writing against debilitating conventions, such texts address precisely the problem that I have tried to formulate: the absence, in the older Anglophone repertoire, of models of representation that construct the Indian as being inside history. This absence can be demonstrated in an unlikely body of literature: the texts produced by the Federal Writers' Project (FWP), which are at the same time useful insofar as they display with admirable clarity, beyond that absence itself, an important diversity of modulations and modifications even among the traditional (largely debilitating) discourses about Native Americans.[3] Furthermore, and this I found surprising and interesting, they occasionally appear to anticipate two basic strategies of writing Native Americans back into (written) history that have dominated the scene since the Native American Renaissance: what one might provisionally call a discourse of cultural change, of cultural loss, and of cultural (re)construction — or briefly, a *discourse of identity*—and a discourse of quotidian survival, or of *exchange*.[4] (What precisely distinguishes the two directions of "rehistoricization" will become clearer in the course of this analysis.) To postulate a contextual relationship between the 1930s and the Native American Renaissance is not to suggest that the FWP texts have produced the literary discourses; no single source, however complex, produces a literary discourse. But what the similarities at the very least suggest is that the discursive changes were a considerable time in the making and that the Native American Renaissance has a genealogy we can begin to trace.

The Indian is present in most of those state and local (county or city) guides that are everywhere acknowledged as the "literary" products of the FWP.[5] The general structure of the guides prefigures (or is based on) a separation between the representation of Indians and history. After a general introductory chapter there normally comes one on geology, physical geography, flora, and fauna: on nature as the "substratum" of civilization.[6] Next comes a chapter on the first human inhabitants, which in turn is followed by one on history or (a frequent phrasing) "the beginning of history," which is thereby made synonymous with white occupation. Indians are thus placed essentially between natural history and history. They can be historicized by being described in terms of a series of first encounters or dehistoricized as having basically static cultures, but they are never properly part of the historical account, in which they tend to provide at best the material for the first two or three paragraphs.[7] If history is the discipline that deals with white people, "prehistory" or archaeology is the discipline that deals with Indians. (Under certain circumstances the French and Spanish or, more rarely, the English can be prehistoricized in a similar way, which creates nice and potentially fruitful ambiguities.)

In many respects, such separation is obviously debilitating—particularly insofar as it evolves into an implicit story that extends across the guide as a whole, in which there first comes a more or less positive image of past Indian civilizations, then a first phase of history that is largely without Indians, then (if anything at all) the description of their "degenerate" state in the present. There is little or no need in such cases to establish explicit continuity between the phases and images; the implicit story of the (naturalized) course of history is clear enough. In some instances, however, the separation is to a degree also enabling. In some guides (such as the California one) it makes possible the creation of a very detailed account of past Indian societies and of their destruction, often naming the destroyers very explicitly. The same agents of history, however, appear in the next chapter as the builders of the present society.[8] Here, as elsewhere, it is possible in one chapter to validate Indian cultures, to tell the truth about the displacement and murder of Indians, and to indicate how little is left "these days" of their original societies, and then in the next chapter to write a history of the heroic struggle of Western powers over possession of the North American continent, in which the Indian appears as no more than a pawn. The themes, the frames of reference, and the discourses and perspectives are so different as to be totally incompatible. What such guides, as a whole, do is create a gap that one can read differently: as hypocrisy, as fragmentation, as more or less intended subversion or deconstruction, or as the manifestation of a discursive problem that in our post-deconstructionist perspective leads to the more or less automatic self-subversion of the discourses employed.

All of this takes place within the framework of the concern of the Work Projects Administration (WPA) and the Federal Writers' Project (FWP), which in 1939 became the Writers' Program (WP), for minorities that has to do with their New Deal origins and contexts. There was an apparent attempt underway in them to do justice — in whatever sense and with whatever means — to disadvantaged minorities. We know in a general way — too general to be satisfactory — that the (self-)representation of some minorities in the United States has profited from WPA/FWP work. We know, for example, that white ethnics achieved greater visibility from folklore projects and from both prairie small-town and big-city interest in the succeeding waves of immigration.[9] But at the same time, the WPA effort was *solidarity* oriented. All discussions of the FWP/WPA agree on what they frequently term its *Americanism*: its celebration of America in the spirit of an ongoing search for a usable past.[10] The American Guides had first priority in the FWP, and if in turn, in making the state guides, "first priority went to the history essay," this was because their aim, as formulated by Katherine Kellock, was "to educate Americans to an evaluation of their own civilization" (Penkower 81, 32).[11] Both *evaluation* and *their own* are slippery terms: How close is *evaluate* to *assess* or *cherish*? In reference to *their own*, what is the relation between group and culture? How monolithic are the two supposed to be? The interpretation of these terms patently changed in the course of the FWP's work, particularly as World War II approached: patriotism was foregrounded.[12] If the project could, and obviously did, thematize ethnicity and class, because it could not afford to deny the problematic aspects of history, the bottom line, from the beginning and with increasing force toward the end, seems to have been that it could above all not afford to become too divisive, either ethnically or along class lines.

The Americanism of the FWP texts thus highlights the simple fact that they had to face, once again, the perpetual problem of the United States: the *e pluribus unum* problem; and they had to face it as a programmatically bi-directional question — for with the concern for justice, there was a tacit corollary that

could be summarized as *plures in uno*, almost an early form of multiculturalism that vanished quickly, however, as WWII crept nearer and as the crisis
that it constituted was increasingly interpreted as a patriotic one. What has just
provisionally been termed *justice* will be sacrificed to solidarity in situations
where conflict arises. The minority will be sacrificed to the majority, and unity
will come before multiplicity. In the FWP texts, accordingly, narrow notions of
use took precedence over the originally more open search for a usable past: very
simple forms of patriotism seemed to require denials of patent problems.[13]

It was also true that from the beginning the project had to combat "the
country's affinity for boosterism" (Penkower 75–76) and that there was a real
danger of censorship at the local or state level: "directors eventually found that
local sponsors would rather forgo the benefit of a guidebook than accept one
containing any controversial material" (99), and "most omissions resulted
from a strict adherence to the chamber of commerce tradition. Blacks and the
massacre of Indians received little mention" (78). There were radical impulses
in the FWP, and if the Washington office, on the one hand, had to tone down or
delete the worst exhibitions of provincialism and bigotry, it also, on the other
hand, worked hard to prevent critical local writers from offending local sensibilities too much. Penkower has an entire chapter (96–116) on the various
forms of censorship that therefore ran at cross-purposes through the production of the project's texts, and although he believes that "censorship was the
greatest danger" to these texts developing their own perspective, he also concludes that the final interference with content was minor so that the project
"struck a successful balance between radical propaganda and chamber of commerce boosterism" (Penkower 96, 113–14).

The term *balance* here hides an uncertainty and ambivalence, or a conflict,
in the material that is carried over into Penkower's own evaluation.[14] If the
project as a whole, indeed, did show a "critical approach to the celebration of
America" and, at the same time in the late 1930s (a period of increasing "cultural nationalism"), managed only to preserve it *comparatively* (Penkower 115),
the question is precisely what a "good" balance between criticism and affirmation is, and behind Penkower's phrases there emerges an ongoing battle, in
the 1930s and in the project, over the definition of a *usable past* — specifically
whether the notion of *use* could be made to integrate a critical perspective on
basic historical problems of American society or whether it had to be restricted
to outright affirmation.

In this field of contestations the representation of minorities takes place,
and the WPA texts have particularly acute problems with visible minorities.
They do not yet know how to consistently write *The Indian*, in their contemporary *present*, as a historical (and hence political) animal, just like all other

members of the species *homo sapiens*. Writers of the period had, indeed, just begun to write *The Negro* as such a historical animal, and the record of the FWP with regard to the two minorities is different, which needs some consideration.

The difference is so obvious that it leads to invidious comparisons between the two groups in the scanty criticism on the topic. Briefly put, Indians received considerable treatment in the guides while African Americans were neglected, and African Americans received the attention of special FWP programs, both as subjects of study and as workers that needed to be employed. This is why Weisberger has a point, but one of very limited validity only when, in the introductory materials to his selections from the "American Guides," he puts forward a longish complaint on racial prejudice in the representation of African Americans in the guides, not even mentioning Indians in this context.[15] This creates the unnecessarily lopsided impression that Indians were consistently represented there with less prejudice. That this is far from true is borne out by his own isolated and uneven comments later on in the book.[16]

Though it is probably not very fruitful to play the two disadvantaged minorities off against one another in this way, Weisberger does pinpoint a real problem, but it can be seen differently. In Mangione, for instance, the topic of African Americans and their contribution both to the project and to American civilization is prominent in the chapter "Varieties of American Stuff" (241–85), which in many ways, of the entire book, is the part most clearly concerned with writerly production, rather than administration and politics. Mangione points out that "perhaps the greatest beneficiaries of the Project were its black employees," that several major African American writers emerged from it, and that it "helped to promote the first Negro studies to be conducted in the United States on an extensive scale" (255–57). He sees that the state guides are uneven in their inclusion and treatment of material on African Americans but also concludes that Sterling A. Brown (then "national editor of Negro affairs") and his staff "achieved their goal of including honest and accurate material about the Negro in most of the state guidebooks," which then "represented, in effect, the first objective description of the Negro's participation in American life," and he adds information on several individual publications on African Americans (Mangione 259–65).

Taken together, Weisberger's and Mangione's opinions probably mean no more than that African Americans, as the larger and more visible minority, in the perspective of the administration of the WPA/FWP, constituted the more urgent social, economic, and cultural problem — and therefore had those special programs assigned to them — and that in the eyes of countless writers, editors, sponsors, and administrators concerned with the guides, African Americans were so touchy a subject that they were overlooked wherever it was possible. It is recognition of the minority as "a problem" that produces both re-actions, even if they are diametrically opposed to one another. It is from such an ambivalent perspective, too, that Penkower strikes something of a balance. He regards the FWP's record in the employment of African Americans on the project as less positive than Mangione, saying that there were comparatively few, and these unevenly distributed, but he, too, finds that Black Studies be-came "the most pioneering of all the project's subsidiary efforts," and his dis-cussion of this aspect winds up with the statement that the project, "in re-jecting the message of [the Harlem Renaissance], abandoned the exotic and the primitive to sharpen its readers' concern for and understanding of the Negroes past" (Penkower 66–67, 140–47).[17]

The representation of Native Americans, in comparison, according to both Mangione and Penkower, suffered neglect in the FWP as a whole — though at times benevolent and fruitful neglect. If we can trust the implications of Man-gione's account, there was simply no perception of Native Americans as a topic of comparable interest or sensitivity in the FWP central administration's day-to-day work, and this reduces the presence of Indians in his text almost to zero. He does not have either McNickle or Kennard (professional staff members of the FWP who are further identified below) among the hundreds of names in his index, and he merely mentions "*Indians of the United States*, a contemporary picture and historical account of what happened to the first Americans under the rule of the white man," as being "among the unborn books" of the FWP (346). Penkower, too, who does at least keep them in sight, has disappointingly little on the FWP's treatment of Indians, beyond the fairly late and general statement

that special studies relating to Indians and their culture failed to realize their potential. Minor school bulletins on Indian legends in South Dakota, New Mexico, and Arizona represented the most that could be done after the path-breaking state guide essays on Indians were completed. Lack of information and the bias of project workers militated against further study. Relief cuts terminated a fieldwork project carried on among sev-eral tribes under the outside supervision of Franz Boas and Ruth Benedict. In Trenton a state official refused to sponsor a series of Indian school bulletins because the first one had dealt with an Indian legend of creation and he feared youngsters would begin to ask about childbirth. (149)[18]

Even with regard to "the path-breaking state guide essays on Indians," what there is in Penkower by way of appreciation of representations of The Indian are isolated remarks that "many Indian 'legends' were merely white men's in-ventions, every state having its 'lovers' leap,' " or "Washington did correct the dominant notion that what Indians did to whites was frightful, but the reverse noble: frontier cruelty was portrayed as commonplace on both sides" (77). Thus, on the whole, Penkower creates an image that supports the impression that the dominant interest of the project lay in solving the urgent questions of the present, and that The Indian was not one of them — much less so than The Negro.

The disparity is apparent in many places, but nowhere as clearly as in the Washington DC guide. Where other state guides react to the shock of the new discourse about African Americans by excluding them from their bodies as comprehensively as possible, it addresses with competence, in its chapter titled "The Negro in Washington," the realities of slavery and discrimination and then discusses the present with equal competence in terms of ongoing viable constructions of ethnic identity.[19] This is in stark contrast to its adherence to the pattern of dehistoricization of The Indian, which it employs, though, with an interesting twist. That, as I have argued, the procedure of separating The Indian from history tries to do two incompatible things at once — to legitimize the conquest and to develop a "good" view of history — is quite apparent, when it here again becomes at least partly enabling, though in a rather unorthodox place. Among the guide's descriptions of buildings (in the "Points of Interest" section that in other guides would have been called the "Tours" section) there is a very detailed account of the South Interior Building (276–81), built in 1935–36 and presented as a symbol of the nation at this point in history. It is full of Indian references and would well merit a full reading that would demonstrate the ambiguity of The Indian as a cultural signifier for the nation: the (if one wishes: imperialist) appropriation as background "indigene" and (in the same process or gesture) the thorough validation of The Indian as culturally valuable that directly contradicts all discourses of delegitimation encountered in the apology of imperialism. (The tension continues, particularly in discourses about the West, to this day.) Earlier, the same Washington guide has an extraordinarily brittle (and brief) chapter entitled "The Indian Background" (17–20), indicating that to know how to deal with one problem (the national one) does not help when dealing with the other (the local one).[20] The cases of The Negro and The Indian are obviously not fully comparable to the writers of the Washington guide; the diversity of rhetorical approaches indicates, rather, that the basic historiographic problem only appears to be the same, and that pragmatically and politically the situations of African Americans and Native Americans are perceived as radically different.

Within this framework, one can isolate a further, specifically ideological rationale for the comparative neglect of The Indian that we find in the FWP as a whole. If we assume — and I think it is legitimate to do so — that the WPA was in a general way (and quite apart from those leftist influences that Penkower does not quite know how to place) interested in class phenomena, we can also say that African Americans, like white immigrants, must have profited from this interest insofar as there is a patent link between class and ethnicity with both sets of minorities. The category of class worked for these groups, who were fully integrated into the economic system as workers and consumers, better than for Native Americans. It also worked better for industrial contexts than for rural ones. But the main factor is probably that as a theoretical tool, *class* relies largely on notions of surplus value and exploitation, both of which rely on work, and the most visible dispossession of Indians has historically been less that of exploitation than a purer, more radical one: deprivation of the means to livelihood. (The fur trade was a classical case of exploitation, but it gave out before a class had been formed.) This is to say that the notion of class would only have appeared applicable to Native Americans if its link with the notion of work could have been severed, but that would have been a "liberation" type of analysis in which the wPA could not be interested.

A number of factors thus militate against the creation of "good" representations of Native Americans. On the other hand there is the fact — pointed out above — that within the FWP material a number of interestingly "good" texts and passages can be identified. The picture is not uniformly black, but quite uneven, as the following section briefly attempts to show. That there should be at least some "good" materials is almost to be expected once one realizes that on the Washington staff of the project, which was largely composed of professional writers and where "different topics were assigned to separate editors throughout the project's existence," there were first "D'Arcy McNickle, author and member of the *Encyclopaedia Britannica* editorial staff, and then Edward Kennard, specialist on the Hopi and Sioux, [who] handled Indians and archaeology" (Penkower 36). The coupling of Indians with archaeology is ominous, once again tending to write, as it generally does, The Indian into prehistory. But these two names make one wonder how far it may have been possible to work against this tendency. It may not be insignificant, for instance, that Arizona's *The Hopi* and *The Navaho* — exemplary, within the context here established — thank "Dr. Edward A. Kennard, Editor of Indian and Archaeological Material for the Federal Writers' Project" for his help.

The two selections from (as they claim) the "American Guides" that have already been mentioned — Hobson and Weisberger — really restrict themselves to the state and a few big-city guides, excluding the majority of city and county ones. With their sweeping perspective, though, they do provide a convenient shortcut to a general idea of the representation of Native Americans in the FWP.[21]

Weisberger's anthology, which includes more material on Native Americans, indicates the unevenness of the guides, and in particular it suggests that as a (very) general rule the West is more complex in its representation of Native Americans than the East. This may simply be due to the presence of more and larger reservations in western (and particularly Midwestern) states than elsewhere. Concretely, some of the western texts (never more than a few) try to address some of the complexities of Indian-white relations and the mechanisms of obscuring them;[22] they try to establish continuities between past and present, rather than making the Indian the object of archaeologic study;[23] and they try to represent fairly the clash between modernizers and traditionalists in Indian communities and their ongoing life.[24] Thus the representation of the Bois Fort Indian Reservation in Minnesota stresses self-organization and self-help, has blueberry marshes and wild rice, and knows of ceremonial dances that occur in connection with the rice gathering. About a third of the text (as reprinted) is dedicated to a credible attempt at an accurate and sympathetic representation of what to the writer is totally strange (278–79). The Fort Apache Reservation in Arizona is represented by a well-arranged and well-edited selection from Arizona's Apache booklet, with all the positive qualities of that evenhanded text (432–33). The description of Acoma focuses on the village's situation and composition, gender roles, and the production of pottery; it is neutral in tone and both informed and informative (433–34). The representation of Taos Pueblo is made up of short characterizations of how "they" live, with a focus on the preservation of traditions — almost as if the writer wished to shield them, too, from outside influence. And the description of Hubbell's Trading Post is entirely factual, focusing on economic mechanisms; what emerges is a working relationship between the trader and the Indian community (434–35).

Again and again, however, even in the best texts, "good points" are mixed with "bad" ones. The Menominee Indian Reservation in Wisconsin (Weisberger 87–88) is described as a viable economic and social enterprise but primarily on the basis of adaptation to the white system. These Indians' system of forestry works well, but they live in "huts, poorly painted, often squalid and unsanitary"; "deep in the forest live some 100 pagans — solitary, shy, and a bit unfriendly," who "every spring . . . hold their own ancient and secret Mitawin ceremony." In the following description, some attempt at fairness is clearly being made, but the whole is written without real understanding — let alone sympathy, which one might argue is essential to the adequate representation of any religious custom — so that as "the tribal dance begins," it is "with moccassined feet shuffling to the slow monotonous drum beats." Interestingly enough, when the writer uses "pagan" a second time, he glosses it as "non-Christianized," as if he suddenly realized the discriminatory implications of the term and wished to neutralize them. There is a struggle against negative cliché going on here, as there comes the inevitable remark that "the women like bright colors," and the struggle is being lost (88).

It also looks as if the descriptions of reservations, in the "Tours" sections of guides, were in general more carefully written (and perhaps more carefully or successfully vetted by Washington) than the general discussions of Indians in the bodies of texts. For example, the description of a nonwestern community, the Catawba Indian Reservation in South Carolina (Weisberger 233–34), attempts to couple an image of racial, cultural, and economic "degeneration" with the description of a turn for the better in the present and the sardonic comment: "The former steady decline can be ironically traced in part to their loyalty to their white brothers: they supported them in all wars, and furnished troops to the Confederacy. In return, the whites have expropriated the lands of the Indians, in spite of George Washington's promise of protection" (234).[25]

Hobson's selections that deal with Indians are less numerous but add to the picture. A description of the lodge used by "the Missouri Valley tribes" basically follows one of Catlin's pictures and toward the end remarks on the "imperfections of the crude tools and equipment at their command" and on the lodge being "a humble covering that guarded with all its passive, effective impenetrability against [the weather]" (28–29). That the characterization of the lodge replicates the stereotype of the Stoic Indian is obvious. The New Mexico guide uses the same technique: adobe is described as an aesthetically pleasing material, and yet the houses in Taos "have a gloomy look. They seem to be crouching close to the ground for protection from some unknown thing, and seem little taller than the hollyhocks screening their tawny walls" (30). The positive value associated with tallness in WASP culture and the traditional "tawny-ness" of Indian maidens and youths are both stereotypically present. Against this, the Navajo hogan is described in those ethnographic terms that the *Navaho* booklet also uses: "Although the hogan is but a mud hut, its mythical prototype is thus described by the Navajo: Built of poles of white shell, turquoise, etc." (35). And there is a good, detailed, respectful account of a Shoshone Sun Dance (325–26), some general information on it in the past tense, and then the present ("revived" and "Christianized") form in the present tense. The text signals understanding and wishes to communicate it.

Among Eastern texts, Weisberger's South Carolina guide appears to be an exception. With regard to Native Americans, his introductions often do not do much more than summarize the selections he offers, so a sampling of them suffices to characterize the general spirit.[26] The New England section, for instance, begins with the myth of the discovery of her "wild shores" by Europeans and "her people [being] among the earliest Americans to wring a living from farm, forest and sea" (3). (The selections appropriately include an Indian love-death legend.) A later section entitled "E Pluribus Unum" has in its introduction the sentence that "on an upstate New York reservation, Indians still lived according to tribal governance — and wore blue jeans" (153); elsewhere, "the Southern Indians were distinctive, for they included the Five Civilized Tribes, who had, by deliberate government policy, been expelled from their ancestral lands and forced to move westward in the 1830s. A few remnants of those who had not gone into exile still could be found" (224). The section on the Midwest is at best uneven. On the one hand it states that "even while axes were leveling the forests and gunshots were driving away the panther and the Indian [an association that goes back at least to Charles Brockden Brown], cities were growing almost next door" (39). But the introduction to a subsection on "The Ethnic Midwest" (80) suddenly establishes a critical perspective on the material,[27] and Weisberger fully shares the ambivalences and insecurities of his material, in which we also find that "mounted Plains Indians fiercely defended their turf" (247), that people could remember "seeing Indians selling the scalps of their tribal enemies as souvenirs in the streets" (248), and that "from 1819 to 1917, much of Oklahoma was Indian Territory, home to the dislocated tribes of the Southeast, and supposedly protected forever from white encroachment" (289). It is perhaps in keeping with this ambivalence that Weisberger does not even acknowledge the existence of Indians in the introduction to the "Mountain States" (339–40).

The discursive problem these texts attempt to solve with such widely differing success is how to avoid, in the representation of Native Americans, the reinscription of patterns of othering, whether in the form of Indian hating or of primitivism. It is not in the major texts, though — not in the state and (big) city guides excerpted by the collections quoted — that the more interesting solutions to the problem are found, but rather in the much more voluminous and diversified minor materials. In some (once again, not more than a few) of these, solutions become apparent that go in the direction of what have already provisionally been called *discourses of identity* and *discourses of exchange*. One needs to begin by showing that the two are not mutually exclusive — that one can actually observe them in interaction in some of the best FWP texts, such as the Arizona booklets — but that their tendencies are ultimately different.

The Arizona booklets begin with the programmatic introduction to the Hopi volume, which is referred to in a footnote in the introduction to the next booklet, the Navajo one, and which is then apparently lost sight of.[28] Or rather, the program itself is to a degree lost sight of; for within the then current framework of thinking the Hopi booklet aims at non-ethnocentric representation, under the aegis of a universalist question that could be phrased something like "How do humans manage to live socially?" and tacitly presupposes (at least until the opposite has been proven) that the solutions found by different cultures are roughly equal in value and dignity. This question itself engenders or fosters more or less nonhierarchical strategies of representation, though within a framework dominated to a considerable degree by the axiom of urgent ethnography: that the pressure toward "assimilation" will destroy traditional lifeways. A general tendency to focus on work, on culture, as a solution to problems establishes a perspective that will easily accommodate cultural relativism and that is being used in all the Arizona pamphlets, though (I find) with lessening clarity and intensity, to engage and counter stereotyping.

Thus, the apparent borrowings from life cycle texts — not in the first-person form of the contemporaneous life history but in a fictionalized third-person form that comes close to it in narrative effect — not only serve to provide the perspective from within that ethnographers need to "complete" their "pictures" of other cultures, but beyond that create a sense of the social as a network of obligations, of power relations, and of work. Thus, for instance, the young Hopi child is placed in a network of multiple personal relations that are (in the spirit of universalism) seen in terms of power but at the same time are appreciated in their specificity:

As he grows older, he will learn his relationship to the various members of his household, how they should be addressed, and what kind of treatment he may expect from them. He will be bossed, disciplined, and reprimanded by his mother's brother, played with by his grandparents, brought presents by his father. His mother will care for all his wants until his position in the family is displaced by the birth of another baby, when he may be turned over to his older sister. He will become accustomed to being ordered around by his older brothers and sisters, and will in turn take advantage of his age with the brothers and sisters who follow him. (*Hopi* 15–16)

These are perspectives that enable translation (between the culture that is being "read" and the reader's own culture) with comparatively little distortion or loss, since what is translated is not the full complexity of solutions, with all their lived realities, implications, and complications, but their pragmatic value in the attempt to survive. Here is a discourse that manages comparatively well to preserve the difference between self and Other (rather than permitting simple appropriation) and to make the Other comprehensible as another human being with essentially the same problems as oneself. It is a discourse that strikes a useful balance between universalism and respect for the absolute uniqueness of the local. Here is, if you will, a strategy of translation that is (paradoxically) predicated on the ultimate untranslatability of the culturally specific.

There are here, thus, two tendencies at work. There is a stress on identity as difference, as is to be expected within the ethnographic environment from which the booklets come, and within this concern cultural difference and its forms of representation — above all stereotype — are programmatically worked through. This is not always explicitly so, but the entire writerly strategy, with its programmatic series of references to universal human problems and with occasional statements on the superiority of Indian solutions to white ones, is designed to create a positive image of Native American sociocultural identity and to counter negative stereotypes. (It is in this sense that I am using the term *programmatically* above: it refers to a not necessarily explicit program that is perceptibly at work all through the texts.) Within this framework, the life cycle patterns, and particularly the rituals of initiation, play a prominent role as "other" patterns of identity formation that are both individual and group-related. On the other hand, and out of the same source, there is the possibility of using the theme of survival as a universally human task that at least can support an attitude of exchange. This perspective avoids overt questions of difference and dealing with stereotype: the reader is again and again drawn into a recognition of the basic similarity of concerns by being made to slip into the Indian perspective. (This is apparently the second contribution of the life-history-like sections in some of these booklets.)

The two possibilities are here mutually involved with one another, but they also represent widely divergent attitudes to and ways of dealing with stereotype and thus a different way of placing the minority vis-à-vis the majority culture. And one needs to remember always that from within the pattern of the one discourse, the "base question" of the other looks different: from within a discourse of identity the question of universal human survival takes on certain valences and aspects that it does not have from within a discourse of exchange, and from the latter's perspective established images of group and personal identity, stereotypes, and role patterns will generally appear much more momentarily negotiable than from the perspective of identity.[29]

We are, of course, fully familiar with the discourse of identity, which has in a way — or rather in several very different ways — become the dominant discourse of contemporary Native American writing. The negotiation and deconstruction of stereotype, of too well established patterns of representation, has been going on in the ways in which I am interested here at least since the publication of Momaday's *House Made of Dawn*. It has been carried forward by many (by now canonical) authors, among the first of whom was Leslie Silko, and both these authors' oeuvres have moved on to very different ways of dealing with the problem. Among the more radical transformations of the problematics has been that self-declaredly postmodernist turn that we find in

Vizenor and others. This literature has engendered its own criticism, with an equally far-ranging variety of perspectives that can perhaps be indicated by contrasting the (to my mind frequently essentialist) criticism of Paula Gunn Allen to Krupat's poststructuralist criticism. This much is obvious. And so is the fact that all of these — and particularly the creative texts — have at the same time had to engage the stereotypes, implicitly or explicitly, that in a sense largely form their material. It is such engagement of the historical patternings of Indian hating and glorification of the Indian, of the Daemonic Savage and the Noble Savage, that largely constitutes their recovery of a viable discourse.

Among the "older" heroes of the Native American Renaissance, Welch is different. A brief comparison of the beginning of *The Death of Jim Loney* with the beginnings of Momaday's and Silko's first novels will indicate the kind and extent of the difference[30]: "*Dypaloh*. There was a house made of dawn. It was made of pollen and of rain, and the land was very old and everlasting. There were many colors on the hills, and the plain was bright with different-colored clays and sands. Red and blue and spotted horses grazed in the plain, and there was a dark wilderness on the mountains beyond. It was beautiful all around" (Momaday, *House* 1).

The first word and the two following sentences set the theme of linguistic and cultural difference, of an ethnicity that is easily recognized as Indianness by anyone with even the most remote knowledge of the Indian cultures of the Southwest. The ensuing descriptions of the land, which in isolation could have come out of Faulkner, for instance, within this context and the perspective created by it need to be taken to refer to The Land, or Mother Earth, as part of the general image of "Indian" worldviews. By the end of the first paragraph of the prologue, a general thematic horizon of narrative perspective and discourse has been established, a horizon of identity. The discourse has taken a direction and could only with difficulty be wrenched around in a different direction.

Or, from Silko:

Ts'its'tsi'nako, Thought-Woman,
　　is sitting in her room
and whatever she thinks about
　　appears.
　　She thought of her sisters,
Nau'ts'ity'i and I'tcts'ity'i,
and together they created the Universe. . . .
(*Ceremony* 1)

To begin with a creation myth is certainly among the most economical and efficient ways to signal ethnocultural difference, since it implies what the representation and reconstruction of such difference is all about: a difference in epistemologies and worldviews, a difference in "realities." A text that begins in this way could only with difficulty be directed away from that horizon of identity that is here created and that gives specificity ("Indianness") to the ensuing poem "Ceremony" and the notions of story and ritual that it advances and that would, without the preceding etiological myth, be much more open to interpretations in terms of a generally "spiritual" or "religious" worldview.

In the beginning of Welch's novel, "Loney watched the muddy boys bang against each other and he thought of a passage from the Bible: 'Turn away from man in whose nostrils is breath, for of what account is he?' The boys stood up, some walking back to the huddle, others standing with hands on hips and heads bent. The rain fell, but more lightly now. Beyond the arc lights the world was black. The shiny helmets lined up against each other" (*Death* 1).

This beginning is programmatically universalist — as is a lot of Welch's poetry. (This aspect may have facilitated explicit and implicit charges of a lack of "Indianness" against Welch.) It takes some time even to identify the scene as a football game: the "muddy boys" and the "huddle" do not necessarily have to be placed on a football field. It is only the sum of these elements plus the postures of those players not in the huddle and the arc lights and the helmets that clarifies the image as one of a specific, and specifically North American, scene. That scene becomes clearer in the rest of the chapter, but Loney's Indianness does not become an implicit theme, it seems to me, until the third chapter. And from there onward, it cannot help but be developed differently — more implicitly and indirectly — so that in point of fact one could trace all through the three texts, down to their endings, the differences that here have only been suggested. The point is not to suggest that the theme of identity is not a relevant one in Welch's early works, but rather that it is treated in significantly different ways. Discourses of identity foreground identity and to a degree theorize it, so that it becomes a matter of knowledge which can be acted out freely and in a sense "abstractly," as if it were a thing so separate from any concrete situation that it can again and again be injected into a multiplicity of situations in essentially the same way. The other type of discourse leaves it embedded in representations of everyday practices and shows it to be inextricably embroiled and implicit in them. Both views of identity are "true," of course, but in different ways, and it appears that no single discourse can realize and communicate both at once.

One might ask why the second discourse should here be called a "discourse of exchange." The term is dispensable. It has been suggested by the thought that in focusing on the everyday (and, as will become apparent, on the irresolvable) this discourse tends to represent interaction across ethnic boundaries in terms of similarity rather than dissimilarity and with a focus on shared problems that may be capable of resolution more easily through exchange than through separation. The discourse of identity cannot but raise the question whether a degree or period of separation is needed in certain situations — in order, for instance, to save a form of ethnic identity from "vanishing." (It should be clear in view of these situational implications that the designations do not imply any preference for the one discourse or the other.)

The term has also been suggested by the specific appearances of this type of discourse in the minor FWP texts. Even in cultural situations that in a general way are burdened by an overwhelming presence of stereotypes, it is possible there to have discourses that will at most by implication acknowledge them, in the interest of exchange. These are discourses that emerge from lived situations in which other considerations are more important than those embodied in and referred to by the stereotypes. The question of survival in a difficult environment tends to take precedence over questions of personal or group identity that under the circumstances appear as marginal and abstract. Thus, for instance, where the Iowa material is good, there is a stress on the hardship faced by all living in this land, hence on the multiplicity of contacts and contact forms, and ultimately this creates a multiplicity of perceptions, of images. What emerges in the best moments (and only then) is something like a true people's history that at least incidentally also admits how recently (less than 150 years back) white supremacy has been established.[31] It is in this spirit that the *Ringgold County History* (1942) integrates Indian individuals into a series of anecdotes of comparative normalcy: everyday life is characterized by a degree of cooperation (one Indian helps a white widow get her horse back, another helps a group of white men bluff a group of aggressive Sioux so they leave peacefully); conflict can remain unbloody (the same widow and her son encounter Indians who want whiskey), but it does become visible when an Indian ineptly tries to make use of the white system of land ownership, and even more so when an Indian is accused of murdering a white man and is not lynched (the narrative insinuates clearly enough that the victim was in fact murdered by his white companion) (5–7).

Conflict becomes even more visible in the very detailed *Buena Vista County History* (1942), which attempts to trace historical processes: settlers (usually called pioneers in what after all is a validating term) keep filtering into Indian Country, Indians keep coming back into "white" areas, and the U.S. government is again and again helpless. To both affected groups, or "the populace," no coherent policy is visible, but only a state of lawlessness that endangers the security of all. The text tries to render the resulting insecurities as story but has great problems containing the tensions it (re)produces discursively. It tries to solve those through recourse to dramatization and a discourse of heroism that can be applied to both groups, but it fails.[32] The discourse of exchange breaks down, and the text has recourse to cliché, so that although there is a tendency to recognize the validity of grievances of individuals on both sides, there is also a very simple validation of the white victims who "left not even the record of their names behind them" (11) and a symmetrical denigration of Indians who do not kill anyone in a certain situation only because they are afraid, and who even communicate "with angry grunts and signs" at the same time that they act "with ruthless waste" (10).[33]

Both the dramatization and the stereotyping that come together here as elsewhere may have something to do with a simple lack of concrete knowledge. The *Scott County History* (1942), after a very balanced account of Mound Builders and the question of whether they were Indians, has a professionally written history of Indian-white contact and conflict from the beginning, with a solid ethnographic description of Indian civilizations as complex entities (Saukenuk, the principal "village" of the Sacs, in 1825 had eight thousand inhabitants) of political alliances among Indians and with outside forces (here, the British, particularly in 1812–14) that drew them into conflicts not their own.[34] The account at least makes the ways in which the populace was affected reconstructable, even if it does not in fact reconstruct it to the extent that the Ringgold County history did. It does stress that things went fairly well for a period between Indians and immigrants, with well-established figures of authority on both sides functioning as mediators, but that as the influx of settlers crowded Indians out, conflict increased and led to Black Hawk's War of 1832 (14–15).

This view — of a period in which patterns of coexistence and mutually profitable exchange appeared to emerge from or next to or within conflict — is interesting because it is reminiscent of the "middle ground" pattern that White has explored. And it does occur in some material from the region covered by that designation. In Ohio, the *Urbana and Champaign County Guide* (1942) is among the few texts that in a detailed way write the Indian into the history of the place. It begins with two pages on "Mound Builders and Indians" that stress the continuity of the two groups and continuous (if "migratory") Indian land use. It has an extended discussion of "Pioneer Forays" — really the 1770s to 1790s — which manages to focus on white military movements and successes without obscuring or denigrating Indians (8–15). The figure of Tecumseh is almost as prominent as that of the central white figure here, Simon Kenton. And there is no questioning of Indian agency, as there is in so many other texts.

The chapter "Frontier County Seat" (16–28) is particularly interesting in this context. It develops an image of intermixed exchange and confrontation between Indians and whites: among the first settlers is one with an Indian wife (16); settlers follow Indian trails and have some of their cabins erected by Indians. "The Miami . . . were working for the settlers only three years after the bitter defeat at Fallen Timbers. A demijohn of Marietta rum and a plentiful supply of roast pork secured the help of an entire village, and the Indians gave a good account of themselves as workers." (21) But the account also indicates that "boundary disputes . . . developed as early as 1798" and were settled peacefully through the authority of Tecumseh and other chiefs (21).[35] Also in Ohio, the (more uneven) *Lake County History* (1941) has what amounts to an exemplary middle ground anecdote. A certain David Abbott settled in a place called Chagrin Mills, and "an interesting story is told in connection with the baptism of his daughter, born in 1797. On the east side of the Chagrin River there lay an Indian village. [In the absence of a parson] the Indian chief . . . called upon his medicine man to perform the ceremony. . . . the medicine man had been educated at a French mission and consecrated as a Catholic priest. The ceremony took place, and the child was christened 'Flower of the Forest' " (30–31).

There seems to be much less material of this type from Illinois, and even though Ohio and Iowa (as well as Minnesota) do provide some examples, the regional configuration does not appear to be perceptible enough in the FWP material to argue convincingly that its rhetorical recovery of a middle ground takes place predominantly as a recovery of the historical knowledge and historical experience of White's middle ground.[36] It is probably preferable to operate with the notion of a general *rhetorical* middling that occurs through dissociation from burdened "grand" or master discourses and that solves the question of general value by not asking it. Such discourses would go into historical depth and discover that history (as fact and as problem) will undermine the simpler types of rhetoric: that it will to a degree make irrelevant and in this manner undermine the impact of stereotype.

In the FWP materials, whose overall aim is to produce a story that gives a good account of "America," or the United States, this serves a function. Such an account needs to claim that it will help to "solve" the basic conflicts of U.S. society as a whole by accounting for *them* — for the conflicts and thereby also for the minorities. A "good" account may monologically focus on one "side" and render its perspective. But it may also attempt to accommodate all the "facts" that are part of contradictory stories about the past, or to negotiate those contradictions among stories. This is in fact what happens in the material as a whole all the time and occasionally in individual texts, when they fuse the contradictions into a single discourse of exchange. Frequently they do not manage to go all the way. To use an extreme example: the term *Indian massacre* is employed to designate both the indiscriminate killing of Indians by white settlers or soldiers and the indiscriminate killing of white settlers by Indians, but it is too disruptive to be employed in both functions within one single text. With its denunciatory impact it contains *in nuce* the two basic versions of the story of "the frontier": the finding of a home by displaced white populations and the displacement and destruction of Indian societies.[37] The term too obviously conjures up stereotypically frozen representations of the two sides. It is only in a later text like Welch's *Killing Custer* that the doubleness of the term is thematically and terminologically engaged, and it is perhaps the merit of that work that it does not evade the clash of stories. It manages to do so by going for detail, by avoiding precisely the level of the well-established grand story, the already known — just like the best among the minor FWP texts.

A good account, in this framework, would be one that accommodates the components of as many of these stories as possible, or that at least does not exclude the possibility of taking cognizance of them. But it is impossible to fuse all the stories into a master one, or to integrate them all within one of the existing stories: not only would the contradictions destroy the coherence of such a story, but the schematic character of any story excludes the possibility of any single one ever containing the whole truth.[38] This suggests that maybe there were then (and possibly are now) no proper or just discourses at the writer's disposal: discourses that would bring the full description of a past society *and* of its destruction together with a validation of the sociocultural continuities that do, after all, exist between the past life of the group and its present one, *and* with a critique of the dominant society that has profited from those destructions, *and* with an acknowledgment of that society's (or its members') "value."[39] The fragmentation of discourses that we see in the FWP guides as a whole may suggest as much. And if there is no single discourse that will competently deal with (these) historical realities, the act of putting them into language will always demonstrate its own deficits and acknowledge that *in a sense* those realities may be outside of discourse, outside of culture.

Within this framework of dubious discursivity, there are open and closed stories, inclusive and exclusive ones. Discourses of identity tend toward the latter and have developed their own strategies to counter their own built-in tendency to write and rewrite, from the past on into the future, those conflicts that they simultaneously recognize and indict as destructive. It is the open story that will try to "resolve" the basic conflicts of a society by giving a good account of them — not by aiming for simple mediation or reconciliation, but by attempting to face the contradictions of history. In a sense, the discourse of exchange, which tends to produce open stories, is then a discourse of disorientation. If discourses of identity have attempted to account for or represent conflicts of norms, of realities, and to establish a type of orientation within, between, above, or beyond them, discourses of exchange have focused on individual fates and perhaps implied the unresolvability of the overall problem. They have been closer to that discourse of outright disorientation that one might need in order to truly represent the devastations of history — but that is not available because it would not be a discourse but gibberish, for there is reason to believe that the devastations of history are properly unrepresentable.[40]

NOTES

I am concerned with the public image here, hence I use both the term "The Indian" and the double capitalization. Where I speak about the people, I use *Native American* and *Indian* indiscriminately to mirror the historically burdened multiplicity of usages that appear to be current in the United States today. I am indebted to the Roosevelt Study Center at Middelburg (The Netherlands) — not only for a three-week study grant that has made possible the initial research on the Federal Writers' Project material on which this paper is based but also and above all for providing an environment conducive to reflection.

1. See especially Kenneth Burke's *Grammar of Motives*.

2. This essay attempts to fill the empty term *useful* with some contents in the subsequent discussion.

3. See the Harvester microfilm archives of the Federal Writers' Project. Series One: Printed and Mimeograph Publications in the Surviving FWP Files, 1933–1943, excluding State Guides. These materials undoubtedly are not complete. Arthur Scharf, "Selected Publications of the WPA Federal Writers' Project and the Writers' Program" (in Mangione, 375–98), shows clearly the difficulty of even compiling a full listing of publications: it misses three out of the four bulletins on Arizona Indians that are referred to later in this essay. As the printed guide to the Harvester microfilms — referring, in this context, to Ann Banks and Robert Carter, *Survey of Federal Writers' Project Manuscript Holdings in State Depositories* — points out, "state Depositories often have further records relating to their own state FWP project" (9). Penkower speaks of forty state depositories that ultimately received materials (233).

4. Both my choice of the term *exchange* and (more importantly) my recognition of those tendencies that I am addressing through it may very well have been influenced by David Murray's current work on questions of exchange, but I am unable to specify the debt. One might also remember here James Clifford's attempt to conceive theoretically of different stories of contact between cultures in terms of the same distinction of identity and exchange and to find a basis for them in different group values (*Predicament* 344). The evidence of the FWP material suggests that this is at least as much a conflict of principles of subjectivity formation *within* cultures as *between* them.

5. That the guides were going to be the major products was clear from the beginning, though whether these would be regional or state guides was for a time uncertain. For the general history of the FWP and its successor (under state supervision and sponsorship), see the Writers' Program: Penkower, esp. 30–31. See also Jerre Mangione's semiautobiographical account of the FWP, esp. 5–6.

6. The individual segments of the guides are often called *essays* in the critical literature — probably to accentuate the fact that they were written by different persons, which tended to increase the divergences in point of view among them.

7. An arbitrary example: The Illinois state guide progresses from "The Illinoisian, His Background" (an anticipatory comment on the making of the present that here, as in some other guides, sets the tone for the whole volume) via "The Land Itself" and "Before the White Man" to "The Land and the People," with subdivisions. But the tendency is often not pure, and this, too, becomes visible in the Illinois guide: the second historical chapter, "French and British (1673–1818)," refers to the "tragic episode" of Black Hawk's War and in so doing does leave access to the historical facts open to the reader (29–31). It thus does not completely effect the separation of Indians and history.

8. California has a similar problem with the representation of the way the land was wrested from the Spanish, who are prehistoricized with a vengeance, after the U.S. takeover.

9. See Hobson.

10. Like many others, Weisberger, in his selection from the guides, predominantly celebrates the Americanism of the enterprise, though not using that term; but he, too, has the ubiquitous use of "Whitmanesque" (xv) to characterize the project's approach to America.

11. And the guides were read accordingly: "the rediscovery [and reaffirmation] of America, a note running through much of the literature of the late thirties, provided most critics with their prevalent theme in reviewing [the first guides]" (Penkower 132).

12. Stott, in his general introduction to Hobson (1–11), also goes for the celebration aspect and stresses the international background of the rise in patriotism (4–7). At the same time, he also endorses "what was felt to be uniquely American: our diversity and our tolerance of diversity" (6), thereby trying to reconcile the two aspects. The entire book tends, throughout, to go for the American, frequently in the shape of local color and the odd event or feature.

13. See Penkower (230–32) on the integration of the project into the war effort in 1942. An arbitrary example is Illinois' *Chicago Mobilized*, 1942.

14. See Penkower's uneasy return to the topic (241–45).

15. "Out of necessity comments that could be politically construed were rare. Comments that displayed offensive racial and ethnic prejudices were unfortunately not. This was particularly true where blacks were concerned. It was most noticeable in the Southern guides. . . . but it was a national phenomenon. Though Alsberg sponsored a

number of distinguished projects in black history and folklore, using black scholars and writers, black men and women appeared in the guides only as whites of the times perceived them. Some guides touched on the harsh conditions of life in the urban ghettos, but throughout the guides as a whole, black family life was not explored, black folkways were rarely described with any penetration, and only fleeting mention was made of black professionals and property owners" (Weisberger xiv).

16. The unfortunate effect is enhanced when Weisberger complains that "the guides tended to overlook the black presence in the Northern Plains states. But, as usual, they did consider the lasting presence of the Indians worthy of record" (275; cf. the longer version of the same complaint, 323), or that "it was not blacks or Europeans who caught the guides' attention, [but rather] the Chinese and Japanese, the Mexicans and the Indians" (429) and accounts for the fact in terms of the rarity value of these minorities.

17. Further, Penkower indicates that Jews "suffered less discrimination," and "with regard to other minorities, the project had a mixed record" (67, 68). Indians are not even mentioned as a separate group by Penkower in this context.

18. I have found no reference in my materials to the Boas-Benedict project.

19. The reference throughout is to the one-volume 1942 edition of *Washington, D.C.: A City and Capital*.

20. The beginning of the essay entitled "History" is similarly uncertain in tone, and Indians, who are initially present in it, vanish from it very quickly.

21. The selections, which look back on the 1930s from the mid-1980s, present things at a double historical remove, which can obscure one of the salient questions the guides must have faced — or ignored: the question whether it suffices to establish whatever one might regard as the truth of the past. Already the notion of a *usable past* implies that one might want to establish some connection with the present, and quite generally there is the question of how far the representation of Native Americans is being extended into the present. And how does the representation address the always implied further problem of the possibility of a future? In many areas, now, the Native American is not dealt with at all, obviously either because the minority is below the threshold of perception or because it is regarded as "extinct." This appears justified, until one recognizes that the perspective of the entire guides project is really national: the local is to legitimate the national. If that is so, then the national problem must also be dealt with at the local level; otherwise (in local texts that ignore their own national horizon) we have provincialism: the perception of the world through the lens of the local. At the same time, undeniably those states with large visible Indian populations must deal with them more obviously: with their histories, the histories of inter-Indian and Indian-white contact and conflict, and their present lives.

22. The Oregon excerpt has this interesting paragraph: "The fur traders who came after Lewis and Clark were as realistic in their approach to the country as were Cortez to Mexico and Pizarro to Peru. They plagued the Indians with whiskey and social diseases,

salted the very beaver skins with corruption, and yearned to be quit of the savage land as quickly as possible. The missionaries who followed were, in the main, devout if somewhat severe men who strove mightily to invest the natives in spirituality and trousers; but even among these a few learned to sing upon both sides of the Jordan, and to deal more briskly in real estate than in salvation. While the great overland migration to Oregon has been sanctified by tradition it seems foolish to presume that the covered wagons carried nothing but animated virtues to Oregon" (Weisberger 345).

23. From the New Mexico guide — whatever the deficiencies of the particular phrasing: "New Mexico is a favorite camping-ground of the anthropologist because here they can study the living Indians in connection with their ancient, unbroken past and possible future" (Weisberger 387).

24. The best comment on the situation is probably the one-paragraph sketch of the complex situation in Oklahoma, and for the Far West, another guide advances a similar argument (Weisberger 323, 372).

25. Further material in Weisberger is as heterogeneous as a description of Oklahoma as a state into whose fabric "this red thread of the Indian" is "steadily . . . being woven": but it is "the influences of Indian blood" that are thereby acknowledged, rather than culture and history (292); sketches of the comparatively affluent Osages in Bartlesville, Oklahoma, of a Creek and Euchee Busk ceremony in Kellyville, Oklahoma, and of Choctaw Funeral Cries in Boswell, Oklahoma (329–30); a detailed account of an O-Kan celebration among the Montana Blackfeet that strives for ethnographic accuracy and sympathy, and a much briefer description of an Indian Shaker service in Washington State (375–76); an Idaho Nez Perce coyote story, a Wyoming Shoshone creation myth, the story of a Sioux landmark (377–78); the "Contemporary Scene" essay from the Arizona guide that pervasively writes the Indian into its image of the present, even though as a comparatively "foreign" figure — not a negatively connoted term, here, one might argue (388–90); Tucson is represented as a highly colored but conflict-free and problem-free environment (405–07). Various stories are relayed: from New York State the story of the Indian wife discarded after decades by her white husband (1161) and an admiring story of an Indian-killer (165); from Florida a description of today's Seminoles coming to Fort Lauderdale as brilliantly exotic figures (234); from Pascagoula, Mississippi, a legend of the honorable death of an entire tribe whose death song can be heard to this day (238–39); from South Dakota a general description pointing out that "there are as many Indians as there were a hundred years ago," but that they have adapted to the white economy (250); from Fort Yates, North Dakota, a description of colorful Indians at fairs and on feast days, which also remarks on their patriotism (279–80); from North Dakota another story of a mistreated Indian wife and her revenge (285).

26. This treatment of Native Americans contrasts, once again, with the more con-

sistently critical perspective developed with regard to the representation of African Americans.

27. "Some pages — especially those on the Menominee Reservation in Wisconsin — took note of the small remnants of the tribes of Indians that had once been sole lords of the land. By the 1930s, they had begun to adopt the white men's ways, but a few holdouts clung to the habits that their ancestors had bequeathed them. The guide referred to these last, with casual insensitivity, as 'pagans' " (Weisberger 80). And similarly, under the heading "Tales of Westward-Moving Folk": in "legends of the Midwest . . . Indians still appeared in landscape fantasy — rocks and waterfalls represent chieftains turned to stone or bereaved maiden's [sic] tears. Rarely did they figure as individuals in their own right, although Tecumseh makes a brief and unstereotyped appearance in the Indiana guide" (89). This last phrase refers to an anecdote that is really not much to write home about — it is a personal sidelight on a model Indian, who "with simple dignity" refused to follow love rather than honor (89–90).

28. *The Hopi*, Arizona State Teachers College Bulletin (1937); *The Navaho*, Arizona State Teachers College Bulletin (1937); *The Apache*, Arizona State Teachers College Bulletin (1939); *The Papago*, Arizona State Teachers College Bulletin (1939); *The Havasupai and the Hualapai*, Arizona State Teachers College Bulletin (1940).

29. One might again want to contrast the two "problematic" minorities in the FWP texts: black and red. Their sociocultural conditions are minimally similar, insofar as both are visible minorities that have been historically suppressed. They are dissimilar in several respects, among which the most important in the present context is that the double imagery of The Indian has traditionally been different from the double image of The Negro in America. (Europe and European colonies in Africa are a different matter.) On the one hand, we have the Noble Savage versus the Daemonic Savage, and on the other hand, we have the Childlike Black versus the Black Rapist. (The latter phrasing indicates a perverted "family" perspective that one need not go into here.) African Americans had recently (in the Harlem Renaissance) developed a positive primitivist image that was close to the Noble Savage image, but because of its recency it may have been more contested, and certainly it was more subject to short-term change — and this is what happened, according to Penkower. The older image of the Noble Indian has remained available, with some modification (the Spiritual Indian, the Ecological Indian), to this day as the core of one of several strategies of positive representation; the Daemonic Indian is obviously not usable for such purposes, except in the attempt to distinguish "good" from "bad" Native Americans, usually as a distinction among groups (and thus as a double cliché, by virtue of both its historical immutability and its denial of individual difference). This is a strategy that was written into the classical canon by Cooper and is still to be found, for instance, in *Dances with Wolves*.

30. The beginning of *Winter in the Blood*, on the other hand, is similar, and it may

be significant that Welch's later novels appear to lean more toward a discourse of identity. For my comparisons I am disregarding paratextual material, such as acknowledgments, mottos, and dedications.

31. At the same time, wherever the topic is settlement as progress, which it again and again becomes (though differently: in Illinois, as cooperation among different groups, above all immigrant; in Iowa, as dispossession of the Indian), there is a tendency to prehistoricize the Indian. And as patriotism increases, so does the identification of America with progress.

32. The most important piece of this sort of writing is probably the "Sioux Memorial Issue" of *Nebraska History*, which was "prepared with the aid of workers of the WPA Writers' Program." It is largely dedicated to the project of creating a Sioux memorial ("on Highway No. 19 near Chadron State Park"), advocated here by John Gutzon de la Mothe Borglum, "Creator of Mount Rushmore Memorial" (252). The issue contains ample attacks on the treachery of white dealings with the Sioux and describes them in a discourse of ennoblement that is particularly apparent in Borglum's own "Memorials to the Sioux Indians" (253–55): "it is a particularly gracious act for us, as the victorious nation, to put up a memorial to those who preceded us here — not merely as a historical record, but to honour them as a brave and valiant race" (254). Everything is in the past tense, and though there is great sympathy for the suffering of Indians, one also detects a notion of historical necessity in the background that becomes more explicit elsewhere in the volume (273). Cf. George A. Beecher, "Why Remember the Indian?" (277–79), with its stress on similarity between "good" Indians and white civilizations, and: "Little has been said or done to perpetuate the memory of those who made the great sacrifice in a lost cause. It is fitting and proper, therefore — indeed, it is true sportsmanship — that . . . we should erect a suitable memorial for the deeds of valor, endurance and heroism which have become an Indian tradition rapidly fading from memory" (278).

33. The Buena Vista history acknowledged that: "To [many of the settlers] all Indians were bad. The settlers made no effort to understand their grievances or to make friends with them, but drove them off with curses or clubs. The Indians on their part believed in revenge. . . . One such revengeful Indian was Inkpaduta, the renegade Sioux chief. He was a big man, six feet tall and strongly built. The smallpox scars on his face made his expression look only the more cruel. For several years he had hated the whites and regarded them as his greatest enemies. They had taken the hunting grounds of his people, they had murdered his brother Sidominadotah, on the banks of Bloody Run, and slain many of his kinsmen. Squaws who went begging for food had been driven off with whips. Now after the cold hungry winter of 1856, Inkpaduta felt that the time had come to get even" (9–10).

34. The British "told the Indians that the Americans were cheating them and also hoping to destroy them, so that later they might occupy their tribal lands. Since much

of this was true, it was very easy for Black Hawk . . . to ally his people with the British" (10).

35. "The Indians could not understand why they no longer owned their tribal lands. They did not consider the signing of a treaty sufficient reason for moving. Nor did their defeat at Fallen Timbers make them regard themselves as a conquered people. They had, as was natural, a strong hatred of the white men, and only the counsel of their leaders kept them from open conflict. Tecumseh and other chiefs wanted the Indians to remain peaceful until a confederation of Indian tribes was established" (22). The battle of Tippecanoe (1811) then "eliminated the last great Indian peril," though after it came the War of 1812 (29).

36. One should also probably insist, once again, on the heterogeneous nature of the material even from those regions that provide the "good" texts. In Iowa, for instance, there is also the *Franklin County History* (1941), which begins with an Edenic scene that is interrupted by Indian hunters, so that soon "there is blood on the Prairie and the grass is trampled down. . . . A white man visiting the camp would find the smell of the bloody skins and the decaying bones intolerable. But the Indians do not mind. . . . After eating, stuffing and then starving, for three or four days or a week, they move on. But the smell of old buffalo and elk hides is still bad. Even the white man's horse would shy away from it. [But then] Fall comes and the prairie is clean again" (3). After this racist beginning, the historical account it gives in "The Indians in Franklin County" (4–8) cannot but proceed in terms of order being imposed on warring Indians by white authority, especially between the Sioux (who are evil and aggressive) and the Sac and Fox (who are less so).

37. If one looks closely, also in the FWP materials, there are, of course, more than these two stories: there is, for instance, also the speculator's story or the story of how one tribe or tribal faction made use of Indian-white conflict to annihilate another; and there is always in the background the story of the conflict among European powers over the colonial domination and partition of the world.

38. On this axiom see Ingarden and Iser.

39. Or, to put it differently, perhaps there exists no single discourse that will integrate a factual knowledge of the past and the present, of both groups and their actions (in so far as groups can act), and that does not simultaneously deny, explicitly or implicitly, either the one or the other group the right to exist in the territory that both are, in fact, inhabiting at the moment in ways that are implicated with their right to exist at all.

40. That, of course, is one well-established view of the Holocaust.

At the initial point of contact, we were on the Eastern shore of North America. Since then, there has been a great decimation of our numbers, language, and culture. In the average American citizen's mind, there is no Indian existence on the eastern shore any longer, which is sad, because once people get out and find the reality of our existence and see that it is there, they are amazed at the durability, survivability, and sustainability of people who have been able to continue after so many hundreds of years and after so many attempts at devastation.

Donna Chavis [Lumbee],
in *Women of the Native Struggle*

Reversing the Gaze

Early Native American Images
of Europeans and Euro-Americans

A. LAVONNE BROWN RUOFF

The mythology of a nation is the intelligible mask of that enigma called the "national character." Through myths the psychology and world view of our cultural ancestors are transmitted to modern descendants, in such a way and with such power that our perception of contemporary reality and our ability to function in the world are directly, often tragically affected.

Richard Slotkin, *Regeneration through Violence: The Mythology of the American Frontier 1600–1860*

The images of the American Indian, noble or savage, and of the mixed-blood, liaison between two cultures or outcast, have fascinated Western Europeans since their arrival on this continent. The evolution of these images and their impact on the American mind have been studied by such scholars as Philip Deloria, Albert Keiser, Roy Harvey Pearce, Elémire Zolla, Richard Slotkin, Robert F. Berkhofer Jr., Klaus Lubbers, and Helen Carr. Although most of these scholars have focused on the image of the full-blood Indian, William B. Scheick has concentrated on that of the half-blood or mixed-blood. As scholars have frequently pointed out, Western Europeans' images of the Indian and the mixed-blood derived from the ambivalence felt by settlers about their own societies and cultures rather than from an objective analysis of the complexity and diversity of those of the American Indians. Western European preconceptions determined the attitudes expressed in government policies toward Indians. In their study of these attitudes and policies, scholars have ignored the images reflected on the other side of the American cultural mirror: Indian images of non-Indians and mixed-bloods.

Postcolonial criticism offers insights into the impact of Western Europeans' perceptions of the Other on both them and those they marginalize. Writer bell hooks comments that she found in that criticism much "writing that bespeaks the continued fascination with the way white minds, particularly the colonial imperialist traveler, perceive blackness, and very little expressed interest in representations of whiteness in the black imagination" (339). Benita Parry argues that anti-colonist writings challenged, subverted, and undermined the ruling ideologies, especially by "overthrowing the hierarchy of coloniser/colonised, the speech and stance of the colonised refusing a position of subjugation and dispensing with the terms of the coloniser's definitions" (176).[1] Such approaches offer helpful insights into the complexities of Native/non-Native discourse.

Fundamentally, what is at issue in perceptions of the image of the Other is power. Michel Foucault's definition is useful because of its emphasis on the multiplicity of form process, interaction, and strategies. He defines power as:

the multiplicity of force relations immanent in the sphere in which they operate and which constitute their own organization; as the process which, through ceaseless struggles and confrontations, transforms, strengthens, or reverses them; as the support which these force relations find in one another, thus forming a chain or a system, or on the contrary, the disjunctions and contradictions which isolate them from one another; and lastly, as the strategies in which they take effect, whose general design or institutional crystallization is embodied in the state apparatus, in the formulation of the law, in the various social hegemonies. (*History* 1:92–93)

At the heart of the consequences of contact between Western Europe and Native America are the Europeans' concepts of power and perception of the Other. Tzvetan Todorov argues that the fact that the Native American populations lacked writing was crucial to how the Western Europeans and the indigenous populations perceived each other. Todorov concludes that since writing cannot assume the role of memory support, speech must do so. The essential feature of Native discourses, called the "speech of the ancients," was that they came from the past, both in interpretation and production. The conquest was an "unpredictable event, surprising and unique," that brings with it a new conception of time (*Conquest* 84). Todorov also emphasizes that "prophecy is rooted in the past, since time repeats itself. . . . Prophecy is memory" (85). He argues that the presence of writing favors improvisation over ritual, "just as it makes for a linear conception of time or, further, the perception of the other"

(252). Dominated by memory, Native Americans lacked the power to manipulate the present. Their conceptual inadequacy, according to Todorov, prevented them from accurately perceiving the Western Europeans. The culture that possessed writing could accurately represent to itself and manipulate the culture without writing. The reverse could not occur. Greenblatt argues that Todorov undervalues the writing that existed at the time of contact. He correctly points out that Todorov fails to show the link between the Aztecs' lack of writing and the Spanish invaders' success in conquering the Natives, which was more attributable to competent translators than to the possession of writing (*Marvelous* 11, 12).

Clearly, the Natives' inability to write or to understand the conquerors' language was a significant factor in how the Europeans perceived them. Henry Louis Gates Jr. suggests that for many Europeans, writing "stood alone among the fine arts as the most salient repository of 'genius,' the visible sign of reason itself. In this subordinate role, however, writing, although secondary to reason, is nevertheless the 'medium' of reason's expression" ("*Race*" 9). With regard to African Americans, there was a direct correlation between economic and political alienation on the one hand and racial alienation on the other, evidenced by the 1740 South Carolina statute making it almost impossible for black slaves to acquire literacy (9). This correlation applies to American Indians as well, though there was more emphasis on teaching Indians to read so that they could read the Bible and become Christian converts.

Essential to any discussion of the image of the Other are concepts of race and racism. Gates argues that because race is applied so arbitrarily, it has become "a trope of ultimate, irreducible difference between cultures, linguistic groups, or adherents of specific belief systems," which often have fundamentally opposed economic interests. Further, we carelessly use language "to *will* this sense of *natural* difference into our formulations, a pernicious act that exacerbates the complex problem of cultural or ethnic difference" ("*Race*" 5). In "'Race,' Writing and Culture," Todorov differentiates between race and racism. The latter he describes as "a type of behavior that consists in the display of contempt or aggressiveness toward other people on account of physical differences (other than those of sex) between them and oneself." Whereas racism is "a well-attested social phenomenon, 'race' itself does not exist!" Although there are great differences among human groups, these differences cannot be superimposed (370). Gates argues in "Talkin' That Talk" that this definition depends upon the "display" of "contempt" or "aggressiveness" for its effect ("*Race*" 403). While Todorov implies that the only racists are those who act with malice for reasons attributable to essential biological differences, Gates responds that

" 'racism' exists when one generalizes about the attributes of an individual (and treats him or her accordingly)" (403).

As Bill Ashcroft, Gareth Griffiths, and Helen Tiffin point out, the role of the first interpreter in colonial contact is "profoundly ambiguous" because the interpreter "always emerges from the dominated discourse." The transitional moment is always the most difficult to describe (80). Homi Bhabha comments that the social articulation of difference, from the minority perspective, is a complex, ongoing negotiation that seeks to authorize "cultural hybridities that emerge in moments of historical transformation." Social differences, therefore, are "the signs of the emergence of community envisaged as a project." Both a vision and a construction, this project takes one beyond the self in order to return to the political conditions of the present (*Location* 2, 3). Bhabha also criticizes historians for being transfixed by the event and origins of the nation and political scientists for focusing only on the modern of the totalities of the nation. Because they limit their concerns to homogeneity, literacy, and anonymity, they never ask the awkward question of "the disjunctive representation of the social, in this double-time of the nation" (*Nation* 294).

All of these issues are represented in one form or another in Native Americans' perceptions of Western Europeans. Tribal myths explaining the origin of whites on this continent and prophesying their return exemplify Todorov's concept of the power of oral tradition to frame Native reaction to first encounters with Europeans. For a number of tribes, especially those in Mexico, the Southwest, and West, the arrival of Europeans confirmed oral traditions about the existence of non-Indians. The existence of such myths greatly facilitated white conquest of the Indian world. The best known of these is the Toltec myth about Quetzalcoatl. Described as a white, bearded man, Quetzalcoatl taught people all the arts and sciences of civilization, founded a religion, and then disappeared, promising to return someday in the year of his birth, Ce Acatl or 1 Reed.[2]

The most common myth about Quetzalcoatl was recorded by Fr. Bernardino de Sahagún, in the *Florentine Codex: General History of New Spain*, book 3. According to this myth, Quetzalcoatl came to earth during the Toltec period (A.D. 600–1100). He was the ruler of the ancient city of Tollan, the capital of Toltec located near present-day Tula, fifty miles north of Mexico City. Deposed because he opposed human sacrifice, a ritual upheld by the followers of the sorcerer Tezcatlipoca, Quetzalcoatl escaped to the east coast. He sailed away on a raft of snakes after prophesying that he would return in the year of his birth, Ce Acatl or 1 Reed.[3] Sahagún recorded the Indians' reaction to Cortés's arrival in book 12 of his *Florentine Codex*.

Ruth Benedict, in *Tales of the Cochiti Indians*, recorded that tribe's version of the prophecy that whites would come. In this myth, Montezuma, rather than Quetzacoatl, was the figure who left and who was destined to return. A strong Indian leader, Montezuma knew that he would not allow anyone to settle on his land, although he realized that some day he would have to give up his power. He told his people how long he would rule and how he would go away: " 'I am going away, but I do not die. I shall come again. When I have gone home, people from the northeast will come and they will be white. They will rule here' " (qtd. in Benedict 191). Dressed in ceremonial costume of buckskin and feather headdress, he went down with Malinche to a lake and told the people to chose as their leader Watumasi, his brother-in-law and an Aztec chief. Watumasi took Montezuma's place but was not the real Montezuma. When Cortés arrived, he did great damage to the country and turned the Mexican tribes against each other. Defeated by the Indians, Cortés returned to Spain for more soldiers. While he was gone, the Indians continued to fight. Watumasi's wife dreamed that there would be four wars with Cortés and that in the fourth, her husband would be captured. During this fourth war, Watumasi was captured and imprisoned. Cortés took all the gold and treasures of Montezuma to Spain and set up another powerless leader like Montezuma to rule Indian pueblos (191–92).

The creation myths of several other Southwestern Indian tribes contain explanations for the existence of whites. Helen Sekaquaptewa gives one explanation in the version of the Hopi emergence myth she narrates in her autobiography, *Me and Mine* (1969). Originally one people, whites and Indians separated after emergence. The chief then asked mockingbird to give each clan a language. The older son of the chief received the first language, which is the language of the white man; the younger, the Oraibi chief, received the Hopi language. When the clans went in separate directions, the older son went to the east — the origin of the whites. The younger brother went to live in Oraibi but was to send for his older brother in time of trouble. If the older brother should return and find the Oraibi people backsliding or departing from the traditions, he should behead the Oraibi chief to end the trouble. In time the white chief brother would come to bring peace and right living (227).

The origin myth of the Laguna Indians (Keres language family) also contains an explanation for the existence of white people. However, they are not seen as saviors. According to one origin myth published by Boas in *Keresan Texts*, the separation of people into whites and Lagunas occurred after emergence. The creator is Ts'ts'ts'ina'k'o, Thought Woman or Spider Woman, who has both male and female characteristics. Whatever she thinks, is. Her assistants are I'tc'ts'it'i, the father (mother) of whites, and Nau'ts'it'i, mother of the

Lagunas. At the place of emergence, there were too many people. The two quarreled about who should go out first. When they came out, the sun shown on I'tc'ts'it'i, rather than on Nau'ts'it'i, indicating he had the greater power. Next they competed about who had magical power. Nau'ts'it'i completed her work of creating animals on earth before I'tc'ts'it'i completed his of creating whites. I'tc'ts'it'i suggested they play with yellow and blue kicking sticks all around the world. After four days, Nau'ts'it'i kicked out the kicking stick and sent her children, the Indians, out of the Place of Emergence. They went northwest with the Storm Clouds. I'tc'ts'it'i kicked out his kicking stick and sent his people southwest. While they ran and kicked the stick, it began to rain, and they were drowned. I'tc'ts'it'i acknowledged the superiority of Nau'ts'it'i. Whites were piled up and Nau'ts'it'i revived them with a song. They vomited foam; small water animals were in their hair, and weeds were on their faces. This is why whites and Mexicans have beards (Boas 8.1: 6, 232–33).[4]

Such myths were not limited to the Southwest. In *Life among the Piutes* (1883), Sarah Winnemucca (Paiute, ca. 1844–91) re-creates a scene in which her grandfather, Truckee, reminds his people of their origin myth, which foretold the coming of whites. There were only four people, two girls and two boys, a dark boy and girl and a white boy and girl. Because they quarreled, Indians and whites split. Grieved, their parents separated the children. The Paiutes believed that the white nation would send someone to meet the Native people and heal the old trouble. Old Winnemucca felt sure the whites they saw in 1844 must be their returned white brothers (6–7).

What all these stories have in common is the emphasis on the original unity of red and white peoples, which made the Western Europeans' sudden arrival appear to be the long-awaited fulfillment of mythic prophesy.

In some cases, stories about the origin of whites evolved after their appearance. For example, John T. Sprague records in *The Origin, Progress, and Conclusion of the Florida War* (1848), the account given by Coacooche, a Seminole chief who fought fiercely against white encroachment of his people's lands. His father, King Philip, had told Coacooche that he was made of the sands of Florida. Tribal elders told him that the white man came from the foam of the ocean, thrown up upon the beach. After lying in the heat of the sun, whites assumed human form and walked into the interior of the country (327). Again, however, the myth emphasizes the interrelationship of the two peoples, here depicted in metaphors of nature forever linked in conflict and resolution, as water both erodes and adds to the beach.

The Jicarilla Apaches also associate the creation of whites with water. In their myth, Child-of-the-Water goes east and walks on the ocean, where he finds a female and a male fish with blue eyes. After taking them home to the other side of the ocean, he asks the help of White Hactcin to make them into people. After whites are created, Child-of-the-Water goes up into the sky on a cloud. "That is why the white men say they will go to Heaven when they die. Child-of-the-Water, who made them, is up there. He is living to the east with White-Shell Woman, his mother" (Opler 98).

In their story about the origin of whites, the Northern Paiute incorporate elements of the Bible. After Coyote (their Creator) planted the apple tree, he told all the Indians to come to eat. Unfortunately, the white man, who was a rattlesnake then, was in the tree: "The white people have eyes just like the rattlesnake. When the Indians tried to come to eat the apples, that snake tried to bite them. That's why the white people took everything away from the Indian; because they were snakes" (Kelley 437).[5]

The oral histories of many tribes contained prophecies about the impact of the arrival of Europeans on Indian people. In *A History of the Ojibway Nation* (1885), William Warren (Ojibwe, 1825–53) records an Ojibwe elder's prophesy: "the white spirits would come in numbers like sand on the lake shore, and would sweep the red race from the hunting grounds which the Great Spirit had given them as an inheritance. It was prophesied that the consequence of the white man's appearance would be, to the An-ish-in-aub-ag, an 'ending of the world'" (117). Warren emphasizes that through harping on this prophecy, Tecumseh and his brother, the Prophet, were able to form the coalition to eradicate the white menace (118).[6]

Greenblatt emphasizes that at first contact, both Western Europeans and Native Americans reacted in wonder — "thrilling, potentially dangerous, momentarily immobilizing, charged at once with desire, ignorance, and fear." This quintessential human response signifies all that cannot be understood or scarcely believed (*Marvelous* 20). Some of the Native Americans' reactions to the Europeans reveal that they too felt they observed the marvelous. In 1633, a Montagnais Indian in eastern Canada related to French Jesuit priests his grandmother's story about his ancestors' reaction the first time they saw a French ship, which they thought was a floating island. When the French offered the Montagnais biscuits and wine, the Indians threw the items overboard because they thought "the Frenchmen drank blood and ate wood" (*Jesuit Relations* 5:119–21). In 1869, Josiah Jeremy (Micmac) recounted to the Rev. Silas Rand the Micmacs' encounter with a French ship. Colin G. Calloway notes that members of this tribe, which lived in the area of present-day Nova Scotia, Prince Edward Island, Cape Breton, and northern Maine, were "among the first of the original inhabitants of North America to encounter seagoing Europeans" (*Crown* 33). In this story, a young woman dreamed that a small island, with tall trees and living beings on it, floated toward the land. The wise men could not understand the dream until the next day when what appeared to be an island drifted to the land and became stationary there. There were trees on it and "a number of bears, as they supposed, were crawling about. They all seized their bows, arrows, and spears, and rushed down to the shore, intending to shoot the bears; what was their surprise to find these supposed bears were men" (Rand 225–26).[7]

The inability to understand one another's language, much less one another's culture and religion, strongly influenced Western Europeans' and Native Americans' images of each other. After encountering the Arawak and claiming their land, Columbus commented in his letter to Santangel that "y no me fué contradicho" ("and I was not contradicted"). The fact that the Native people did not contradict Columbus's claim to their land became important because it enabled Spain to claim that the Natives voluntarily wished to transfer title to their lands to their conquerors (qtd. in Greenblatt, *Marvelous* 58). If the consequences were not so horrendous for Native people, the exchange and the presumptions on which it is based would be ridiculous. Unable to communicate with words nor to understand Native speech, Columbus resorted to the use of music.

However, such linguistic confusion affected Native people's perceptions of Western Europeans as well. Hernando de Escalante Fontaneda, shipwrecked in Florida and held captive by the Carlos (Calusa) Indians for seventeen years, records that the Spanish had a similar linguistic opacity. In a "memorial" transcribed in approximately 1575, he reports that the Natives ordered some captured Spanish to dance and sing. Convinced that the Christians refused to do so because they were obstinate, the Natives planned to kill their prisoners. The cacique, puzzled by their strange behavior, asked Escalante for an explanation: "When we require these, your companions, to dance and sing, and do other things, why are they so dissembling and obstinate that they will not? or is it that they do not fear death, or will not yield to a people unlike them in their customs?" (qtd. in Greenblatt, *Marvelous*, 96). Escalante, who had learned the natives' language, intercedes on their behalf, explaining that the captives cannot understand the commands. Persuaded, the cacique then orders his "vassals" that "when they should find Christians thus cast away, and take them, they must require them to do nothing without giving notice, that one might go to them who should understand their language" (qtd. in Greenblatt, *Marvelous*, 97).[8]

Many of the early accounts written by Native Americans about their first news of or interactions with whites emphasize their wonder and terror, as they attempted to understand the totally alien culture of the dominant society. Describing his trip east after he surrendered, Black Hawk (Mesquakie, 1767–1838) both marvels at and rejects some of the wonders of civilization. Though he called the railroad "the most astonishing sight" he ever saw, Black Hawk preferred riding on horseback (145). He and his companions were astonished to see a man go up in the air in a balloon. One of the young men asked the balloonist "if he was going up to see the Great Spirit" (147).

Charles Eastman (Santee Dakota, 1858–1939) describes in *Indian Boyhood* (1902) his uncle's attempts to explain to him the settlers' greed: "The greatest object of their lives seems to be to acquire possessions — to be rich. They desire to possess the whole world. For thirty years they were trying to entice us to sell them our land." The 1862 Minnesota Uprising provided the settlers with the opportunity to seize the Santees' land and drive them away. "'I am also informed,' said my uncle, 'but this I hardly believe, that their great Chief (President) compels every man to pay him for the land he lives upon and all his personal goods — even for his own existence — every year!' (This was his idea of taxation.) 'I am sure we could not live under such a law'" (187–88).

Encounters with whites also terrified Indians. Despite her grandfather's assurances that the whites were good people, young Sarah Winnemucca was so frightened by these strange men that she screamed whenever they approached. Because of their big white eyes and hairy faces, she called them "owls." The Paiutes also believed that the whites were killing everybody and eating them. When the family heard whites were coming, her mother and aunt buried Winnemucca and her sister up to their heads, covered their faces with sage bushes, and left them all day. Winnemucca vividly expresses her fear: "Oh, can any one imagine my feelings buried alive, thinking every minute that I was to be unburied and eaten up by the people that my grandfather loved so much?" (12).

As they traveled abroad, Native Americans observed the weaknesses in Western European civilizations, which they discussed in their lectures and in their written works. Wonder is replaced by repulsion. Increasingly disillusioned with assimilation, they express their resistance by emphasizing cultural difference. According to Homi Bhabha, the concept of cultural differences focuses on the problem of the ambivalence of cultural authority in "the attempt to dominate in the *name* of a cultural supremacy which is itself produced only in the moment of differentiation" (*Location* 34). The enunciation of cultural difference "problematizes the binary division of past and present, tradition and modernity, at the level of cultural representation and its authoritative address" (35). Samson Occom (Mohegan, 1723–92), expresses this sense of difference in his comments about England, where he went in 1765 to raise money for Eleazar Wheelock's Indian Charity School in Connecticut. He was both awed and appalled by London: "such Confusion as I never Dreamt of — there was Some at Churches, Singing and Preaching, in the Streets some Cursing & Laughing, & Coaches and footmen passing and repassing. Crossing and Criss-crossing, and the Poor Beggars Praying, Crying, and Begging upon their knees" (qtd. in Blodgett 88). During his two-year stay, Occom preached over three hundred sermons and raised over £12,000. Occom also expressed his antagonism to the British class system in his address to the Christian Indians (ca. 1775–76), urging them to remain neutral in the Revolutionary War: the "Nobles and the great, and they are very Proud and they keep the rest of their Brethren under their Feet, they make Slaves of them. The great ones have got all the Land and the rest are poor Tenants — and the People in this Country live more upon a leavel [sic] and they live happy." Further, the King of England wants to make Americans slaves, so they are obliged to defend themselves. Although he tells those who feel they must participate in the war to join the Americans, he concludes with a strong plea for neutrality: "use all your Influence to your Brethren, so far as you have any Connections, to keep them in Peace and quietness, and not to intermeddle in these Quarrels among the White People" (qtd. in Love 228–29).

His disillusionment is echoed by Joseph Brant (Mohawk, 1742–1807), who supported the British in the Revolutionary War and who visited England. Brant forcefully outlined the superiority of Native to European life in a letter written in 1786, in which he stresses that in civilized government, the happiness of people is constantly sacrificed to the splendor of empire. In contrast, the Indians have no prisons, pompous parade of courts, written laws, or splendid villains above the law: "The estates of widows and orphans are never devoured by enterprising sharpers. In a word, we have no robbery under the color of the law." He strongly attacks the contrast between civilization's palaces and prisons, which are more cruel than torture. He especially criticizes imprisoning a man for debt (Stone 2:481–83).

Their reactions to white culture and the response of later nineteenth-century Indians exemplify Frantz Fanon's comment that Native intellectuals inventory bad habits drawn from the colonial world and remind people of the good customs of their own people. Fanon suggests that Native writers move through three stages: 1) they provide proof of assimilation; 2) they return to their roots, despite the fact that they have only exterior relations with their people, and focus on recalling their lives; 3) they fight or resist (221, 222). One such writer is George Copway (Kahgegagahbowh, Ojibwe, 1818–69), a Methodist missionary, lecturer, and author. He records his observations on white civilization in his *Life, History and Travels* (1847), revised and expanded in 1850 as *The Life, Letters and Speeches* (New York) and as *Recollections of a Forest Life* (London). In his autobiography, Copway walks a fine line between praising and rejecting the values of his Ojibwe heritage and those of the dominant society. Trained to become a Methodist missionary, Copway visited the East in 1839 on his way back from Illinois to his tribal home in Canada. Though little impressed by Boston, he was overwhelmed by the prosperity of white civilization. His reaction exemplifies the double vision of one who is attempting to assimilate but still identifies with his Native culture. From the top of the statehouse, he saw the steeples, vessels, wharves filled with merchandise, towns, steam cars: "Here were factories in different directions. As I saw the prosperity of the white man, I said, while tears filled my eyes, 'Happy art thou, O Israel, who is like unto the[e], *O people saved by the Lord!*'" At the same time, he laments the losses suffered by the "noble race of red men who once lived and roamed in all the land, and upon the waters as far as my eye could reach" (*Life* 123).

Not all of his experiences in white society were positive. Though he received many acts of personal kindness from his white benefactors, Copway also encountered prejudice. The Yankees of Buffalo annoyed him with their curiosity about his marriage to a white woman, Elizabeth Howell, asking how many Indians married white women and whether or not his white father-in-law approved of the union. Copway neatly reverses the gaze and criticizes whites' behavior. He is shocked at the hypocrisy of American whites who, instead of spending Christmas in prayer as did the Indian converts, spent it "gadding about from house to house, and indulging in luxuries to excess. Nay, more; I have been informed that not a few professors entertain their visitors with firewater or devil's spittle on that day. What a contradiction this would be in the estimation of converted Indians, were they to witness these scenes" (*Life* 126–27). He also reminds his audience that swearing or profaning the name of the Great Spirit was unknown among Indians: "I often swore, when I knew not what I said. I have seen some white faces with black hearts, who took delight in teaching them to profane the name of God. O merciless, heartless, and wicked white men, may a merciful God forgive you your enormous turpitude and recklessness" (88).

In the nineteenth century, three Native Americans recorded their reactions to visiting England. Their remarks are reminiscent of the literary tradition of the foreigner abroad, exemplified by the hugely popular travel literature of the period as well as of the fictional accounts of visits to strange places in Oliver Goldsmith's *Citizen of the World* or even Swift's *Gulliver's Travels.* Instead of Europeans' commenting on the quaint customs of the Natives, the indigenous people remark on the bad manners and bizarre habits of the Western Europeans. Copway's *Running Sketches of Men and Places* (1851) is the first full-length travel book by an Indian. Although it contains portraits of famous people he met, he has written it in the voice of the awed spectator, anxious to impress both those about whom he writes and his readers. Unfortunately, because of the haste with which he put the volume together, it contains long quotations from travel books.

Far more interesting are the accounts by the Rev. Peter Jones (1802–56), who was half white but raised until adolescence as a traditional Ojibwe. Jones, the first Indian Methodist minister in Canada, visited England in 1831 to raise money for his people. During his trip to London, Jones wrote his brother on December 30, 1831, that he found the English to be "a noble, generous-minded people — free to act and free to think." However, Jones disliked being regarded as an object of great curiosity:

No nation, I think can be more fond of novelties than the English; they will gaze upon a foreigner as if he had just dropped down from the moon. . . . When my Indian name, Kahkewaquonaby, is announced to attend any public meeting, so great is the curiosity, the place is sure to be filled. They are truly industrious, and in general very honest and upright. Their close attention to business produces, I think, too much worldly-mindedness, and hence they forget to think enough about their souls and their God; their motto seems to be "Money, money; get money, get rich, and be a gentleman." With this sentiment they fly about in every direction, like a swarm of bees, in search of the treasure which lies so near their hearts. (221)

Jones was fascinated by women's clothes. "I will only say, that the ladies of fashion wear very curious bonnets, which look something like a farmer's scoop-shovel; and when they walk in the tiptoe style they put me in mind of the little snipes that run along the shores of the lakes in Canada. They also wear sleeves as big as bushel bags, which make them appear as if they had three bodies with one head" (221–22). Jones, who married a white woman he met on his London visit, spent most of his life acting as a liaison between his people and the Canadian government. After his death, his wife published his journals and *History of the Ojebway Indians* (1861).

George Henry or Maungwudaus (Ojibwe, b. 1810) was Peter Jones's half brother. A Methodist missionary, Maungwudaus mortified his half brother in 1844 by leaving the ministry, abandoning his Christian name, leading a wild Indian troupe to tour Great Britain, and converting to Catholicism.[9] Maungwudaus's observations were published in *An Account of the Ojibway Indians* (1848). He visited the palace of Queen Victoria, which was so big the Indians got tired before they finished visiting all the rooms. Although he pronounced her handsome, Maungwudaus also made clear that "there are many handsomer women than she is" (Henry, 4). Many of the customs pertaining to women puzzled Maungwudaus. He noted that there are eighty thousand common wives in the City of London, who are allowed to "walk in the streets every night for the safety of the married women" (5). English ladies were very talkative while eating, "like ravens when feasting on venison" (5). Although English women were pretty, they could not walk alone: "they must always be assisted by the men. They make their husbands carry their babies for them when walking" (4). With tongue-in-cheek humor, he recorded the insistence of some officers' wives that the Indian men kiss them. When the natives kissed them Indian-style on both cheeks, the ladies protested that they should be kissed on their mouths (5). At an officer's request, the Indians dutifully kissed the women on their mouths. The war chief then said in Ojibway to the ladies: "That is all you are good for; as for wives, you are good for nothing" (6). Asked for a translation, Maungwudaus quickly replied that the chief wished the officers would invite him often so that he could kiss the handsome ladies. He also commented that "many of the Englishmen have very big stomachs, caused by drinking too much ale and porter. Those who drink wine and brandy, their noses look like ripe strawberries" (5).

Maungwudaus encountered prejudice in England. When the Indians stopped to watch a monkey dressed like a man, performing on a music box in the street, a young man asked the Indians "which of the two strangers will think the most civilized, you or the monkey" (Henry, 9). Maungwudaus put the young man in his place by replying, "You may consider yourselves better and wiser than those strangers, but you are very much mistaken. Your treatment to them tells them that you are not, and you are so foolish and ignorant, you know nothing about it. I have been traveling five years amongst these people in their own country, and I never, not once, was insulted, but I was always kindly treated and respected by every one of them" (9). His wife and several of his children died in England. He left London in 1848 to return to North America.

By 1854, he was back in Europe. In a letter to Peter Jones, written in Paris and dated 19 October 1854, Maungwudaus described the appearance of French men: "The French people wear much hair about the mouth, which makes them look bold and noble; but our friend Sasagon, who has no taste for beauty, says it would puzzle any one of our people to find where the Frenchman's mouth is; and that a person having much hair round his mouth makes him look like one of our Indian dogs in North America when running way with a black squirrel in his mouth" (qtd. in Jones 220). Sasagon observed that because the French women carry big and heavy loads on their backs, they would make "good wives for the Ojebway hunters" (220). Maungwudaus concluded that the French were not so "selfish and proud as most of the English" (220).

At the beginning of the twentieth century, E. Pauline Johnson (Mohawk, 1861–1913) used a more literary and sophisticated reversal of the gaze in "A Pagan in St. Paul's Cathedral."[10] She uses Native terms to describe London and to compare Canadian Indian and British concepts of government, lifestyle, and worship. For Johnson, London is a campground for the "paleface," the Parliament is the council, and Buckingham Palace is the "Teepee of the Great White Father" (139). The sights and sounds of London do not awe Johnson. Instead, they evoke memories of and nostalgia for the Native people and landscape of Canada. The music of St. Paul's Cathedral, for example, beats in her ears "like the far-off cadences of the Sault Ste. Marie rapids" (141). Her allusions to the Iroquois of the Northeastern woodlands, the prairie tribes of Saskatchewan, and the rapids of Sault Ste. Marie remind the reader of the variety of Indian nations and the vast geography of her homeland.

Johnson also demonstrates her staunch commitment to Canadian and Indian nationalism. She stresses the king's special links to her people, who supported Great Britain in the Revolutionary War and the War of 1812. While the British may call him the "King of England," the Iroquois refer to him as the "Great White Father," who visited Canadian reserves and decorated the oldest chiefs because they fought for England. Her use of the term "Great White Father," a term common in Native oratory referring to the king of England in Canada or the president in the United States, reinforces the colonizer's emphasis on the king's paternal relationship to the childlike Natives. At the same time, however, Johnson undercuts this paternalism by stressing the king's dependence upon Native people, who helped Great Britain fight against the Americans.

Johnson's rejection of the role of the "colonized" is reflected as well in her insistence on the equality of Native and British religious customs. She asks, "Why may we not worship with the graceful movement of our feet? The paleface worships by moving his lips and tongue; the difference is but slight" (142). To exemplify this equality, Johnson uses the device of a scene within a scene. Moving from the present to memory, she creates a vignette in which an Onondaga firekeeper explains the importance of the White Dog Sacrifice, one of that nation's most sacred rites. The firekeeper emphasizes that the children of "The Great Spirit" must sacrifice what is nearest to their hearts and lives. Because "only the spotless and stainless can enter into His presence," the Onondagas must sacrifice a white dog, a "member of our household, a co-habitant of our wigwam, and on the smoke that arises from the purging fires will arise also the thanksgivings of all those who desire that the Great Spirit in His happy hunting grounds will forever smoke His pipe of peace" (142). Johnson limits her depiction of this sacrifice to the speech by the firekeeper, excluding the ritual killing of the dog. Despite its romantic tone, the essay is an effective example of Johnson's resistance to the dominant society's efforts to eradicate or ignore Native culture. By describing their reactions to the dominant society, Johnson and other early Native writers defy colonialist authority, which Bhabha states "requires the production of differentiations, individualizations, identity effects through which discriminatory practices can map out subject populations that are tarred with the visible and transparent mark of power" (*Location* 111).

Native writers, however, increasingly shifted their discourse from wonder to resistance to the unjust policies affecting their people. Clearly, they became convinced of the principle, delineated in the twentieth century by Michel Foucault, that the agency of domination resides "in the one who listens and says nothing." As Foucault comments, the "discourse of truth" takes effect in the "one from whom it is wrested" (*Archaeology* 62). They combated European dominance with the word rather than the arrow. This harsher stance is exemplified by Peter Jones's letter of August 23, 1830, describing his perception of white Americans' philosophy about Indians: "Come let us make a *law*, and let us drive them away from their little reserves, and from the graves of their fathers, and send them away to the northern regions, or beyond the Rocky mountains, and let them there perish by their own countrymen in bloody Indian wars, or let them starve to death. Then we shall have their fine rivers and their rich flats, so we shall eat, drink, and be merry" (qtd. in Smith 124).

In the early nineteenth century, the strongest published voice of Native American resistance was William Apess (Pequot, 1798–1839), whose literary career follows the three stages outlined by Fanon. Apess wrote *A Son of the Forest* (1829), the first full autobiography written by an Indian to be published. His use of irony exemplifies Linda Hutcheon's assertion that "irony is a trope of doubleness" that characterizes the "two-fold vision of post-colonial." It is not only the doubleness of the colonial culture imposed upon the colonized but also the "doubleness of the colonized in relation to the colonizer, either as model or antithesis" (134).

Apess introduces the reversed gaze in his "An Indian's Looking-Glass for the White Man," appended to the 1833 edition of *Experiences of Five Christian Indians of the Pequot Tribe*. Murray perceptively comments that even the title is ambiguous: do Indians look at themselves for the benefit of whites so that they can see themselves? What Apess forces his white audience to look at, according to Murray, is the image of degenerate and demoralized Indians who are equally a creation of white civilization. "In this way the whites are forced to see in the mirror the results of their *own* acts, their own creations, rather than the 'other,' the natural Indian" (61). This forceful polemic demonstrates the author's commitment to fighting back. Here Apess skillfully uses irony to argue for Indians' racial equality with whites: "If black or red skins, or any other skin of color is disgraceful to God, it appears that he has disgraced himself a great deal — for he has made fifteen colored people to one white, and placed them here on this earth" (157).

An even more powerful reversal of the gaze is his *Eulogy on King Philip* (1836), which Barry O'Connell correctly says "proposes a fundamental revision of the conventional patriotic narrative of the creation of the United States" (28). Maureen Konkle argues that in the *Eulogy*, Apess rejects the notion of an innate Indian consciousness because he "understands that the positing of inherent difference between Indians and Europeans is a crucial step in denying Indians' political status" and that the legitimacy of the state depends on that denial (458). Konkle reads Apess's *Eulogy* in the light of Supreme Court decisions respecting Indians in the 1820s and 1830s and Edward Everett's *Address at Bloody-Brook* (1835), a speech commemorating King Philip's War published in Boston a month before Apess delivered his *Eulogy* in January 1836. Konkle concludes that both Chief Justice John Marshall and Everett demonstrate that legitimate control of land in North America requires both the recognition and the denial of Indian political autonomy. They also demonstrate, Konkle argues, that the best means of denying that "dangerous autonomy" is the production of knowledge that reduces "resistant Indian political entities to an assemblage of inferior, soon-to-be-extinct individuals" (459). Konkle emphasizes that Apess denies the "validity of the concept of inherent Indian difference in order to reassert the primacy of Indian politics, negating the self/other dynamic of colonial discourse by introducing a third term, the Indian nation, the existence of which the U.S. concedes in the treaties" (459–60). As O'Connell points out, Apess speaks in the *Eulogy* for a concept of nationhood founded on "struggle, contradiction, and the presence of many nations with different and often irreconcilable interests" (28).

Apess's forceful use of the reversed (or double) gaze is reflected in his emphasis that there were two "fathers" of the country: George Washington and King Philip (Metacomet), the seventeenth-century Wampanoag chief. In the *Eulogy*, Apess reverses the view of King Philip propounded by those in the dominant society by rewriting the history of the Puritan conquest and of the Pequot War against Philip. To counteract the demonization of the Pequots by Cotton and Increase Mather, Apess emphasizes that the cause of the wars between the Pequots and whites was "good usage": the whites, not the Indians, were the aggressors, and "the wars, cruelties, and bloodshed is a job of their own seeking, and not the Indians" (307). There are, he argues, a thousand witnesses to the fact that the Indians never hurt those who were kind to them (307). One example of his effective use of doubleness and irony is his account of how the starving whites, who had hired themselves as servants to the Indians in order to live, stole the Indians' corn. Another is his description of how Captain Miles Standish and his men prepared a feast for the Indians and massacred their Native guests when they sat down to eat. Apess's comment that "their conduct being more like savages than Christians" underscores the doubleness of this episode, as does his comment that "we wonder if these same Christians do not think it the command of God that they should lie, steal, and get drunk, commit fornication and adultery" (281, 282). He cites other examples of white savagery, such as their robbing Indian graves and murdering Indians without provocation, when the Natives came to visit white ships.

In their speeches, oral stories, and writings, Native Americans strongly attacked the hypocrisy of white Christians. Indians actively opposed efforts to convert them and were particularly appalled by the conduct of the clergy. These attacks also reflect their resistance to assimilation. Fr. Paul Le Jeune recorded in his *Relation* of 1639 the sharp questioning of Catholic doctrine by teenage Indian seminarians, who questioned the necessity of the good man's being sent to hell because he had not been baptized. If this is true, the seminarians argued, then "God does not love all good people, since he throws that one into the fire." They also asked where God existed before the creation of heaven and earth and how the angels who sinned before the creation of heaven and hell could be cast into hell as punishment (*Jesuit Relations* 16:183, 185). The *Relation* of 1642–43 describes the disgust of a group of Algonquians about what Catholicism had done to their tribe. Prayer spoiled everything for them because their dreams and prophecies were no longer true. Before the priests came, the French were not so religious: "They did not have all those prayers which you are introducing; it is you who have brought in all these novelties, and who teach them to Savages, and overturn their brains and make them die" (24:211).

Especially fascinating is the two-hour religious debate held on July 31, 1844, between two Ojibwe leaders and a Jesuit priest. The account is contained in a letter written six months later by a participant, Father Pierre Chazelle.[11] Chief Oshawana tells the priest not to "believe that savages are fools. . . . The Great Spirit has not left them in ignorance: . . . he has given them Wisdom" (Delâge 303). He also chides the priest that God sent Christ to the whites because they had fallen away from their religion: "He gave great gifts to your ancestor. But you did not know how to take advantage of these precious gifts and you rejected the blessings of your ancestor. That must be why the Great Spirit sent his son to the white man; but the white man chased him away" (304). God did not send Christ to the Indians because it was not necessary, "because we did not despise the customs of our ancestor" (304).[12] He reminds the priest of the consequences the Indians have suffered as a result of white conquest: "And today, his race has multiplied on our great island and has established its customs here. But we, we have become fugitives, destitute and almost annihilated" (305). The chief concludes his first speech with a strong statement about his tribe's determination to retain their culture: "Therefore, my brother, do not flatter yourself that we will change. No, never will I, a savage man, forget the Great Spirit by whom all things exist. I know what he has given to me, and I will preserve it carefully. I feed my fire, it will not go out" (305). Chief Petrokeshig not only seconds these sentiments but also urges the priest not to build a cabin on the island and to leave.

That Native Americans frequently criticized the hypocrisy of the clergy demonstrates their disillusionment with European culture. In a letter written after he returned to America, Samson Occom contrasted the English bishops, who, he felt, were a good deal like the "Anti-Christian Popes." He praised, however, the "Gospel Bishops," who were meek, humble, gentle, and kind, like their "Good Master" — "compassionate and merciful unto the miserable and charitable to the poor." The behavior of the bishops reveals no such compassion. When Occom described the miserable and wretched situation of the Indians and asked assistance in "evangelizing these poor heathen," "they never gave us a single brass farthing" (qtd. in W. B. Sprague 3:193).

Native people were enraged by priests' sexual liaisons with Indian women. Ruth Benedict collected a story about such an incident involving the first priest at Cochiti. When the governor refused to send the priest away as the woman's husband urged, the Indians planned to kill the priest. Hearing of the plan, the priest escaped to San Felipe. People there refused to surrender him to the Cochiti men, who had persuaded the men of Santo Domingo, Tesuque, and San Ildefonso to join them. The priest then fled to Mexico. After some time elapsed, the pope sent him back to San Felipe, and the governor, out of gratitude to the pueblo, gave San Felipe all the land they asked for. The people of Cochiti sent a message to Rome asking not to be Catholics (Benedict 193–95).

Edmund Nequatewa tells of a similar incident among the Hopi. The Spanish priest undercut the traditional power structure of the Hopi and got them to do his bidding by convincing them they had more power than the chiefs. He subsequently sent the husbands of the prettiest women away from the pueblo to get him water so that he could visit the wives. Circumvented by the husbands, the priest ordered all the pre-adolescent girls brought to him. After learning what he had done, the Hopis plotted to kill him. When the chief came to the priest's house, the priest defied him: "'You have no power to kill me. If you do, I will come to life and wipe out your whole tribe'" (Nequatewa 45). The unarmed chief challenged the priest to blow the chief into the air because the

Hopi gods were stronger than the priest's god. The priest cut down the chief with his sword but was soon overpowered, hung from a beam, and burned (Nequatewa 42–45).

Native American writers also depicted nonclerical white men as sexual predators. In *Life among the Piutes*, Winnemucca emphasizes what Birgitte Georgi-Findlay calls "the outrageous issues of sexual violence and miscegenation revealed in the violation of native women's bodies by white men" (229).[13] Winnemucca learned this danger as a child when settlers came into her family's camp asking that her mother give one of her daughters to them. Later the author describes how white men kidnapped two twelve-year-old Paiute girls and how, during the Bannock War of 1878, male settlers lassoed Paiute women and did "fearful" things to them (228). In dealing with this threat, Winnemucca stresses her role as a resistor, a warrior woman determined to keep her virtue intact. When she and her sister shared a room with eight cowboys, a man touched her during the night. Winnemucca punched the offender in the face and warned, "Go away, or I will cut you to pieces, you mean man!" (231). Through her depiction of the sexual violence that Indian women suffered at the hands of male settlers, Winnemucca, like the slave narrators, reverses the gaze by reminding whites of their own brutality. Such narratives emphasize how the conquest of Indians, like the slave system, destroyed the morality of whites. In contrast to the predatory behavior of the white men, Winnemucca portrays herself as a proper Paiute woman whose morals correspond to the code of conduct of mainstream women in the nineteenth century.

The betrayal of Indian women by white males is a thread that runs through two short stories by E. Pauline Johnson (Mohawk, 1861–1913), "A Red Girl's Reasoning" and "As It Was in the Beginning," collected in *The Moccasin Maker* (1913). Both combine the plot of mixed-blood women betrayed by weak white lovers, with forceful attacks on settlers' religious hypocrisy. In the first story, Johnson not only reverses the gaze by emphasizing the dominant society's lack of respect for Indian culture but also depicts her heroines as strong, independent women who ultimately reject their white lovers. "A Red Girl's Reasoning" focuses on non-Indians' refusal to accept the sanctity of the tribal marriage ceremonies of settlers to Indian women. The heroine, Christine Robinson, leaves her husband, Charles McDonald, because he does not honor the Indian marriage ceremony of her white father and Indian mother. In "As It Was in the Beginning," Esther takes physical and verbal revenge against her unfaithful white lover, Lawrence. Johnson uses the plot of victimization of a young mixed-blood girl who has been taken from her family by Father Paul, an Episcopalian priest, to be stripped of her cultural heritage and educated in white ways. The author combines this with the domestic romance of the scorned woman. Esther is ready to give up family and heritage when Lawrence professes his love for her. After overhearing her beloved Father Paul dissuade his nephew from marrying her, an enraged Esther kills her lover, whom the clergyman dearly loved. In this story, Johnson abandons the verbal combat used by Christine in "A Red Girl's Reasoning" for physical violence.[14]

Native writers also depicted the settlers as corrupters of Indian family life through the introduction of alcohol. In *A Son of the Forest* and *Five Christian Indians*, Apess describes how his alcoholic grandmother beat him and broke his arm, an act he blamed on the whites: "inasmuch as they introduced among my countrymen that bane of comfort and happiness, ardent spirits — seduced them into a love of it, and, when under its unhappy influence, wronged them out of their lawful possessions — that land, where reposed the ashes of their sires; and not only so, but they committed violence of the most revolting kind upon the persons of the female portion of the tribe." (*Son* 7). Copway describes how a trader who wanted to keep the Ojibwes addicted to liquor and away from the missionaries told the Natives that the black coats invited the Natives to a camp meeting in order to kill them (*Life* 97). The destructive impact of white-introduced alcohol is a theme that runs throughout Native American written literature.

Native authors attacked the settlers for their greed and corruption as well. John Rollin Ridge (Cherokee, 1827–67) depicts the criminal behavior of the settlers in the California gold fields in *The Life and Adventures of Joaquín Murieta, the Celebrated California Bandit* (1854), a romance that established the image of Murieta as a Byronic folk hero and ushered in a flood of stories, dramas, and films that made the bandit a popular figure in Mexican and California legend. Fired with enthusiastic admiration of the American entrepreneurial character, Murieta, who is a mixed-blood of Spanish and Indian descent, moves to California, where he becomes successful. American injustice turns this peaceful miner into a daring desperado after Murieta is beaten and bound, his mistress raped, his half brother hanged, and his land stolen.

Among the strongest indictments of the settlers' corruption are Winnemucca's attacks on the agency system in *Life among the Piutes*. She castigates W. V. Rinehart, the Paiutes' venial agent at the Malheur Reservation in Oregon. Rinehart sold rations to the Indians, almost beat a tribesman to death, and threatened to shoot a young boy for talking back. She is equally critical of the Rev. James H. Wilbur, agent of the Yakima Reservation. Winnemucca attributes the maltreatment of Indians by agents to the corrupt agency system, known for its misuse of funds.

Native writers also criticized the settlers for their treatment of children. In *A Son of the Forest*, Apess describes his conflicts with the master to whom he was bound out because the man would not allow his apprentice to attend Methodist camp meetings. Apess is bitter about the fact that his various masters did not care enough about him to see he had a religious education and that they and other non-Indians filled his head with stereotypical stories about savage Indians, making him fear his own people.

The strongest resistance to how the settlers treated children appears in the numerous accounts of Indian boarding schools. Especially poignant is Zitkala-Ša's "The School Days" (1901).[15] This chapter in Zitkala-Ša's autobiography portrays the author's traumatic transition from traditional Yankton Sioux childhood to the harsh world of the White Manual Labor Institute. She depicts this experience as a cultural fall from a Dakota Eden into a hellish non-Indian school that neither nurtured the Indian children nor respected their cultures. Zitkala-Ša loses her spirit when, after hiding to escape her tormentors, she is tied to a chair and has her hair cut in a style only cowards wore: "In my anguish, I moaned for my mother, but no one came to comfort me. Not a soul reasoned quietly with me, as my own mother used to do; for now I was only one of many little animals driven by the herder" (56). In the course of this essay, the child moves from being a terrified victim to an active rebel who, when instructed to mash turnips, pounds them so hard she breaks the bottom of the bowl and who scratches out the eyes of Satan's pictures in *The Stories of the Bible*.

In "As It Was in the Beginning," Johnson gives an equally devastating account of the impact of the boarding school system on an Indian child. Taken from her half-blood father and full-blood mother, Esther is forbidden to speak her language and denied permission to return home for a visit, lest she regress to her Indian ways. She is miserable: "I wanted my own people, my own old life, my blood called out for it, but they always said I must not return to my father's tepee. I heard them talk amongst themselves of keeping me away from pagan influences" (147).

Not all portrayals of non-Indians by Indian writers are negative. In *Life, Letters and Speeches*, Copway recalls the many kindnesses he received from strangers. When, while traveling on a boat, the wind blew away his handkerchief containing all his money, a kindly Quaker gave him enough money to continue his journey. He meticulously records the generous acts by the Methodists he met in the course of his journey. Winnemucca also records in *Life among the Piutes* the generous treatment she received from various whites. Her loving portrait of Samuel B. Parrish, the agent at Malheur, counters her attacks on Rinehart and Wilbur. A gentle, loving man, he genuinely cared about the welfare of his charges, who prospered under his care. Charles Eastman, in *From the Deep Woods to Civilization*, pays tribute to Mr. and Mrs. Frank Wood, with whom he roomed and "who were a father and mother to me at this period of my life" (71). Johnson's "Mother o' the Men" and "The Nest Builder," both in *The Moccasin Maker*, celebrate Canadian women settlers for their bravery, stamina, and love of family. In "My Mother," also in *The Moccasin Maker*, she pays tribute to her parents, Chief George H. M. Johnson and Emily Susanna Howells, in a fictional account of their marriage. She depicts their relationship as an ideal union between a noble, educated, and heroic Indian male and a gentle, generous, and devoted white woman.

Despite these positive portrayals, the image of the non-Indian in Indian oral and written literature through the nineteenth century was negative. Native authors frequently appealed to the humanity of their audience in order to get them to understand the humanness of Indian people. Kwame Anthony Appiah describes this technique as challenging the dominant society "in the name of the ethical universal; in the name of humanism" (152). Although early Native American writers appealed to a broader humanism, usually through references to Christian principles, they did not believe that non-Indians would treat Indians as fellow Christians. The philosophical chasm that separated the cultures of Indians and non-Indians is summarized in a speech by Sitting Bull, leader of the Hunkpapa Teton division of the Sioux, who fought the whites almost constantly between 1869 and 1876, in his speech at the Powder River council in 1877:

we have now to deal with another race — small and feeble when our fathers first met them but now great and overbearing. Strangely enough they have a mind to till the soil and the love of possession is a disease with them. These people have made many rules that the rich may break but the poor may not. They take tithes from the poor and weak to support the rich who rule. They claim this mother of ours, the earth, for their own and fence their neighbors away; they deface her with their buildings and their refuse. That nation is like a spring freshet that overruns its banks and destroys all who are in its path. (qtd. in Turner 255)

NOTES

1. In his *The Colonizer and the Colonized*, Albert Memmi powerfully describes the personal and social impact of colonialism on both the colonizer and the colonizer.

2. Quetzalcoatl's Nahuatl name derives from *quetzal*, a rare green bird found only in the highlands of Chiapas and Guatemala, and *coatl*, a serpent or plumed serpent. *Coatl* is also defined as the Maya term *co* for serpent and the Nahuatl word *atl*, for water. Quetzal feathers were a symbol of something precious. *Coatl* can also mean "twin brother," so that Quetzalcoatl can also be translated as "Precious Twin"; another of his star is often represented by Quetzalcoatl and the evening star by Xolotl names. He has many names. Among the Nahuas, he was known also as the Plumed Serpent, Lord of

the Land of the Dead, God of Wind, personification of the planet Venus, Lord of Dawn. Because the morning (*shoo-lotl*) is his twin brother, Quetzalcoatl is also called Xoltol, Ce Acatl (from the time of his birth). Sahagún gives the name as Quetzalcotal. See Waters (122) and Sahagún (1:2–3).

3. According to Frank Waters, this version of the myth is based on the belief that Quetzalcoatl was the historical Topiltzin, who ruled Tula and was priest of Quetzalcoatl. Deposed from his throne, he escaped from Mexico during the twelfth century. He presumably arrived in Yucatan, where he was known as Kukulcan, and initiated a renaissance of Maya culture in Chicen Itza, which duplicated that of Tula (122–24). For Sahagún's version, see book 3, chapters 3, 4, 12, and 13.

4. I have followed the simplified orthography Leslie Marmon Silko uses in *Ceremony*.

5. See also Jarold Ramsey's "The Bible in Indian Mythology" (*Reading*) for an excellent account of biblical influences in Native oral literature.

6. *Ojibwe* is the spelling currently used by the tribes in Minnesota, Wisconsin, and Michigan. Other spellings are *Ojibway, Ojebway,* and *Ojibwa*.

7. Calloway excerpts the story on 33. William S. Simmons comments that "floating islands and island canoes are familiar motifs in the Algonquian folklore of northern New England and eastern Canada" (65).

8. Todorov suggests that Columbus "did not succeed in his human communications" with the Arawak because he "is not interested in them" (*Conquest* 33). In "Learning to Curse," Greenblatt concludes that "Indians were frequently either found defective in speech, and hence pushed toward the zone of wild things, or granted essentially the same speech as the Europeans" (572). Eric Cheyfitz argues that Todorov and Greenblatt acknowledge a third relationship in the European understanding of American languages that is simultaneous with the other two: "that Columbus and subsequent voyagers did indeed recognize that they were dealing with different languages that they didn't understand" (106). To produce the "elegant opposition" described above, Todorov and Greenblatt marginalize this third term in their arguments (106). David Murray gives an excellent discussion of the complexities of the representation of Indian languages in *Forked Tongues*.

9. On the cover of his *Remarks concerning the Ojibway Indians*, George Henry describes himself as a second cousin of Jones. Donald Smith is convinced, however, that he was Jones's half brother (317 n. 78).

10. "A Pagan in St. Paul's Cathedral: Iroquois Poetess' Impressions in London's Cathedral" originally appeared in the *London Express* (August 3, 1906) and was reprinted in *The Moccasin Maker* (1913; all citations are to the 1998 reprint).

11. The letter was originally published in *Lettres des Nouvelles Missions du Canada, 1843–1852*, edited with commentary and annotations by Lorenzo Cadieux in 1852. Fa-

ther Chazelle's letter has been translated by Denys Delâge and edited by Helen Hornbeck Tanner in "The Ojibwa-Jesuit Debate at Walpole Island, 1844."

12. In "The Bible in Western Indian Mythology," Ramsey notes that tribes from this area had similar reactions. They were puzzled or repelled by certain moral interpretations insisted upon by the Christian narrators. The missionary Asa Smith observed that "as long as they listened to the interesting historical parts of the Bible, they were pleased, but the great truth that all are under condemnation to the penalty of the law while in their present situation, is very offensive to them" (qtd. in Ramsey 171). Ramsey emphasizes that the Western Indians operated under a "shame-culture morality, by and large, enforced mainly by fear of public shame for wrongdoing rather than private guilt in the sight of a god" (171).

13. See also Cheryl Walker (139–63). Both Walker and Ruoff, in "Early Native American Women Authors" (85–90), discuss Winnemucca's use of the sentimental tradition as a means of reversing the gaze of her audience.

14. In "The Derelict," Johnson creates a white lover who achieves heroic status by sacrificing himself for his beloved. In this story, Charles Cragstone, a handsome Episcopal priest, settles in Canada because his English family considered him a failure. In love with Lydia, a mixed-blood, Cragstone plans to marry her even though he knows he should not. Not only is she Indian but she also has been accused of theft and fired from her job as a maid. When Medicine Joe confesses on his deathbed that he was the thief, Charles violates the sanctity of the confession by revealing that Joe is the real thief. Though his act results in his being dismissed from the clergy, he nevertheless has redeemed himself as worthy of the ever-loyal Lydia. In *Cogewea* (1927), Mourning Dove vividly depicts male settlers' despicable treatment of Indian women. The story of Green Blanket, whose husband planned to kill her before she fled, is particularly powerful. Cogewea's white father abandoned his Indian family, and the heroine herself narrowly escapes from the greedy and wily Alfred Densmore, who plans to kill her for her money.

15. Zitkala-Ša published three autobiographical essays in the *Atlantic Monthly* in 1900 and 1901, which were subsequently reprinted in *American Indian Stories* (1921).

The country can't make up its mind. One decade we're invisible, another dangerous. Obsolete and quaint, a rather boring people suitable for schoolkids and family vacations, then suddenly we're cool and mysterious. Some now regard us as keepers of planetary secrets and the only salvation for a world bent on destroying itself. Heck, we're just plain folk, but no one wants to hear that.

Paul Chaat Smith,
in "What Do You Think of When You Think of Indians?"

Metacritical Frames of Reference
in Studying American Indian Literature
An Afterword

KATHRYN SHANLEY

Representation tends to mean two different things, but what is most often meant by the term rests with the virtual more than with the actual — of course, all terms having to do with "the real" slip around. The first meaning simply denotes the act of one thing standing in the place of another, speaking for that other or others, while the second meaning, as I employ it, calls for exactitude of presence. At heart both meanings result from the same process, a process I define as a spiritual — or, if you prefer, aesthetic — proceeding having nothing to do with the dualism of sacred and profane. The act of *re*-presentation (my way of differentiating the first meaning from the meaning I favor) poignantly pulls together time and presence, much as opening a medicine bundle pulls power from another time into the present moment through its carefully acquired and assembled contents. Each object in the bundle can be seen as a synecdoche in relation to a whole cultural repository of power; yet each piece, not just the most symbolically powerful pieces, is whole in itself and is essential *to* the whole. Words carried in living memory as stories, songs, poems, chants, jokes, and so on are necessary for enlivening the whole. Given that the act of reading is solitary and that medicine power bundled, then opened ceremonially, is communal, it is hard to imagine collections such as this and tribal medicine bundles as bearing similarity in their effects, and nearly impossible to assess literary effects in ways that suggest they approach *re*-presentation. The multidimensional dynamics of *re*-presentation abound on the fringes of knowing the self and the Other and fall into misrepresentation and stereotype when imagination fails, fear enters, and domination rears up. Textual representation, therefore, requires a depth of full-bodied experience to bring it to life as understanding. Nevertheless, efforts to create a metacritical frame of reference for understanding American Indian life, literature, and thought serve a purpose in that they evoke further reflection and experience.

In the recent writings of Gerald Vizenor, Louis Owens, Arnold Krupat, and others, *frontier* has come to designate that dynamic space where two selves, two

Others, meet. The potential for a *re*-presentational moment, as when ceremonial participants experience simultaneous recognition (are "of one mind") always exists. Often, when westerners attempt to evoke images of tribal peoples, they envision a people "of one mind" who approach Others with awe and wonder. But what we really know, and as Gerald Vizenor so aptly claims about tribal narratives, is that power words "are discourse and in this sense tribal literatures are the world rather than representation" (*Narrative* 4). Excepting those rare moments, cross-personal and cross-cultural exchanges and impressions involve misperceptions of the Other and improvisational representations of the self. If the two individuals involved (let's just say there are only two) remain respectful and openhearted, they will create something new out of their encounter that is nonetheless full of misperceptions and inept self-performances — a joke, perhaps, or merely a word, but nevertheless an unforgettable thing, even an authentic thing, however fleeting.

For American Indian people, stories can cure or kill. Within American Indian tribal communities the power to cure or kill through words has its greatest effect, since tribally specific beliefs flourish in collectivity. Within American Indian literature, writings read mostly by non-Indians, perhaps the most one can hope for is "to change a reader's habits of interpretation[, a gesture that] amounts to a subtle, counter-colonial, and reappropriative act" (Rainwater 30–31). Changing the hearts and minds of readers habituated to see "Indians" as exotic Others requires a shift in mainstream worldview, the paradigm through which social interactions and cross-cultural perceptions fall categorically into place. The problem with representations of American Indians, in other words, frequently results from reliance on a dualistically organized worldview; though it may hardly be recognized as *religious* in nature, to designate it as *secular* is to speak out of the dualistic thinking that would divide the world into sacred and profane. As Lynda Sexson puts it: "Religion is not a discrete category within human experience; it is rather a quality that pervades all of experience. Accustomed as we are to distinguishing between 'the sacred' and 'the profane,' we fail to remember that such a dividing up of reality is itself a religious idea. It is often an awkward idea, rather like someone trying to carry himself over a stream in his own arms — a confusion of part and whole, form and function" (*Ordinarily* 7) In the divided-up reality that prompts readers to understand American Indians and their literatures (indeed, the very word *literature* implies a divided-up world) in contrapuntal ways, re-presentation in the religious sense can hardly be achieved, even modestly.

This collection of essays, as discussions of first encounters, distorted images, and literary appropriations, must therefore fit within the first stages of ideal representation, where recognition and apology begin the process of understanding. At the same time, we must be careful not to take liberties in creating metaphors from living Native American traditions, not to assume we are speaking for American Indians, and not to claim more power for literature than it deserves. I would not, for example, make the metaphorical leap from medicine bundles to word bundles, even though I believe in the power of words to shape realities. "*Re*-presentation," as I define it above, does not occur in this collection; its lesser cousin "representation" does, yet the ideal must be born in mind.

The recognition and apology essential to a full accounting of the process of *re*-presentation is something akin to the Oglala Lakota holy man Black Elk's apology to the birds, that part of the Sun Dance ritual involved with cutting down the sacred tree. As Black Elk says, "You are a kind and good-looking tree; upon you the winged peoples have raised their families; from the tip of your lofty branches down to your roots, the winged and four-legged peoples have made their homes" (Brown 74). In the respectful place of encounter, each recognizes the other's value and values, and a thing taken or received is acknowledged. This is no less true for the authors of these essays, as each takes on the task of recognition of American Indian peoples' value and values at the same time as each author attempts to give back, as a sort of apology, the dignified voice or space that has been usurped from American Indians through stereotypes and misrepresentations. American Indian writers do and will continue to represent tribal worldviews through the myriad of literary and artistic forms that capture their imaginations, beginning in oral traditions and with family stories, and those writings will do more than any metacriticism can.

Often American Indian writings will take up the task Jace Weaver characterizes as "the ongoing and continual healing of ... grief" (34), because much needs to be grieved yet. American Indian history tells stories of such egregious injustices that can no longer be denied — ranging from callous indifference to American Indian suffering to blatant acts of genocide. In the growth of a written literary tradition, there must always be room for all sorts of expressions — the full range of human experience expressed through art — if we ever expect to gain understanding. But first, the way needs to be cleared for a new kind of hearing. I agree with Robert Warrior when he says, "it is now critical for American Indian intellectuals committed to sovereignty to realize that we too must struggle for sovereignty, *intellectual sovereignty*, and all the definition and articulation of what that means to emerge as we critically reflect on that struggle" (97–98). American Indian intellectuals, in dialogue with others and aided significantly by various popular and scholarly movements, are beginning to break open the dualistic paradigm of mainstream Euro-American thinking. We would be naive to believe the end result will be bring us into "one mind" — that rarely happens in the world. What we can hope for is productive and respectful exchanges, and even a few good jokes along the way.

Contributors

Gretchen M. Bataille is senior vice president for academic affairs at the University of North Carolina. Previously, she was provost and academic vice president at Washington State University and served as an administrator and professor at the University of California, Santa Barbara, Arizona State University, and Iowa State University. She has lectured in Italy, Switzerland, and Portugal and has presented lectures on Native American literature for USIA scholars studying at UCSB. Her most recent books are *Native American Women: A Biographical Dictionary* and *Ethnic Studies in the United States*. With Kathleen M. Sands, Bataille published *American Indian Women: Telling Their Lives* and *Native American Women: A Guide to Resources*. For six years she served as editor of *Explorations in Ethnic Studies*, an interdisciplinary journal published by the National Association for Ethnic Studies.

Hartwig Isernhagen teaches American literature and other literatures in English at the University of Basel and is past president of the Swiss Association for North American Studies. He has organized conferences in Switzerland on American literature and particularly on American ethnic literatures. His publications include *Momaday, Vizenor, Armstrong: Conversations on American Indian Writing* and over a dozen articles on indigenous writing in English from the South Pacific to Native American literature. His most recent book project is "Difference and Value: Theoretical Perspectives of the Indigene." He has lectured in the United States, Canada, France, and Italy.

David L. Moore is assistant professor in English at the University of Montana and has taught at Cornell University and Salish Kootenai College. He has published on Native literary history and critical legal theory in relation to tribal sovereignty, American and Native American identity issues, and cultural property. His current book project is entitled "Native Knowing: American Identity and Native American Sovereignty." He lives with his family in Missoula, Montana.

David Murray teaches American Studies and Critical Theory at the University of Nottingham. He is the author of *Forked Tongues: Speech Writing and Representation in North American Indian Texts* and has written articles on Frank Hamilton Cushing, Indian autobiography, Gerald Vizenor, Okkah Tubbe, and Tony Hillerman. His most recent book is *Indian Giving: Material and Discursive Economies in Indian-White Exchanges*.

Louis Owens is professor of English at the University of California, Davis. He has published extensively on American and Native American literature, including such works as *Other Destinies: Understanding the American Indian Novel*; *Mixed Messages: Literature, Film, Family, Place*; and *The Grapes of Wrath: Trouble in the Promised Land*.

John Purdy teaches Native American literature and is chair of the Department of English at Western Washington University. He has written two significant critical books, *The Legacy of D'Arcy McNickle* and *Word Ways: The Novels of D'Arcy McNickle*, as well as numerous articles on Native American literature. His anthology *Nothing but the Truth* was published in 2000. He is the editor of the preeminent journal in the field, *Studies in American Indian Literatures*. Purdy has been a Fulbright scholar in Germany and New Zealand and has lectured throughout Europe.

Jarold Ramsey was raised on a ranch in central Oregon, near the Confederated Warm Springs Reservation, and was educated at the Universities of Oregon and Washington. Until his retirement in 1997, he was a member of the English faculty at the University of Rochester, where he first taught a course in Indian literature in 1970. In addition to four books of poetry, he has written or edited the following books on American Indian literatures and western folklore: *Coyote Was Going There* (1977); *Reading the Fire* (1982; new expanded edition, 1999); *Nehalem Tillamook Tales* (1990); and (with Suzi Jones) *The Stories We Tell: An Anthology of Oregon Folk Literature* (1994). He is a past chair of the MLA Committee on the Literatures and Languages of America.

Bernadette Rigal-Callard is professor of North American Studies at the Université Michel de Montaigne–Bordeaux III and is a specialist in contemporary North American religions and Native literatures. She studied at Bordeaux and at the University of California, Santa Barbara, where she frequently returns, and taught in Edinburgh. She taught the first masters and doctoral seminars in France on Native literatures, focusing on the modes of adaptation and representation of traditional myths, on intermythology and postcolonialism. She is known both in Europe and the United States through publications on Gerald Vizenor (six studies) and N. Scott Momaday (including a book in English, *Scott Momaday, House Made of Dawn*, and a collection of articles on this novel, both in 1997), as well as on James Welch, Louis Owens, Louise Erdrich, Thomas King, Paula Gunn Allen, Indian autobiography, and various aspects of American and Canadian Native cultures. She serves on the editorial board of *ernas* (*European Review of Native American Studies*).

A. LaVonne Brown Ruoff, professor emerita of English at the University of Illinois at Chicago, is the author of significant texts on Native literature, among them *American Indian Literatures* and *Redefining American Literary History*. She edited *Literature of the American Indian* as well as *Wynema* by S. Alice Callahan, *Life, Letters and Speeches* by George Copway, and *The Moccasin Maker* by E. Pauline Johnson. She has been honored by the American Book Awards for life-time achievement, the MLA Division of American Indian Literatures, and the Association for Study of American Indian Literatures for her work in that field, and MELUS (the Association for Multi-Ethnic Literatures in the United States) for her contributions to ethnic studies. Native Americans in Chicago recognized her with a distinguished service citation from the Indian Council Fire. She is general editor of the American Indian Lives Series at the University of Nebraska Press and a member of the North American Indian Prose Award Selection Committee. Ruoff directed four NEH Summer Seminars for College Teachers on American Indian Literatures.

Kathleen M. Sands has published on and taught a broad range of ethnic literatures at Arizona State University. With Gretchen M. Bataille, she published *American Indian Women: Telling Their Lives* and *Native American Women: A Guide to Resources*. Her books *The Autobiography of a Yaqui Poet* and *Charreria Mexicana: An Equestrian Folk Tradition* have been favorably received by the indigenous communities. Her most recent book is *Telling a Good One: The Process of a Native American Collaborative Biography*, coauthored with Theodore Rios and published by the University of Nebraska Press. Sands has been a Fulbright scholar in Greece and Portugal and has lectured in those countries as well as Italy, France, and Switzerland. Her publications include numerous articles on folk traditions, Native American literatures, and cross-cultural studies.

Kathryn Shanley is associate professor and chair of Native American Studies at the University of Montana. She has published widely in the field of Native American literature on authors such as Leslie Marmon Silko, James Welch, N. Scott Momaday, Linda Hogan, Thomas King, and Beth Brant. Her book *Only an Indian: Reading James Welch* is forthcoming.

Bibliography

Adams, Hank. "The Golden Indian." *Akwesasne Notes* 16 (Summer 1984): 10–12.

Aeppel, Timothy. "At One with Indians, Tribes of Foreigners Visit Reservations." *Wall Street Journal* 6 Aug. 1996: A1, A6.

Alcoff, Linda. *Real Knowing: New Versions of the Coherence Theory.* Ithaca NY: Cornell UP, 1996.

Aleiss, Angela. "Prelude to World War II: Racial Unity and the Hollywood Indian." *Journal of American Culture* 18.2 (1995): 25–34.

Alexie, Sherman. *Reservation Blues.* London: Minerva, 1996.

Allen, Paula Gunn. "Kochinnenako in Academe: Three Approaches to Interpreting a Keres Indian Tale." *North Dakota Quarterly* 53.2 (1985): 84–106.

———. "The Psychological Landscape of *Ceremony.*" *American Indian Quarterly* 5 (1979): 7–12.

———. *The Sacred Hoop: Recovering the Feminine in American Indian Traditions.* Boston: Beacon, 1986.

———. "Special Problems in Teaching Leslie Marmon Silko's *Ceremony.*" *American Indian Quarterly* 14.4 (1990): 379–86.

———, ed. *Studies in American Indian Literature: Critical Essays and Course Designs.* New York: MLA, 1981.

Anderson, Jack. "Lots of Smoke Rises around This 'Indian.'" *Washington Post* 16 Feb. 1984: 11.

Andrews, Wayne, ed. *Concise Dictionary of American History.* New York: Scribner's, 1962.

Andrist, Ralph K. *The Long Death: The Last Days of the Plains Indians.* New York: Collier, 1964.

The Apache. Arizona State Teachers College Bulletin [Flagstaff] 20.1 (1939).

Apess, William. *On Our Own Ground: The Complete Writings of William Apess, a Pequot.* Ed. Barry O'Connell. Native Americans of the Northeast: Culture, History, and the Contemporary Series. Amherst: U of Massachusetts P, 1993.

Appiah, Kwame Anthony. *In My Father's House: Africa in the Philosophy of Culture*. New York: Oxford UP, 1992.

———. "Is the Post- in Postmodernism the Post- in Postcolonial?" *Critical Inquiry* 17 (Winter 1991): 336–57.

Archives of the Federal Writers' Project. A Study in Government Patronage of the Arts. Urbana: U of Illinois P, 1977.

Archives of the Federal Writers' Project. Series One: *Printed and Mimeograph Publications in the Surviving FWP Files, 1933–1943, excluding State Guides*. Microfilm. 35 reels. Brighton, Sussex, England: Harvester Microform, 1986– .

Ashcroft, Bill, Gareth Griffiths, and Helen Tiffin, eds. *The Empire Writes Back: Theory and Practice in Post-Colonial Literatures*. New Accents Series. London: Routledge, 1989.

Association of Aboriginal Post-Secondary Institutions (AAPSI). "Copyright Law and Traditional Indigenous Knowledge of First Nations Peoples: A Resource and Information Guide." AAPSI: Westbank BC, n.d.

Bakhtin, Mikhail. *The Dialogic Imagination: Four Essays by M. M. Bakhtin*. Ed. Michael Holquist. Trans. Caryl Emerson and Michael Holquist. Austin: U of Texas P, 1981.

Banks, Ann, and Robert Carter. *Survey of Federal Writers' Project Manuscript Holdings in State Depositories*. Washington DC: AHA, 1985.

Barkan, Elazar, and Ronald Bush, eds. *Prehistories of the Future: The Primitivist Project and the Culture of Modernism*. Stanford CA: Stanford UP, 1995.

Barnett, Louise K. *The Ignoble Savage: American Literary Racism, 1790–1890*. Westport CT: Greenwood, 1975.

Barreiro, Jose, ed. *Indian Roots of American Democracy*. Ithaca NY: Akwe:kon, 1992.

Barrett, S. M., ed. *Geronimo's Story of His Life*. New York: Duffield, 1906.

Barry, Roxana. "Rousseau, Buffalo Bill, and the European Image of the American Indian." *Art News* 74 (Dec. 1975): 58–61.

A Basic Call to Consciousness: The Hau de no sau nee Address to the Western World. Mohawk Nation, Rooseveltown NY: Akwesasne Notes, 1978.

Bataille, Georges. *La littérature et le mal*. Paris: Gallimard, 1957.

Bataille, Georges, et al., eds. *Encyclopaedia Acephalica*. London: Atlas, 1995.

Bataille, Gretchen M., and Charles L. P. Silet. *Images of American Indians on Film: An Annotated Bibliography*. New York: Garland, 1985.

———, eds. *The Pretend Indians: Images of Native Americans in the Movies*. Ames: Iowa State UP, 1980.

Beck, Peggy, Anna Lee Walters, and Nia Francisco. *The Sacred: Ways of Knowledge, Sources of Life*. Tsaile AZ: Navajo Community College P, 1992.

Behar, Ruth. *The Vulnerable Observer: Anthropology That Breaks Your Heart*. Boston: Beacon, 1996.

Bell, Elizabeth, Lynda Hass, and Laura Sells. *From Mouse to Mermaid: The Politics of Film, Gender, and Culture*. Bloomington: Indiana UP, 1995.

Benedict, Ruth F, ed. *Tales of the Cochiti Indians. Bureau of American Ethnology Bulletin* 98 (1931). Rpt., introd. Alfonso Ortiz. Albuquerque: U of New Mexico P, 1981.

Berkes, Fikret. "The Common Property Resource Problem and the Creation of Limited Property Rights." *Human Ecology* 13.2 (1985): 187–208.

Berkhofer, Robert F., Jr. *The White Man's Indian: Images of the American Indian from Columbus to the Present.* New York: Knopf, 1978.

Bhabha, Homi K. *The Location of Culture.* London: Routledge, 1994.

———, ed. *Nation and Narration.* London: Routledge, 1990.

Bierhorst, John, ed. *Four Masterworks of American Indian Literature.* Tucson: U of Arizona P, 1974.

Billington, Ray. *Land of Savagery, Land of Promise: The European Image of the American Frontier in the 19th Century.* Norman: U of Oklahoma P, 1985.

Bird, S. Elizabeth, ed. *Dressing in Feathers: The Construction of the Indian in Popular Culture.* Boulder CO: Westview, 1996.

Black Hawk. *Black Hawk: An Autobiography.* Ed. and introd. Donald Jackson. Urbana: U of Illinois P, 1955. Rpt. of *The Life of Ma-ka-tai-me-she-kia-kiak or Black Hawk.* Trans. Antoine Le Claire. Ed. John B. Patterson. 1833.

Bloch, Ernst, et al., eds. *Aesthetics and Politics.* London: Verso, 1977.

Blodgett, Harold. *Samson Occom.* Dartmouth College Manuscript Series, no. 3. Hanover: Dartmouth College P, 1935.

Boas, Franz, ed. *Keresan Texts.* 2 vols. Publication of the American Ethnological Society, 8.1 and 8.2 (1928). New York: AMS, 1974.

Boehme, Sarah E., Museums West Consortium, and Gerald T. Conaty. *Powerful Images: Portrayals of Native America.* Seattle: U Washington P, 1998.

Bordewich, Fergus M. *Killing the White Man's Indian: Reinventing Native Americans at the End of the Twentieth Century.* New York: Doubleday, 1996.

Browder, Laura. *Slippery Characters: Ethnic Impersonators and American Identities.* Chapel Hill: U of North Carolina P, 2000.

Brown, Frank. *Canoe Nation Newsletter.* Seattle, 1995. [Remarks at 1993 Qatuwas in Bella Bella BC]

Brown, Joseph Epes, recorder and ed. *The Sacred Pipe: Black Elk's Account of the Seven Rites of the Oglala Sioux.* Norman: U of Oklahoma P, 1953.

Bruchac, Joseph, ed. *The Next World: Poems by Third World Americans.* Trumansburg NY: Crossing P, 1978.

———, ed. *Survival This Way: Interviews with American Indian Poets.* Tucson: U of Arizona P, 1987.

Brumble, H. David, III. *American Indian Autobiography.* Berkeley: U of California P, 1988.

———. "Anthropologists, Novelists and Indian Sacred Material." *Canadian Review of American Studies* 11.1 (1980): 31–48.

Burke, Kenneth. *A Grammar of Motives.* New York: Prentice, 1945.

Cadiux, Lorenzo, ed. *Lettres des Nouvelles Missions du Canada, 1843–1852*. Montreal: Les Éditions Bellarmin; Paris: Maisonneuve et LAROSE, 1973.

Calder, Jenni. *There Must Be a Lone Ranger: The American West in Film and in Reality*. New York: Taplinger, 1974.

Calloway, Calvin G., ed. *The World Turned Upside Down: Indian Voices from Early America*. Bedford Series in History and Culture. Boston: St. Martin's, 1994.

Calloway, Colin G. *Crown and Calumet: British-Indian Relations, 1783–1815*. Norman: U of Oklahoma P, 1987.

Carr, Helen. *Inventing the American Primitive: Politics, Gender and the Representation of Native American Literary Traditions, 1789–1936*. New York: New York UP, 1996.

Carter, Forrest. *The Education of Little Tree*. 1976. Albuquerque: U of New Mexico P, 1993.

Castro, Michael. *Interpreting the Indian: Twentieth Century Poets and the Native American*. Albuquerque: U of New Mexico P, 1983.

Catulle. *Poésie*. Trans. George Lafaye. Paris: Société d'édition "Les Belles Lettres," 1922.

Chakrabarty, Dipesh. "Postcoloniality and the Artifice of History: Who Speaks for 'Indian' Pasts?" *Representations* 37 (Winter 1992): 1–26.

Chapman, Abraham, ed. *Literature of the American Indians: Views and Interpretations*. New York: New American Library, 1975.

Cheung, King-Kok. *Articulate Silences: Hisaye Yamamoto, Maxine Hong Kingston, Joy Kogawa*. Ithaca NY: Cornell UP, 1993.

Cheyfitz, Eric. *The Poetics of Imperialism: Translation and Colonization from* The Tempest *to* Tarzan. New York: Oxford UP, 1991. Expanded ed., Philadelphia: U of Pennsylvania P, 1997.

Chiappelli, Fredi, ed. *First Images of America: The Impact of the New World on the Old*. Vol. 2. Berkeley: U of California P, 1976.

Christian, Barbara. *Black Feminist Criticism: Perspectives on Black Women Writers*. New York: Pergamon, 1985.

Churchill, Ward. *Fantasies of the Master Race: Literature, Cinema, and the Colonization of the American Indian*. Monroe ME: Common Courage, 1992.

———. "Generations of Resistance: American Indian Poetry and the Ghost Dance Spirit." *Contemporary Native American Literary and Political Mobilization*. Ed. Bo Scholer. Aarhus, Denmark: SEKLOS, 1984. 160–79.

———. *Indians Are Us? Culture and Genocide in Native North America*. Monroe ME: Common Courage, 1994.

———, ed. *Marxism and Native Americans*. Boston: South End, 1982.

———. "The Tragedy and the Travesty: The Subversion of Indigenous Sovereignty in North America." *American Indian Culture and Research Journal* 22.2 (1998): 1–69.

Clements, William M. *Native American Verbal Art: Texts and Contexts*. Tucson: U of Arizona P, 1996.

Clifford, James. *The Invented Indian: Cultural Fictions and Government Policies.* New Brunswick, NJ: Transaction, 1990.

———. "On Ethnographic Allegory." *Writing Culture: The Poetics and Politics of Ethnography.* Ed. James Clifford and George Marcus. Berkeley: U of California P, 1986. 98–121.

———. *The Predicament of Culture: Twentieth Century Ethnography, Literature, and Art.* Cambridge: Harvard UP, 1988.

Clifford, James, and George Marcus, eds. *Writing Culture: The Poetics and Politics of Ethnography.* Berkeley: U of California P, 1986.

Clifton, James A., ed. *Being and Becoming Indian: Biographic Studies of North American Frontiers.* Chicago: Dorsey, 1989.

Coleman, Michael C. *Presbyterian Missionary Attitudes towards American Indians, 1837–1893.* Jackson: U of Mississippi P, 1985.

Coltelli, Laura. *Winged Words: American Indian Writers Speak.* Lincoln: U of Nebraska P, 1990.

Comstock, W. Richard. "On Seeing with the Eye of a Native European." *Seeing with a Native Eye: Essays on Native American Religion.* Ed. Walter Capps. New York: Harper, 1976. 58-78.

Cook-Lynn, Elizabeth. "American Indian Intellectualism and the New Indian." *American Indian Quarterly* 20.2 (1996): 57–76.

———. "Who Stole Native American Studies?" *Wicazo Sa Review* 12.1 (1997): 9.

———. *Why I Can't Read Wallace Stegner and Other Essays: A Tribal Voice.* Madison: U of Wisconsin P, 1996.

———. "You May Consider Speaking about Your Art . . . ." *I Tell You Now: Autobiographical Essays by Native American Writers.* Ed. Brian Swann and Arnold Krupat. Lincoln: U of Nebraska P, 1987. 57–63.

Copway, George. *Life, Letters and Speeches.* American Indian Lives Series. Ed. A. LaVonne Brown Ruoff and Donald B. Smith. Lincoln: U of Nebraska P, 1997. Rev. ed. of *The Life, History and Travels of Kah-ge-ga-gah-bowh (George Copway), a Young Indian Chief of the Ojebwa Nation, . . . with a Sketch of the Present State of the Ojebwa Nation, in Regard to Christianity and Their Future Prospects* (Albany: Weed and Parsons, 1847); *The Life, Letters and Speeches of Kah-ge-ga-gah-bowh or, G. Copway, Chief Ojibway Nation* (New York: Benedict, 1850); and *Recollections of a Forest Life; or, The Life and Travels of Kah-ge-ga-gah-bowh, or George Copway, Chief of the Ojibway Nation* (London: Gilpin, 1850).

———. *Running Sketches of Men and Places, in England, France, Germany, Belgium, and Scotland.* New York: Riker, 1851.

Cruikshank, Julie. *Life Lived Like a Story: Life Stories of Three Yukon Elders.* In collaboration with Angela Sidney, Kitty Smith, and Annie Ned. Lincoln: U of Nebraska P, 1985.

Culler, Jonathan. *Structuralist Poetics: Structuralism, Linguistics and the Study of Literature.* Ithaca NY: Cornell UP, 1975.

Cultural Property Rights. Spec. issue of *Tribal College: Journal of American Indian Higher Education* 8.2 (1996).

Davis, Shelton H. "Hard Choices: Indigenous Economic Development and Intellectual Property Rights." *Akwe:kon Journal* 10.4 (1993): 19–25.

Deane, Seamus. Introduction. *Nationalism, Colonialism, and Literature.* Minneapolis: U of Minnesota P, 1990.

Delâge, Denys, and Helen Hornbeck Tanner. "The Ojibwa-Jesuit Debate at Walpole Island, 1844." *Ethnohistory* 41.2 (1994): 295–321.

Deloria, Philip J. *Playing Indian.* New Haven: Yale UP, 1998.

Deloria, Vine, Jr. "Comfortable Fictions and the Struggle for Turf: An Essay Review of *The Invented Indian: Cultural Fictions and Government Policies.*" *American Indian Quarterly* 16.3 (1992): 397–410.

———. "Commentary: Research, Redskins, Reality." *American Indian Quarterly* 15 (Fall 1991): 457–68.

———. *Custer Died for Your Sins: An Indian Manifesto.* 1969. Norman: U of Oklahoma P, 1988.

———. *We Talk, You Listen; New Tribes, New Turf.* New York: Macmillan, 1970.

Deloria, Vine, Jr., and Clifford M. Lytle. *The Nations Within: The Past and Future of American Indian Sovereignty.* Austin: U of Texas P, 1984.

Devons, Carol. *Countering Colonization: Native American Women and Great Lakes Missions, 1630–1900.* Berkeley: U of California P, 1992.

Diggins, John Patrick. *The Promise of Pragmatism: Modernism and the Crisis of Knowledge and Authority.* Chicago: U of Chicago P, 1994.

Dilworth, Leah. *Imagining Indians in the Southwest: Persistent Visions of a Primitive Past.* Washington DC: Smithsonian, 1996.

Dippie, Brian. *The Vanishing American: White Attitudes and United States Indian Policy.* Middletown CT: Wesleyan UP, 1982.

Docherty, Brian. *American Crime Fiction: Studies in the Genre.* Houndmills, Basingstoke UK: Macmillan P, 1988.

Donaldson, Laura. "On Medicine Women and White Shame-ans: New Age Native Americanism and Commodity Fettishism as Pop Culture Feminism." *Signs: A Journal of Women and Culture in Society* 24 (Spring): 677–96.

Douglas, Ann. *Terrible Honesty: Mongrel Manhattan in the 1920s.* New York: Farrar, 1995.

Drinnon, Richard. *Facing West: The Metaphysics of Indian-Hating and Empire-Building.* Minneapolis: U of Minnesota P, 1980.

Dubois, William E. *The Souls of Black Folk. Three Negro Classics.* 1903. New York: Avon, 1965.

Dussell, Enrique. *The Invention of the Americas: Eclipse of "the Other" and the Myth of Modernity.* New York: Continuum, 1995.

Eagleton, Terry, Fredric Jameson, and Edward Said. *Nationalism, Colonialism, and Literature.* Minneapolis: U of Minnesota P, 1990.

Eastman, Charles A. *From the Deep Woods to Civilization: Chapters in the Autobiography of an Indian.* 1916. Introd. Raymond Wilson. Lincoln: U of Nebraska P, 1977.

———. *Indian Boyhood.* 1902. New York: Dover, 1971.

Edel, May. "Stability in Tillamook Folklore." *Journal of America Folklore* 57 (1944): 118–27.

———. "The Tillamook Language." *International Journal of American Linguistics* 10.1 (1939): 1–57.

Eliade, Mircea. *The Sacred and the Profane: The Nature of Religion.* New York: Harcourt, 1959.

Elliott, Michael A. "Ethnography, Reform and the Problem of the Real: James Mooney's *Ghost-Dance Religion.*" *American Indian Quarterly* 22.2 (1998): 201–33.

Fabian, Johannes. *Time and the Other: How Anthropology Makes Its Object.* New York: Columbia UP, 1983.

Fanon, Frantz. *Black Skin, White Masks.* New York: Grove P, 1967.

———. *The Wretched of the Earth.* 1961. New York: Grove, 1963.

Farley, Ronnie, ed. *Women of the Native Struggle: Portraits and Testimony of Native American Women.* New York: Orion Books, 1993.

Farrell, Brenda. *Do You See What I Mean? Plains Indian Sign Talk and the Embodiment of Action.* Austin: U of Texas P, 1995.

Feest, Christian. "Europe's Indians." *The Invented Indian: Cultural Fictions and Government Policies.* Ed. James A. Clifton. New Brunswick NJ: Transaction, 1990.

———, ed. *Indians and Europe: An Interdisciplinary Collection of Essays.* Aachen, Germany: Rader Verlag, 1987.

Feraca, Stephen E. *Why Don't They Give Them Guns: The Great American Indian Myth.* Lanham MD: UP of America, 1990.

Ferguson, Suzanne, and Barbara Groseclose, eds. *Literature and the Visual Arts in Contemporary Society.* Columbus: Ohio State UP, 1985.

Fiedler, Leslie. *Love and Death in the American Novel.* New York: Dell, 1960.

Forbes, Jack C. *The Indian in America's Past.* Englewood Cliffs NJ: Prentice, 1964.

Foster, Hal. *Recodings: Art, Spectacle, Cultural Politics.* Port Townsend WA: Bay P, 1985.

Foucault, Michel. *The Archaeology of Knowledge.* Trans. A. M. Sheridan Smith. New York: Harper, 1976.

———. *The History of Sexuality: An Introduction.* 2 vols. 1976. Trans. Robert Hurley. New York: Vintage, 1978.

Francis, Daniel. *The Imaginary Indian: The Image of the Indian in Canadian Culture.* Vancouver: Arsenal Pulp, 1992.

Frayling, Christopher. *Spaghetti Westerns: Cowboys and Europeans from Karl May to Sergio Leone*. London: Routledge, 1981.

Friar, Ralph E., and Natasha A. Friar. *The Only Good Indian: The Hollywood Gospel.* New York: Drama Book Specialists, 1972.

Gaines, Jane M. *Contested Culture: The Image, the Voice, and the Law*. Chapel Hill: U of North Carolina P, 1991.

Gandhi, Leela. *Postcolonial Theory: A Critical Introduction*. New York: Columbia UP, 1998.

Gates, Henry Louis, ed. *"Race," Writing and Difference*. Chicago: U of Chicago P, 1985.

Geertz, Clifford. *Local Knowledge: Further Essays in Interpretive Anthropology*. New York: Basic, 1983.

Georgi-Findlay, Birgitte. "The Frontiers of Native American Women's Writing: Sarah Winnemucca's *Life among the Piutes.*" *New Voices in Native American Literary Criticism*. Ed. Arnold Krupat. Studies in Native American Literature Series. Washington DC: Smithsonian, 1993. 222–52.

Gill, Sam D. *Native American Religions: An Introduction*. Belmont CA: Wadsworth, 1982.

Gilroy, Paul. *The Black Atlantic: Modernity and Double Consciousness*. London: Verso, 1993.

Girard, René. *La violence et le sacré*. Paris: Grasset, 1972.

Glass-Coffin, Bonnie. "Anthropology, Shamanism, and the 'New Age.'" *Chronicle of Higher Education* 15 June 1994: A48.

Graff, Gerald. "Co-optation." *The New Historicism*. Ed. H. Aram Veeser. New York: Routledge, 1989. 168–81.

Graham, Wade. "Cash Cow: It's Buffalo, the Other Red Meat." *New Yorker* 20 and 27 Oct. 1997: 96–98.

Greenblatt, Stephen J. "Learning to Curse: Aspects of Linguistic Colonialism in the Sixteenth Century." *First Images of America: The Impact of the New World on the Old*. Ed. Fredi Chiappelli. Vol. 2. Berkeley: U of California P, 1976. 561–80.

———. *Marvelous Possessions: The Wonder of the New World*. Chicago: U of Chicago P, 1991.

Harlow, Ralph Volney. *The United States: From Wilderness to World Power*. New York: Holt, 1958.

Harris, Cheryl I. "Whiteness as Property." *Harvard Law Review* 106.8 (1993): 1707–91.

Hartley, Marsden. *The Collected Poems of Marsden Hartley, 1904–1943*. Ed. Gail R. Scott. Santa Rosa CA: Black Sparrow, 1987.

———. "Red Man Ceremonials: An American Plea for American Esthetics." *Art and Archaeology* 9.1 (1920): 7–14.

Harvey, David. *The Condition of Postmodernity: An Enquiry into the Origins of Cultural Change*. Oxford: Basil Blackwell, 1989.

Hauptman, Laurence M. *Tribes and Tribulations: Misconceptions about American Indians and Their Histories*. Albuquerque: U of New Mexico P, 1995.

The Havasupai and the Hualapai. *Arizona State Teachers College Bulletin* [Flagstaff] 21.5 (1940).

Henry, George (Maungwudaus). *An Account of the Chippewa Indians, Who Have Been Travelling among the Whites, in the United States, England, Ireland, Scotland, France and Belgium*. Boston: Author, 1848.

Hillerman, Tony. *Talking God*. New York: Harper, 1989.

Highwater, Jamake. *The Primal Mind: Vision and Reality in Indian America*. New York: Harper, 1981.

———. *Shadow Show: An Autobiographical Insinuation*. New York: Alfred Van Der Marck, 1986.

Hobson, Archie, ed. *Remembering America: A Sampler of the WPA American Guide Series*. Introd. Bill Stott. New York: Columbia UP, 1985.

Hogan, Linda. "Return: Buffalo." *Native American Literature: A Brief Introduction and Anthology*. Ed. Gerald Vizenor. New York: Harper, 1995. 265–67.

———. *Seeing through the Sun*. Amherst: U of Massachusetts P, 1985.

Honour, Hugh. *The New Golden Land*. New York: Pantheon, 1975.

hooks, bell. "Representing Whiteness in the Black Imagination." *Cultural Studies*. Ed. Lawrence Grossberg, Cary Nelson, and Paula A. Treichler. New York: Routledge, 1992. 338–408.

The Hopi. *Arizona State Teachers College Bulletin* [Flagstaff] 18.2 (1937).

Howard, James H. "The Native American Image in Western Europe." *American Indian Quarterly* 4.1 (1978): 33–56.

Howard, Kathleen L., and Diana F. Pardue. *Inventing the Southwest: The Fred Harvey Company and Native American Art*. Flagstaff: Northland, 1996.

Huggan, Graham. "Decolonizing the Map." *The Post-colonial Studies Reader*. Ed. Bill Ashcroft, Gareth Griffiths, and Helen Tiffin. London: Routledge, 1995. 407–11.

Hutcheon, Linda. "Circling the Downspout of Empire: Post-colonialism and Postmodernism." *Ariel* 20.4 (1989): 149–75. Excerpted in *The Post-colonial Studies Reader*. Ed. Bill Ashcroft, Gareth Griffiths, and Helen Tiffin. London: Routledge, 1995. 130–35.

Hutchins, Robert. Online posting. 24 June 1994. AMLIT Discussion Group. 10 Nov. 2000 *http://tile.net/lists/amlitlamerican.html*.

Hymes, Dell H. *"In Vain I Tried to Tell You": Essays in Native American Ethnopoetics*. Philadelphia: U of Pennsylvania P, 1981.

———. "In Need of a Wife: Clara Pearson's Split-His-(Own)-Head." *American Indian Linguistics and Ethnography in Honor of Laurence C. Thompson*. Ed. A. Mattina and T. Montler. Occasional Papers in Linguistics, no. 10. Missoula: U of Montana, 1993. 127–62.

Italie, Hillel. "The Many Lives of Sherman Alexie." *Associated Press* 10 May 2000. 12 Nov. 2000 *www.thenavajotimes.com/Sunny/Sherman_Alexie/sherman_alexie.html*.

Jackson, David. "Jamake Highwater's Native Intelligence." *Village Voice* 3 May 1983: 37–38.

Jackson, Michael. *Paths toward a Clearing: Radical Empiricism and Ethnographic Inquiry*. Bloomington: Indiana UP, 1989.

Jacobs, Alex. "The Politics of Primitivism: Concerns and Attitudes in Indian Art." *Akwe:kon* 2.3 (1985): 1–3.

Jacobs, Elizabeth. Tillamook Field Notebooks and Research Notes. Melville Jacobs Collection, U of Washington Archives, Seattle, Washington.

Jacobs, Elizabeth, and Melville Jacobs. *Nehalem Tillamook Tales*. Introd. Jarold Ramsey. Corvallis: Oregon State UP, 1990.

Jacobs, Melville. *The Content and Style of an Oral Literature*. New York: Wenner-Gren, 1959.

———. "Fate of Indian Oral Literatures." *Northwest Review* 3 (Summer 1962): 90–99.

———. *The People Are Coming Soon*. Seattle: U of Washington P, 1960.

Jaggar, Alison M., and Susan R. Bordo. *Gender/Body/Knowledge: Feminist Reconstructions of Being and Knowing*. New Brunswick NJ: Rutgers UP, 1989.

Jahner, Elaine. "An Act of Attention: Event Structure in *Ceremony*." *American Indian Quarterly* 5 (1979): 37–46.

Jameson, Fredric. *Marxism and Form: Twentieth Century Dialectical Theories of Literature*. Princeton NJ: Princeton UP, 1971.

Jaskowski, Helen, ed. *Early Native American Writing: New Critical Essays*. New York: Cambridge UP, 1996.

The Jesuit Relations and Allied Documents. Travels and Explorations of the Jesuit Missionaries in New France, 1610–1761. Ed. Reuben Gold Thwaites. 73 vols. Cleveland: Burrows Brothers, 1896–1901.

Johnson, Charles. *Being and Race: Black Writing since 1970*. Bloomington: Indiana UP, 1988.

Johnson, E. Pauline. *The Moccasin Maker*. 1913. Ed. and introd. A. LaVonne Brown Ruoff. Tucson: U of Arizona P, 1987. Rpt. Norman: U of Oklahoma P, 1998.

Jonaitis, Aldon. "Creations of Mystics and Philosophers: The White Man's Perceptions of Northwest Coast Indian Art from the 1930s to the Present." *American Indian Culture and Research Journal* 5.1 (1981): 1–46.

Jones, Peter. *History of the Ojebway Indians, with Especial Reference to Their Conversion to Christianity*. 1861. Freeport NY: Books for Libraries, 1970.

Kasson, Joy S. *Buffalo Bill's Wild West: Memory, Celebrity, and Popular History*. New York: Hill, 2000.

Keiser, Albert. *The Indian in American Literature*. 1933. New York: Octagon, 1970.

Kelley, Isabel T. "Northern Paiute Tales." *Journal of American Folk-Lore* 51.202 (1938): 363–438.

King, Thomas. *All My Relations: An Anthology of Contemporary Canadian Native Fiction.* Toronto: McClelland, 1990.

———. *Green Grass, Running Water.* New York: Houghton, 1993.

King, Thomas, Cheryl Calver, and Helen Hoy, eds. *The Native in Literature.* Toronto: ECW, 1987.

Kirst, Sean. "Native Leader Appeals for Understanding." *Syracuse Post Standard* 29 Jan. 1999: B1, B5.

Konkle, Maureen. "Indian Literacy, U.S. Colonialism and Literary Criticism." *American Literature* 69.3 (1997): 457–86.

Kroeber, A. L. "Sign Language Inquiry." *Aboriginal Sign Languages of the Americas and Australia.* Ed. D. Jean Umiker-Sebeok and Thomas A. Sebeok. Vol. 2. New York: Plenum, 1978. 185–204.

Kroeber, Karl. "Reasoning Together." *Canadian Review of American Studies* 12.2 (1981): 253–70.

Krupat, Arnold. *Ethnocriticism: Ethnography, History, Literature.* Berkeley: U of California P, 1992.

———. *For Those Who Come After: A Study of Native American Autobiography.* Berkeley: U of California P, 1985.

———. *The Turn to the Native: Studies in Criticism and Culture.* Lincoln: U of Nebraska P, 1996.

———. *The Voice in the Margin: Native American Literature and the Canon.* Berkeley: U of California P, 1989.

Krupat, Arnold, and Brian Swann. *Here First: Autobiographical Essays by Native American Writers.* New York: Modern Library, 2000.

Lacombe, Alain. *Le roman noir américain.* Paris: Union Générale d'Editions, 10/18, 1975.

LaDuke, Winona. "Return of Buffalo Nation: For Native Peoples of the Plains, Visions of a Buffalo Commons." *Native Americas* 15.4 (1998): 10–21.

Larson, Charles R. *American Indian Fiction.* Albuquerque: U of New Mexico P, 1978.

Lears, T. J. Jackson. "The Concept of Cultural Hegemony: Problems and Possibilities." *American Historical Review* 90.3 (1985): 567-93.

Leon-Pórtilla, Miguel. *Endangered Cultures.* 1976. Trans. Julie Goodson-Lawes. Dallas: Southern Methodist UP, 1990.

Leuthold, Steven. *Indigenous Aesthetics: Native Art, Media and Identity.* Austin: U of Texas P, 1998.

———. "Native American Responses to the Western." *American Indian Culture and Research Journal* 19.1 (1995): 153–89.

Lévi-Strauss, Claude. *The View from Afar.* Oxford: Basil Blackwell, 1985.

Lewis, R. W. B. *The American Adam: Innocence, Tragedy, and Tradition in the Nineteenth Century.* Chicago: U of Chicago P, 1955.

Lincoln, Kenneth. *Native American Renaissance.* 1983. 2nd ed. Berkeley: U of California P, 1985.

Lofaro, Michael A. *Davy Crockett: The Man, the Legend, the Legacy.* Knoxville: U of Tennessee P, 1985.

Louis, Adrian C. *Among the Dog-Eaters.* Albuquerque: West End, 1992.

———. *Vortex of Indian Fevers.* Evanston IL: Northwestern UP, 1995.

Love, William Deloss. *Samson Occom and the Christian Indians of New England.* Boston: Pilgrim, 1899.

Lubbers, Klaus. *Born for the Shade: Stereotypes of the Native American in United States Literature and the Visual Arts, 1776–1894.* Amsterdam Monographs in American Studies, no. 3. Atlanta: Rodopi, 1994.

Ludington, Townsend. *Marsden Hartley: The Biography of an American Artist.* Boston: Little, 1992.

Lunn, Eugene. *Marxism and Modernism: An Historical Study of Lukacs, Brecht, Benjamin and Adorno.* London: Verso, 1982.

Lutz, Hartmut. *"Indianer" und "Native Americans": Zur sozial-und literarhistorischen Vermittlung eines Stereotyps.* Hildesheim, Germany: Olms, 1985.

Lyman, Christopher. *The Vanishing Race and Other Illusions: Photographs of Indians by Edward S. Curtis.* New York: Pantheon, 1982.

Lyotard, Jean-Francois. *The Differend: Phrases in Dispute.* Minneapolis: U of Minnesota P, 1989.

———. *Lessons on the Analytic Sublime.* Trans. Elizabeth Rothenberg. Stanford CA: Stanford UP, 1994.

———. *The Postmodern Condition: A Report on Knowledge.* Trans. Geoff Bennington and Brian Massumi. Minneapolis: U of Minnesota P, 1984.

Manganaro, Marc, ed. *Modernist Anthropology: From Fieldwork to Text.* Princeton NJ: Princeton UP, 1990.

Mangione, Jerre. *The Dream and the Deal: The Federal Writers' Project, 1935–1943.* New York: Equinox, 1972.

Masayesva, Victor, Jr., dir. *Imagining Indians.* Film/videocassette. Hoteville, AZ: Isis Productions, 1993.

McBride, Bunny. *Molly Spotted Elk: A Penobscot in Paris.* Norman: U of Oklahoma P, 1995.

McCay, Bonnie J., and Louise Fortmann, eds. *Voices from the Commons: Evolving Relations of Property and Management.* Spec. issue of *Cultural Survival Quarterly* 20.1 (1996).

McClaren, Peter. *Revolutionary Multiculturalism: Pedagogies of Dissent for the New Millennium.* Boulder CO: Westview, 1997.

McKinnon, C. A. "Feminism, Marxism, Method and the State." *Feminist Theory: A Critique of Ideology.* Ed. N. Keohane, M. Rosaldo, and B. Gelpi. Chicago: U of Chicago P, 1982.

McNickle, D'Arcy. *Runner in the Sun: A Story of Indian Maize.* 1954. Afterword Alfonso Ortiz. Albuquerque: New Mexico UP, 1987.

McQuade, Donald, ed. *The Harper American Literature.* 3rd ed. New York: Harper, 1996.

Medium Rare: A Publication of the Native American Journalists Association Winter 1993: 7 [summary of meeting with Ted Turner].

Memmi, Albert. *The Colonizer and the Colonized.* 1957. Trans. Howard Greenfield. Expanded ed. Introd. Jean-Paul Sartre. Afterword Susan Gilson Miller. Boston: Beacon, 1991.

Mihesuah, Devon A. "Suggested Guidelines for Institutions with Scholars Who Conduct Research on American Indians." *American Indian Culture and Research Journal* 17.3 (1993): 131–40.

———. "Voices, Interpretations, and the New Indian History: Comments on the *American Indian Quarterly*'s Special Issue on Writing about American Indians." *Writing about (Writing about) American Indians.* Spec. issue of *American Indian Quarterly* 20.1 (1996): 91–108.

Miller, Jay. "The Matter of the (Thoughtful) Heart: Centrality, Focality, or Overlap." *Journal of Anthropological Research* 36.3 (1980): 338–42.

Miller, Marilyn, and Marian Faux, eds. *The New York Public Library American History Desk Reference.* New York: Macmillan, 1997.

Mitchell, Lee Clark. *Witnesses to a Vanishing American: The Nineteenth Century Response.* Princeton NJ: Princeton UP, 1981.

Moffitt, John, and Santiago Sebastian. *O Brave New People: The European Invention of the American Indian.* Albuquerque: U of New Mexico P, 1996.

Momaday, N. Scott. *The Ancient Child.* New York: Perennial-Harper, 1989.

———. *House Made of Dawn.* New York: Perennial-Harper, 1989.

———. *The Names: A Memoir.* Tucson: U of Arizona P, 1976.

Moore, David L. "Decolonializing Criticism: Reading Dialectics and Dialogics in Native American Literatures." *Studies in American Indian Literatures (SAIL)* 6.4 (1994): 7–35.

———. Introduction. *Cultural Property in American Indian Literatures: Representation and Interpretation.* Spec. issue of *American Indian Quarterly* 21.4 (1997): 545–54.

———. "Myth, History, and Identity in Silko and Young Bear: Postcolonial Praxis." *New Voices in Native American Literary Criticism.* Ed. Arnold Krupat. Washington DC: Smithsonian, 1993. 370–95.

———. "Rough Knowledge and Radical Understanding: Sacred Silence in American Indian Literatures." *American Indian Quarterly* 21.4 (1997): 633–62.

———. "Silko's Blood Sacrifice: The Circulating Witness in *Almanac of the Dead.*" *Leslie Marmon Silko: A Collection of Critical Essays.* Ed. Louise Barnett and James Thorson. Albuquerque: U of New Mexico P, 1999.

Morrison, Howard. *American Encounters: A Companion to the Exhibition at the National Museum of American History.* Washington DC: Smithsonian, 1992.

Mourning Dove [Christine Quintasket]. *Cogewea, the Half-Blood: A Depiction of the Great Montana Cattle Range.* With notes and biographical sketch by Lucullus Virgil McWhorter. 1927. Introd. Dexter Fisher. Lincoln: U of Nebraska P, 1981.

Muratorio, Blanca. *The Life and Times of Grandfather Alonso: Culture and History in the Upper Amazon.* New Brunswick NJ: Rutgers UP, 1991.

Murray, David. *Forked Tongues: Speech, Writing and Representation in North American Indian Texts.* Bloomington: Indiana UP, 1991.

———, ed. *Literary Theory and Poetry: Extending the* Canon. London: B. T. Batsford, 1989.

———. "Racial Identity and Self-Invention: The Red and the Black." *Race and Writing.* Ed. Tim Youngs. London: Longmans, 1997. 80–101.

Nabokov, Peter, ed. *Native American Testimony: A Chronicle of Indian-White Relations from Prophecy to the Present, 1492–1992.* Foreword Vine Deloria, Jr. Expanded ed. New York: Viking, 1991.

Nason, James D. "Native American Intellectual Property Rights: Issues in the Control of Esoteric Knowledge." *Borrowed Power: Essays on Cultural Appropriation.* Ed. Bruce Ziff. New Brunswick NJ: Rutgers UP, 1996. 237–54.

Neihardt, John G. *Black Elk Speaks.* New York: Pocket Books, 1973.

Nequatewa, Edmund. *Truth of a Hopi: Stories Relating to the Origin, Myths, and Clan Histories of the Hopi.* 1936. Flagstaff: Northland, 1967.

O'Brien, Sharon. "Tribes and Indians: With Whom Does the United States Maintain a Relationship?" *Notre Dame Law Review* 66: 5 (1991): 1461–1502.

O'Connell, Barry. Introduction. *On Our Own Ground: The Complete Writings of William Apess, a Pequot.* Amherst: U of Massachusetts P, 1992.

O'Connor, John. *The Hollywood Indian: Stereotypes of Native Americans in Films.* Trenton: New Jersey State Museum, 1980.

Ong, Walter. *Orality and Literacy: The Technologizing of the Word.* London: Routledge, 1988.

Opler, Morris E., ed. *Myths and Tales of the Jicarilla Apache Indians.* Memoirs of the American Folklore Society, vol. 31. 1938. New York: Dover, 1994.

Ortiz, Alfonso. Afterword. *Runner in the Sun: A Story of Indian Maize.* By D'Arcy McNickle. Albuquerque: U of New Mexico P, 1987.

Ortiz, Simon. "Indians Sure Come in Handy." *Fight Back: For the Sake of the People, For the Sake of the Land. INAD Literary Journal* 1.1 (1980): 4. Albuquerque: Institute for

Native American Development, Native American Studies, U of New Mexico, 1980. Reprinted in *Woven Stone*. Tucson: U of Arizona P, 1992. 296–97.

———. "Song/Poetry and Language: Expression and Perception." *Symposium of the Whole: A Range of Discourses toward an Ethnopoetics*. Ed. Jerome Rothenberg and Diane Rothenberg. Berkeley: U of California P, 1983. 399–407.

Owens, Louis. *Bone Games*. Norman: U of Oklahoma P, 1994.

———. *Mixedblood Messages: Literature, Film, Family, Place*. Norman: U of Oklahoma P, 1998.

———. *Nightland*. New York: Dutton, 1996.

———. *Other Destinies: Understanding the American Indian Novel*. Norman: U of Oklahoma P, 1990.

———. *The Sharpest Sight*. Norman: U of Oklahoma P, 1992.

———. *Wolfsong*. Albuquerque: West End, 1991.

The Papago. Arizona State Teachers College Bulletin [Flagstaff] 20.3 (1939).

Parry, Benita. "Resistance Theory/Theorising Resistance; or, Two Cheers for Nativism." *Colonial Discourse/Postcolonial Theory*. Ed. Francis Barker, Peter Hulme, and Margaret Iversen. Manchester: Manchester UP/St. Martin's, 1994. 172–96.

Parry, Elwood. *The Image of the Indian and the Black Man in American Art, 1590–1900*. New York: George Braziller, 1974.

Pearce, Roy H. *Savagism and Civilization: A Study of the Indian and the American Mind*. 1953. Foreword Arnold Krupat. Berkeley: U of California P, 1988. Rpt. of *The Savages of America*. 1953.

Penkower, Monty Noam. *The Federal Writers' Project: A Study in Government Patronage of the Arts*. Urbana: U of Illinois P, 1977.

Penn, William S. *As We Are Now: Mixblood Essays on Race and Identity*. Berkeley: U of California P, 1997.

Pernal, Mary. Letter. *Ithaca Journal* 29 Jan. 1999: 9A.

Peterson, Nancy J. "Introduction: Native American Literature — From the Margins to the Mainstream." *Modern Fiction Studies* 45.1 (1999): 3.

Phinney, Archie. *Nez Perce Texts*. Columbia University Contributions to Anthropology, vol. 25. New York: Columbia UP, 1934.

Pinsky, Robert. *The Situation of Poetry: Contemporary Poetry and Its Traditions*. Princeton, NJ: Princeton UP, 1976.

Potter, Greg. Letter. *Ithaca Journal* 29 Jan. 1999: 9A.

Prats, Armando José. "His Master's Voice(over): Revisionist Ethos and Narrative Dependence from *Broken Arrow* (1950) to *Geronimo: An American Legend* (1993)." *ANQ: Quarterly Journal of Short Articles, Notes, and Reviews* 9.3 (1996): 15–29.

Rainwater, Catherine. *Dreams of Fiery Stars: The Transformations of Native American Fiction*. Philadelphia: U of Pennsylvania P, 1999.

Ramsey, Jarold, ed. *Coyote Was Going There: Indian Literature of the Oregon Country.* Seattle: U of Washington P, 1977.

———. *Reading the Fire: Essays in the Traditional Indian Literatures of America.* Seattle: U of Washington P, 1999.

Rand, Rev. Silas, ed. *Legends of the Micmacs.* Wellesley Philological Publications. New York: Longmans, Green, 1894.

Rawls, James J. *Indians of California: The Changing Image.* Norman: U of Oklahoma P, 1984.

Revard, Carter. "Walking among the Stars." *I Tell You Now: Autobiographical Essays by Native American Writers.* Ed. Brian Swann and Arnold Krupat. Lincoln: U of Nebraska P, 1987. 65–84.

Ridge, John Rollin. *The Life and Adventures of Joaquín Murieta, the Celebrated California Bandit.* 1854. Introd. Joseph Henry Jackson. Norman: U of Oklahoma P, 1977.

Rigal-Cellard, Bernadette. "Analyse de deux mises en scène interculturelles du sujet: Les pactes autobiographiques de Momaday dans *The Names* et de Vizenor dans *Interior Landscapes*." *Annales de* CRAA 18 (1993): 161–74.

———. "*House Made of Dawn* de Scott Momaday: La course d'Abel, ou comment franchir le mur du silence." *Annales du* CRAA 15 (1990): 63–78.

———. "A Reading of the Prologue of *House Made of Dawn*." *Forum: Native American Literatures.* Ed. Laura Coltelli. 2/3 (1992): 39–56.

Rios, Theodore. "Telling a Good One: A Papago Autobiography." *MELUS* 10.3 (1983): 55–65.

Robinson, Harry. *Nature Power: In the Spirit of an Okanagan Storyteller.* Ed. Wendy Wickwire. Seattle: U of Washington P, 1993.

Root, Deborah. *Cannibal Culture: Art, Appropriation and the Commodification of Difference.* Boulder CO: Westview, 1996.

Rosaldo, Renato. *Culture and Truth: The Remaking of Social Analysis.* Boston: Beacon, 1989.

Rubin, William, ed. *"Primitivism" in 20th Century Art: Affinity of the Tribal and the Modern.* New York: Museum of Modern Art, 1984.

Ruoff, A. LaVonne Brown. *American Indian Literatures: An Introduction, Bibliographic Review, and Selected Bibliography.* New York: MLA, 1990.

———. "Early Native American Women Authors: Jane Johnston Schoolcraft, Sarah Winnemucca, S. Alice Callahan, E. Pauline Johnson, and Zitkala-Ša." *Nineteenth-Century American Women Writers: A Critical Reader.* Ed. Karen Kilcup. Malden MA: Blackwells, 1998. 81–111.

———. "History of Written Literature." *American Indian Literatures: An Introduction, Bibliographic Review and Selected Bibliography.* New York: MLA, 1990. 62–115.

Russo, Mel, and Connie Talbot. Letter. *Ithaca Journal* 29 Jan. 1999: 9A.

Ryan, Michael, and Douglas Kellner. *Camera Politica: The Politics and Ideology of Contemporary Hollywood Film*. Bloomington: Indiana UP, 1988.

Sahagún, Bernardino de. *General History of the Things of New Spain: Florentine Codex*. Trans. Arthur J. O. Anderson, Charles E. Dibble, et al. Monographs of the School of American Research, no. 14. 13 vols. in 12. Salt Lake City: U of Utah P, 1950–82.

Said, Edward W. *Culture and Imperialism*. New York: Vintage, 1994.

———. *Orientalism*. New York: Random, 1978.

Sands, Kathleen M. "Collaboration and Colonialism: Native American Women's Autobiography." *MELUS* 22.4 (1997): 39–59.

———. "Telling a Good One: A Papago Autobiography." *MELUS* 10.3 (1983): 55–65.

Sands, Kathleen M., and Allison Sekaquaptewa Lewis. "Seeing with a Native Eye: A Hopi Film on Hopi." *American Indian Quarterly* 14.4 (1990): 387–96.

Santos, Paula Mota. "Good Indians and Bad Indians: The European Perspective of Native Americans as Depicted in 'The Mission' and 'Black Robe.'" *Native American Women in Literature and Culture*. Ed. Susan Castillo and Victor M. P. Da Rosa. Porto, Portugal: Fernando Pessoa University Press, 1997.

Sarris, Greg. *Keeping Slug Woman Alive: A Holistic Approach to American Indian Texts*. Berkeley: U of California P, 1993.

Sauer, Carl Ortwin. *Sixteenth-Century North America: The Land and the People as Seen by the Europeans*. Berkeley: U of California P, 1971.

Savage, William, ed. *Indian Life: Transforming an American Myth*. Norman: U of Oklahoma P, 1977.

Sayre, Gordon M. *Les Sauvages Americains: Representations of Native Americans in French and English Colonial Literature*. Chapel Hill: U of North Carolina P, 1997.

Scheckel, Susan. *The Insistence of the Indian: Race and Nationalism in Nineteenth Century American Culture*. Princeton NJ: Princeton UP, 1998.

Scheick, William J. *The Half-Blood: A Cultural Symbol in 19th Century American Fiction*. Lexington: UP of Kentucky, 1979.

Scheper-Hughes, Nancy, and Margaret M. Lock. "The Mindful Body." *Medical Anthropology Quarterly* 1.1 (1987): 6–41.

Scholer, Bo, ed. *Coyote Was Here: Essays on Contemporary Native American Literary and Political Mobilization*. Aarhus, Denmark: SEKLOS, 1984.

Schrader, Robert Fay. *The Indian Arts and Crafts Board: An Aspect of New Deal Indian Policy*. Albuquerque: U of New Mexico P, 1983.

Schubnell, Matthias. *N. Scott Momaday: The Cultural and Literary Background*. Norman: U of Oklahoma P, 1985.

Sekaquaptewa, Helen, and Louise Udall. *Me and Mine: The Life Story of Helen Sekaquaptewa*. Tucson: U of Arizona P, 1969.

Sexson, Lynda. *Ordinarily Sacred*. New York: Crossroad, 1982.

Shanley, Kathryn. "Bloodties and Blasphemy: American Indian Women and the Problem of History." *Is Academic Feminism Dead: Theory in Practice*. New York: New York UP, 2000. 204–32.

Shoemaker, Nancy. *Negotiators of Change: Historical Perspectives on Native American Women*. New York: Routledge, 1995.

Silko, Leslie Marmon. *Almanac of the Dead*. New York: Penguin Books, 1992.

———. *Ceremony*. New York: Penguin, 1986.

———. "Leslie Marmon Silko Interview." By Kim Barnes. *Journal of Ethnic Studies* 3 (Winter 1986): 83–105.

———. *Storyteller*. New York: Seaver, 1981.

Simmons, William S. *Spirit of the New England Tribes: Indian History and Folklore, 1620–1984*. Hanover: UP of New England, 1986.

Sioux Memorial Issue. Spec. issue of *Nebraska History: A Quarterly History* 21.4 (1940).

Slotkin, Richard. *Regeneration through Violence: The Mythology of the American Frontier, 1600–1860*. Middletown CT: Wesleyan UP, 1973.

Smith, Dinitia. "American Indian Writers Offer Fresh Perspective: New Generation Eschews Traditional Elements in Hard-Edged, Urban Tales." *Minneapolis Star Tribune* 27 April 1997: F15.

Smith, Donald B. *Sacred Feathers: The Reverend Peter Jones (Kahkewaquonaby) and the Mississauga Indians*. American Indian Lives Series. Lincoln: U of Nebraska P, 1987.

Sollors, Werner. *Beyond Ethnicity: Consent and Descent in American Culture*. New York: Oxford UP , 1986.

———, ed. *The Invention of Ethnicity*. New York: Oxford UP, 1989.

Soros, George. "The Capitalist Threat." *Atlantic Monthly* 279.2 (1997): 45–58.

Spivak, Gayatri Chakravorty. *In Other Worlds: Essays in Cultural Politics*. New York: Routledge, 1988.

———, trans. "Translator's Preface." *Of Grammatology*. By Jacques Derrida. Baltimore: Johns Hopkins UP, 1997.

Sprague, John T. *The Origin, Progress, and Conclusion of the Florida War*. New York: Appleton, 1848. Gainesville: U of Florida P, 1964.

Sprague, W. B. *Annals of the American Pulpit*. 9 vols. New York, 1857–69.

Stedman, Raymond William. *Shadows of the Indian: Stereotypes in American Culture*. Norman: U of Oklahoma P, 1982.

Stone, William. *The Life of Joseph Brant-Thayendanegea*. 2 vols. New York, 1838. St. Clair Shores MI: Scholarly, 1970.

Sullivan, Andrew. "There Will Always Be England." *New York Times Magazine* 21 Feb. 1999: 38.

Swann, Brian, and Arnold Krupat. *I Tell You Now: Autobiographical Essays by Native American Writers*. Lincoln: U of Nebraska P, 1987.

Swiderski, Richard M. *Lives between Cultures: A Study of Human Nature, Identity, and Culture.* Juneau AK: Denali, 1991.

Tapahonso, Luci. *Saanii Dahataal, the Women Are Singing.* Tucson: U of Arizona P, 1993.

Tedlock, Barbara. "The Clown's Way." *Teachings from the American Earth: Indian Religion and Philosophy.* Ed. by Dennis Tedlock and Barbara Tedlock. New York: Liveright, 1975. 105–18.

"The Theory of Devolution." Editorial. *Los Angeles Times* n.d. Rpt. *Ithaca Journal* 19 May 1999: 9A.

Thoreau, Henry David. "Walking." *Walden and Other Writings of Henry David Thoreau.* Ed. Brooks Atkinson. New York: Modern Library, 1937. 595–632.

Todorov, Tzvetan. *The Conquest of America: The Question of the Other.* 1982. Trans. Richard Howard. New York: Harper, 1984.

———. "'Race,' Writing and Culture." Trans. Loulou Mack. *"Race," Writing and Difference.* Ed. Henry Louis Gates Jr. Chicago: U of Chicago P, 1985. 370–80.

———. "Typologie du roman policier." *Poétique de la prose.* Paris: Seuil, 1971. 55–65.

Tompkins, Jane. "At the Buffalo Bill Museum — June 1988." *South Atlantic Quarterly* 89.3 (1990): 525–45.

Trend, David. *Cultural Pedagogy: Art/Education/Politics.* New York: Bergin and Garvey, 1992.

Trinh, T. Minh-ha. *Woman, Native, Other.* Bloomington: Indiana UP, 1989.

———. *When the Moon Waxes Red: Representations, Gender, and Cultural Politics.* New York: Routledge, 1991.

Tsosie, Rebecca. "Surviving the War by Singing the Blues: The Contemporary Ethos of American Indian Political Poetry." *American Indian Culture and Research Journal* 10.3 (1986): 25–52.

Turner, Frederick W., III, ed. *The Portable North American Indian Reader.* New York: Viking, 1974.

Umiker-Sebeok, D. Jean, and Thomas A. Sebeok, eds. *Aboriginal Sign Languages of the Americas and Australia.* Vol. 2. New York: Plenum, 1978.

United Nations Information Centre in Sydney for Australia, New Zealand, and the South Pacific. E-mail to David L. Moore. 25 Nov. 1992.

Vickers, Scott B. *Native American Identities: From Stereotypes to Archetype in Art and Literature.* Albuquerque: U of New Mexico P, 1998.

Vizenor, Gerald. *Dead Voices: Natural Agonies in the New World.* Norman: U of Oklahoma P, 1992.

———. *Fugitive Poses.* Lincoln: U of Nebraska P, 1998.

———. "*Harold of Orange*: A Screenplay." *Studies in American Indian Literatures* 5.3 (1993): 53–88.

————. *Hotline Healers*. Hanover NH: UP of New England, 1997.

————. *Manifest Manners: Postindian Warriors of Survivance*. Hanover NH: Wesleyan UP, 1994.

————. *Narrative Chance: Postmodern Discourse on Native American Indian Literatures*. Norman: U of Oklahoma P, 1989.

————, ed. *Native American Literature: A Brief Introduction and Anthology*. New York: HarperCollins, 1995.

————. "The Ruins of Representation: Shadow Survivance and the Literature of Dominance." *American Indian Quarterly* 17.1 (1993): 7–30.

————. *Trickster of Liberty: Tribal Heirs to a Wild Baronage*. Minneapolis: Minnesota UP, 1988.

Walker, Cheryl. *Indian Nation: Native American Literature and Nineteenth-Century Nationalisms*. New Americanists Series. Durham: Duke U P, 1997.

Walters, Anna Lee. *Ghost Singer*. Flagstaff: Northland, 1988.

————, ed. *Neon Pow Wow: New Native American Voices of the Southwest*. Flagstaff: Northland, 1993.

————. *The Sun Is Not Merciful*. Ithaca NY: Firebrand, 1985.

————. *Talking Indian: Reflections on Survival and Writing*. Ithaca NY: Firebrand, 1992.

Warren, William. *A History of the Ojibway Nation, Based on Traditions and Oral Statements*. Collections of the Minnesota Historical Society, no. 5 (1885). Minneapolis: Ross and Haines, 1957. Introd. W. Roger Buffalohead. Minneapolis: Minnesota Historical Society, 1984.

Warrior, Robert Allen. *Tribal Secrets: Recovering American Indian Intellectual Traditions*. Minneapolis: U of Minnesota P, 1994.

Washburn, Wilcomb E. *The Indian and the White Man*. Garden City NY: Anchor, 1964.

Waters, Frank. *Mexico Mystique: The Coming Sixth World of Consciousness*. Chicago: Sage, 1979.

Wax, Murray L. "The Ethics of Research in American Indian Communities." *American Indian Quarterly* 15 (Fall 1991): 413–56.

Weatherford, Jack McIver. *Indian Givers: How the Indians of the Americas Transformed the World*. New York: Crown, 1988.

Weaver, Jace. *That the People Might Live: Native American Literature and Native American Community*. New York: Oxford UP, 1997.

Weisberger, Bernard A., ed. *The WPA Guide to America: The Best of 1930s America as Seen by the Federal Writers' Project. Selections from the American Guide Series, Written by the Federal Writers' Project of the Works Progress Administration, 1935–1941*. New York: Pantheon, 1985.

Welch, James. *The Death of Jim Loney*. New York: Harper, 1979.

————. *Fools Crow*. New York: Viking, 1986.

————. *Winter in the Blood*. New York: Harper, 1974.

White, Richard. *The Middle Ground. Indians, Empires, and Republics in the Great Lakes Region, 1650–1815.* Cambridge: Cambridge UP, 1991.

Whitman, Walt. *Leaves of Grass.* Ed. Sculley Bradley and Harold W. Blodgett. New York: Norton, 1973.

Wilkerson, Charles. *Time, American Indians, and the Law.* New Haven: Yale UP, 1987.

Williams, Robert A. *The American Indian in Western Legal Thought: The Discourses of Conquest.* New York: Oxford UP, 1989.

Wilson, Michael, and David L. Moore. "Staying Afloat in a Chaotic World: A Conversation with Ray Young Bear." *Akwe:kon Journal* 9.4 (1992): 22–26.

Winnemucca, Sarah [Hopkins]. *Life among the Piutes: Their Wrongs and Claims.* Ed. Mrs. Horace Mann. 1883. Bishop CA: Chalfant, 1969.

Womack, Craig. "Howling at the Moon: Queer but True Story of My Life as a Hank Williams Song." *As We Are Now: Mixblood Essays on Race and Identity.* Ed. William S. Penn. Berkeley: U of California P, 1997. 28–49.

Wong, Hertha Dawn. *Sending My Heart Back across the Years: Tradition and Innovation in Native American Autobiography.* New York: Oxford UP, 1992.

Woodmansee, Martha, and Peter Jaszi, eds. *The Construction of Authorship: Textual Appropriation in Law and Literature.* Durham: Duke UP, 1994.

WPA Staff. *Washington, DC: A City and a Capital.* Temecula CA: Reprint Services, 1989.

Xie, Shaobo. "Rethinking the Problem of Postcolonialism." *New Literary History* 28.7 (1997): 7–19.

Young Bear, Ray A. *Black Eagle Child: The Facepaint Narratives.* Iowa City: U of Iowa P, 1992.

———. "Connected to the Past: An Interview with Ray Young Bear." *Survival This Way: Interviews with American Indian Poets.* By Joseph Bruchac. Tucson: Sun Tracks and U of Arizona P, 1987. 337–48.

———. *Remnants of the First Earth.* New York: Grove, 1996.

Zitkala-Ša (Gertrude Bonnin). *American Indian Stories.* 1921. Introd. Dexter Fisher. Lincoln: U of Nebraska P, 1986.

Zolla, Elémire. *The Writer and the Shaman: A Morphology of the American Indian.* Trans. Raymond Rosenthal. New York: Harcourt, 1973.

Index

Adams, Hank, 32, 35, 36

Address at Bloody-Brook (Everett), 213

African Americans: associated with modernity and hybridity, 90; double imagery of, 193 n.29; and FWP and WPA programs, 173, 174–75, 176, 177, 190–91 n.15, 191 n.16, 192–93 n.26, 193 n.29; and literacy, 200; and postcolonial criticism, 199; as symbol of America, 89–90; viewed as domestic animals, 5; viewed as exotic primitives, 84–86, 89, 193 n.29; viewed as primitive in Europe and America, 84–86; viewed by Austin, 88–89; viewed by Hartley, 88

Agriculture Department, 55

A History of the Ojibway Nation (Warren), 204

Ahmad, Aijaz, 21

AIM, 28

Akwesasne Notes (Adams), 32

Alaska, 44

Albert and Elaine Borchard Foundation, vii

alcohol, 217

Alexie, Sherman, 9, 91–92, 93

Algonquians, 214, 220 n.7

Allegheny Reservation, 66

Allen, Paula Gunn, 59, 183; quoted, 99, 167

Almanac of the Dead (Silko), 53, 72–74, 75, 93

America. *See* United States

American Adam, 30, 36, 70

The American Adam (Lewis), 77 n.14

American Constitution, 66

American Encounters (Harjo), 25

American Guides: aim of, 172–73, 187, 190 n.11 n.12, 191 n.21; dehistoricization of Native Americans in, 170, 171–72, 176, 191 n.20; discourses of identity and exchange in, 170–71, 180–82, 185, 187, 188–89, 189 n.4; double historical remove in, 191 n.21; fragmentation of discourses in,

188–89, 195 n.37 n.39 n. 40; Hobson's selections in, 177, 179, 190 n.12; Indian massacres in, 187–88; Mangione's selection in, 174–75; Native Americans neglected in, 175–77, 191 n.20; Native Americans present in, 174, 177–80, 185–86, 187, 190 n.5 n.7, 191 n.16 n.21, 191–92 n.22, 192 n.23 n.24 n.25, 192–93 n.26, 193 n.29, 194 n.32 n.33, 195 n.36 n.37; Penkower's selection in, 173, 175–77, 193 n.29; reservations in, 178–79; strategies of rehistoricization anticipated by, 171–72; structure of, 171, 190 n.6; Weisberger's selection in, 174, 177–78, 179–80, 190 n.10, 191 n.16 n.21, 191–92 n.26, 193 n.27

American Indian. *See* Native American

"American Indian Fiction Writers" (Cook-Lynn), 81

American Indian Journal, 34

American Indian Literatures (Ruoff), 75 n.1

American Indian Quarterly, 60, 76 n.11

American Revolution, 14

The American Rhythm (Austin), 88

Amerika, 86, 89

An Account of the Ojibway Indians (Maungwudaus), 209

Anderson, Jack, 32

Andrews, Lynn, 4

Andrist, Ralph K., 53–54, 57

"An Indian's Looking-Glass for the White Man" (Apess), 212

Anishinaabe, 13

anti-Semitism, 89, 165 n.7

Apaches, 142, 203–04

"A Pagan in St. Paul's Cathedral" (Johnson), 210–11, 220n. 10

Apess, William, 212–14, 217

"A Poet's Lament: Concerning the Massacre of

cide, 54; replaced by castrated Texas steer, 64, 77 n.14; return of, 53–54, 55, 57, 64–65, 67, 70–72, 74; as revisionary of American narrative, 64; as symbol of Native survival and defeat, 63; and tribal sovereignty, 64; in Welch's *Fools Crow*, 74–75

Burke, Kenneth, 168

Bush, Ronald, 84

California: FWP guide to, 171, 190 n.9

Calloway, Colin G., 204, 220 n.7

Calusa Indians, 205

Cannibal Culture (Root), 94

Captain John Smith and Pocahontas, 116

Carr, Helen, 85–86, 89, 137–38, 198

Carter, Asa, 49 n.8

Carter, Dan T., 49 n.8

Carter, Forrest, 49 n.8

"Cash Cow: It's Buffalo, the Other Red Meat" (Graham), 55–56

casinos, 56–57

Castaneda, Carlos, 4, 46

Castro, Michael, 30

Catawba Indian Reservation, 179

Catlin, George, 3, 179

Catullus, 156

Cayuga land claim, 55, 66, 75 n.2

Ceremony (Silko), 51, 73, 96–97 n.14

Chakrabarty, Dipesh, 11, 12, 13

Chandler, Raymond, 153, 158, 165 n.4

Chateaubriand, 4

Chateau de la Bretesche, vii

Chaucer, Geoffrey, 12

chauvinism, 83

Chavis, Donna, 197

Chazelle, Father Pierre, 214–15

Cherokee, 11

Cherokee Nation v. Georgia, 65

Cheyfitz, Eric, 220 n.8

Chief Wahoo, 21

China, 65

Choctaw, 11, 159, 162, 163, 164

Chona, Maria, 134, 137–38

Chow, Rey, 14

Churchill, Ward, 53, 54

Citizen of the World (Goldsmith), 208

Clackamas Chinooks, 125, 127

class, 177

Clements, William, 121

Clement VII, 2

Cleveland Indians, 21

Clifford, James, 56, 60, 137, 139, 189 n.4

Clifton, James, 39

Clinton, Bill, 53

"The Clown's Way" (Tedlock), 38

Cody, Bill, 63

Cogewea, the Half-Blood (Mourning Dove), 20, 221 n.14

cold war, 106

collaborative autobiography, Native American. *See* autobiography, collaborative Native American

collaborative personal narrative, Native American. *See* autobiography, collaborative Native American

colonialism: contemporary interest in, 18, 110; and cultural property, 58–60, 76 n.8; double consciousness produced in, 46; language and history destroyed in, 26–27; and literary texts, 147–48 n.10; and Native American collaborative autobiography, 136, 137, 145, 147–48 n.10

colonial mimicry, 20

The Colonizer and the Colonized (Memmi), 219 n.1

Colson, Elizabeth, 139, 140

Columbus, Christopher, 2, 5, 25, 205, 220 n.8

communitism, 77 n.15

community, 53

Comstock, W. Richard, 28

Concise Dictionary of American History (Scribner), 16

The Condition of Postmodernity (Harvey), 17

Congress, 66

Cook-Lynn, Elizabeth: criticism of, 163; insistence on cultural specificity by, 93–94; mentioned, 46, 82, 83, 90; on Native American representation, 44–45, 81, 95; on Silko's *Almanac of the Dead*, 93

Cooper, Gary, 118 n.8

Cooper, James Fenimore, 30, 115, 193 n.29

Copway, George, 207–08, 217, 218

Cornell University, 59

Corporation for Public Broadcasting, 32

Cortés, Hernan, 2, 201, 202

Costner, Kevin, 63, 110

"Critique of Judgement" (Kant), 76–77 n.12

Crockett, Davy, 103, 106, 107

Crow Dog, Mary, 47 n.2

Cruikshank, Julie, 143–44

Crusoe, Robinson, 96–97 n.14, 114–15

Cultee, Charles, 130

cultural appropriation, 27, 46, 94–95, 153

cultural capital, 36

cultural property: 6, 82; and alternation and

ship in, 172; discourses of identity and exchange in, 180–82, 185; guides produced by (see American Guides); minorities in, 172, 173–75, 176, 190–91 n.15, 191 n.16, 193 n.29

"The Festival of the Corn" (Hartley), 87

Fiedler, Leslie, 77 n.14

film noir, 161

films: 3, 4, 6, 100–101; audience reaction to misrepresentation in, 100, 101, 106–07; cross-cultural romance, and war genres, 109–10, 116; Native Americans reimagining images in, 108; remakes from 1950s and 1960s, 117 n.3

First Amendment, 59

Flaubert, Gustave, 12

Florentine Codex: General History of New Spain (Sahagún), 201

Florida: FWP guide to, 192 n.25

Florida Seminoles, 101

Fonda, Jane, 117 n.2

Fools Crow (Welch), 72, 74–75

Forbes, Jack, 94

Forked Tongues (Murray), 220 n.8

Forrest, Nathan Bedford, 49 n.8

Fort Apache Reservation, 178

For Those Who Come After (Krupat), 142

Foucault, Michel, 12, 70, 199, 212

Franklin County History, 195 n.36

Freneau, Philip, 30

From the Deep Woods to Civilization (Eastman), 218

frontier, 57, 224–25

Frost, Robert, 162

FWP. See Federal Writers' Project

Gandhi, Leela, 11, 14, 15; colonization viewed by, 16, 17, 18, 20

Gates, Henry Louis Jr., 200

Gatsby, Jay, 16

Geertz, Clifford, 60

gender, 41, 49 n.12, 109

"Generations of Resistance: American Indian Poetry and the Ghost Dance Spirit" (Churchill), 53

genocide, 26, 46, 61, 226

Georgi-Findlay, Birgitte, 215–16

Geronimo, 137, 142

Geronomo's Story of His Life (Barrett), 142

Ghost Dance: 56, 58; and cultural property, 63, 68–69; in Hogan's "Return: Buffalo," 71–72; and the return of the buffalo, 53–54; as revision of American narrative, 64; in Silko's *Almanac of*

the Dead, 72–73, 75; solutions within, 67–68; and tribal sovereignty, 64

ghost dance literature, 56, 67, 68

Ghost Dance Religion and the Sioux Outbreak of 1890 (Mooney), 67

Gilroy, Paul, 90

Girard, René, 159, 161, 163, 165 n.2 n.5

Giroux, Henry, 104

Go Down, Moses (Faulkner), 156

Goldsmith, Oliver, 208

Graham, Wade, 55–56

Greenblatt, Stephen J., 200, 204, 220 n.8

Green Grass, Running Water (King), 6, 96–97 n. 14, 114–16, 118 n.14

Grey, Zane, 63

Griaule, Marcel, 85

Griffith, D. W., 63

Griffiths, Gareth, 201

Gulliver's Travels (Swift), 126, 208

Hammett, Dashiel, 153

Hanta Yo (Hill), 116

Harjo, Joy, 14, 25

Harlem Renaissance, 175, 193 n.29

Harold of Orange (Vizenor), 111–14, 116, 118 n.9 n.10 n.11 n.12

Harris, Cheryl I., 76 n.6

Hartley, Marsden, 86, 87–88, 90

Harvey, David, 17

Hawkeye: in King's *Green Grass, Running Water*, 96–97 n.14, 114–15

Heidegger, Martin, 15

Hemingway, Ernest, 13, 169

Henry, George. See Maungwudaus, George

Here First (Krupat and Swann), 49–50 n. 16

Hiawatha, 113, 121

Highwater, Jamake: Castenada excused by, 46; compared to Cook-Lynn, 45; cultural appropriation by, 4; invented ethnicity of, 6, 32–33, 34–35, 36–39, 48 n.6, 49 n.9

Hillerman, Tony, 34, 154, 163

Himes, Chester, 153

historiography, 169–70

History of the Ojebway Indians (Jones), 209

Hobson, Archie, 177, 179, 190 n.12

Hogan, Linda: 14, 62; and cultural exchange, 69; detective story used by, 152; and personal and cultural identity and its boundaries, 82–83; quoted, 119; and the return of the buffalo, 53, 58 (see also "Return: Buffalo" [Hogan])

Hollywood: 61, 63, 102, 117 n.3; Native Americans portrayed by, 108, 109, 115

Holocaust, 61, 62, 195 n.40
hooks, bell, 199
Hopis: emergence myth of, 202; in the FWP guide,
180–82
House Made of Dawn (Momaday): 165 n.6; and
the discourses of identity, 182; managed exoti-
cism of, 23; Pulitzer Prize awarded to, 4, 22, 23,
102
Howard, Victoria, 125, 130
Howells, Emily Susanna, 218
Huggan, Graham, 47 n.1
Hutcheon, Linda, 212
Hutchins, Robert, 58
hybridity, 83
Hymes, Dell, 121, 127

Idaho: FWP guide to, 192 n.25
identity: determined by Indians themselves, 43–
44; romanticized version of Native American,
35
Illinois: FWP guide to, 187, 194 n.31
imagery rehearsal, 108
Imagining Indians (Masayesva), 6, 108–10, 116
imperialist nostalgia, 27–28
Indian Boyhood (Eastman), 206
Indian Country Today, 48 n.7
Indian Gaming Act of 1988, 78 n.21
*Indian Givers: How the Indians of the Americas
Transformed the World* (Weatherford), 1
Indian Health Service, 42
Indian Lawyer (Welch), 152
Indianness, 29, 30, 83–84
Indian Reorganization Act, 45
Indians. *See* Native Americans
Indian Self-Determination Act, 78 n.21
"Indians Sure Come in Handy" (Ortiz), 26
Indian wars, 47 n.2, 213, 216; Black Hawk's, 186,
190 n.7, 194–95 n.34; contemporary, 31, 54–55
indigenes, 81–82
individualism, 31
intellectual property, 58
interculturality, 168
International Colonial Exhibition, 90, 96 n.11
Interpreting the Indian (Castro), 30
Intertribal Bison Cooperative, 55
The Invented Indian (Clifton), 39
Inventing the Southwest (Swentzell), 79
The Invention of Ethnicity (Sollors), 40
Iowa: FWP guide to, 185, 187, 194 n.31, 195 n.36
Ireland, 77 n.17
irony, 212, 213
Iroquois Confederacy, 66, 78 n.19, 211

Isernhagen, Hartwig, 6–7
Ishmael: in King's *Green Grass, Running Water*,
96–97 n.14, 114–15
"Is the Post- in Postmodernism the Post- in Post-
colonial?" (Appiah), 27
*I Tell You Now: Autobiographical Essays by Native
American Writers* (Swann and Krupat), 44

Jackson, David, 34
Jacobs, Alex A., 94
Jacobs, Elizabeth: on Clara Pearson's self-
translation, 122; as collaborator, 128, 130–31 n.4;
and *Nehalem Tillamook Tales*, 120, 121, 125, 126;
and a popular edition of Pearson's stories, 123,
130 n.1
Jacobs, Melville, 120, 123, 125, 130 n.1
James, Henry, 163
Jameson, Fredric, 95 n.2
Jaskowski, Helen, 75 n.1
jazz, 88–89
Jeremy, Josiah, 204
The Jesuit Relations, 214
Jews, 89
Jim, Rex Lee, 19
Johnson, Charles, 33–34, 41, 49 n.13
Johnson, Chief George H. M., 218
Johnson, E. Pauline, 210–11, 216, 218–19, 220 n.10,
221 n.14
Johnson, Robert, 91
Jones, Rev. Peter, 208–09, 210, 212, 220 n.9
Joyce, James, 12

Kant, Immanuel, 76–77 n. 12
Keats, Ezra Jack, 12
Keiser, Albert, 198
Kellock, Katherine, 172
Kennard, Edward, 175, 177
Kenton, Simon, 186
Keresan Texts (Boas), 202
Kesey, Ken, 28–29, 46
Killing Custer (Welch), 188
Killing the White Man's Indian (Bordewich),
77 n.16
King, Thomas: *Green Grass, Running Water*, 6,
96–97 n. 14, 114–16, 118 n.8 n. 14; Native Ameri-
can images reimagined by, 108, 114, 115, 116; and
postmodernism, 96 n.12
King Philip's War, 213
Kinsella, W. P., 34
kinship, 30–31
Konkle, Maureen, 213
Kosovo, 65

Melville, Herman, 13, 115
Memmi, Albert, 219 n.1
Menominee Indian Reservation, 178, 193 n.27
Metacomet, 213
Mexico, 201
Micmacs, 204–05
Midnight's Children (Rushdie), 17
Mihesuah, Devon A., 76 n.11
Miller, Alfred Jacob, 3
Mills, Florence, 84–85
The Mimic Men (Naipaul), 19
Mingus, Charles, 91
Minnesota: FWP guide to, 178, 187
Minnesota Uprising, 206
Minthorne, Gilbert, 129
Mississippi: 11; FWP guide to, 192 n.25
mixed-blood, 198, 199
Mixedblood Messages (Owens), 23
The Moccasin Maker (Johnson), 216, 218–19,
    220 n.10
Modern Fiction Studies, 12
modernism: 96 n.12; and the primitive, 84–86, 87,
    95 n.4
Mohanty, Satya, 11
Momaday, N. Scott: 13, 14, 28, 165 n.6, 168; and the
    discourses of identity, 182, 183; ignored by
    Bhabha, 13; initiated into tribal culture, 22; as
    mimic man, 23; Pulitzer Prize awarded to, 4, 20,
    22, 23, 102; strategic location of, 23
Monroe, Harriet, 88
Montagnais, 204
Montana: FWP guide to, 192 n.25
Montana Department of Livestock, 56
Montezuma, 201–02
Mooney, James, 67, 72–73
Moore, David: 6, 137, 147 n.7, 148 n.11
Morrison, Toni, 13
Mound Builders, 186
Mountainmen Rendezvous, 107–08
Mourning Dove, 20, 221 n.14
movies. *See* films; media
Muratorio, Blanca, 147 n.5, 149 n.14
Murray, David: 6, 121, 189 n.4, 212; mentioned,
    220 n.8
Museum of Modern Art, 95 n.4
The Mysterious Warrior, 116
The Mystic Warrior, 116
mythbody, 124
myths: of American national character, 198; cre-
    ation, 183–84, 202; origin, 165 n.2; on the origin
    of whites on this continent, 201–04, 219 n.2,
    219–20 n.3

Naipaul, V. S., 19, 23
naming, 4–5
National Congress of American Indians (NCAI), 40
nationalism, 6, 43, 65, 106
The Nations Within (Lytle), 77 n.18
Native American Graves Protection and Repatria-
    tion Act of 1990, 60
Native American Identities (Vickers), 49 n.15
"Native American Intellectual Property Rights,"
    75 n.3
Native American Journalists Association, 117 n.2
Native American Renaissance, 170, 171, 183
Native American Renaissance (Lincoln), 75 n.1
Native Americans: American interest in, 1, 28; in
    the American narrative, 18–19; challenging and
    reappropriating representations of, 99, 100–
    102, 108, 117 n.2; and class, 177; constructed by
    Euro-Americans, 15, 17–19, 40, 42; as cultural
    signifiers, 176; defined, 29, 47 n.3; Disney model
    of, 103; double imagery of, 183, 193 n.29; Euro-
    pean interest in, 1–3; experience denied to, 119;
    identity self-determined by, 43–44; and the
    land, 18; legal determination of, 42; mimicking
    Indianness, 19, 133; misrepresentation of, 1–7,
    29, 100, 101, 103, 198; naming of, 4–5; prehistor-
    icization of, 170, 171, 177, 194 n.31; recognition
    and apology in ideal representation of, 225–26;
    as symbol of America, 86–87, 89–90; twentieth-
    century images of, 3–4, 9, 150; viewed as exotic
    primitives, 84–86, 89, 104; views of, 3–4, 7, 90,
    183, 193 n.29, 197, 223
*Native American Women in Literature and Cul-
    ture* (Santos), 151
Native critics, 26, 47 n.1
Native writers. *See* writers, Native American
Native writing. *See* literature, Native American;
    poetry, Native American
Navajoes, 13; in the FWP guide, 179
NCAI. *See* National Congress of American Indians
    (NCAI)
Nebraska History, 194 n.32
Ned, Annie, 143–44
Negritude, 33–34
Nehalem Tillamook Tales (Jacobs and Jacobs),
    120, 120–21, 126, 127; accessibility of, 121–22; as
    collaborative effort, 128, 130–31 n.4; Euro-
    American audience accommodated in, 123–25,
    127, 128–29; interpretive distortions of, 120–21;
    latter-day Native writing anticipated by, 126–
    27; measured-verse retranslation of, 127–28, 130
    n.3; republication of, 127
Nequatewa, Edmund, 215

New Age, 90, 94, 110
New Deal, 172
New Mexico: FWP guide to, 179, 192 n.23
New Yorker, 55
New York State: FWP guide to, 180, 192 n.25
New York State Citizens for Equitable Resolution of the Cayuga Land Claim, 55
New York Times, 49 n.8
New York Times Magazine, 65
Nietzsche, Friedrich, 15
Nightland (Owens), 164
Noble Savage, 4, 30
Norse, 1
North Dakota: FWP guide to, 192 n.25

O'Brien, Sharon, 41
O'Callahan, Jay, 126
O'Connell, Barry, 213
O'Gorman, Edmundo, 7
Occom, Samson, 206–07, 215
Of Grammatology (Derrida), 15
Ohio: FWP guide to, 186–87, 195 n.35
Ohitika Woman (Crow Dog), 47 n.2
Ojibwe, 204, 207, 220 n.6
Oklahoma: 11; FWP guide to, 180, 192 n.24 n.25
Old Shatterhead, 1
One Flew over the Cuckoo's Nest (Kesey), 28–29
Oneidas, 55, 66
Ong, Walter, 128
Onondaga Nation, 66, 69, 211
opinion leaders, 100, 106–07, 117 n.2
Opler, Morris, 38
Opus Posthumous (Stevens), 37
Orality and Literacy (Ong), 128
oral tradition, 199–200, 201 (*see also* storytelling)
Oregon: FWP guide to, 191–92 n.22
Orientalism (Said), 5–6
The Origin, Progress, and Conclusion of the Florida War (Sprague), 203
origin stories. *See under* myths
Ortiz, Alfonso, 69–70
Ortiz, Simon, 13, 26, 28
Oshawana, Chief, 214–15
Other: and the cold war, 106; and colonial history, 106, 110, 117–18 n.6; construction of, 84; and the construction of the Indian, 17, 18, 117–18 n.6; and the frontier, 224–25; and power, 199; Said's warning about, 6; in Whitman's "Facing West from California's Shores," 15, 16
Other Destinies (Owens), 90, 163
Owens, Louis: vii, 6, 90, 118 n.14 (*see also The Sharpest Sight*); autobiographical explorations

of, 157, 163; criticism of, 163; frontier used by, 224; Greek myths appropriated by, 163, 164; and Native appropriation of alien language, 49 n.15; postcolonial agenda of, 153, 163–64; and Steinbeck, 155; strategic location of, 11–12; and violence, 156, 163; works of, classified as mystery, 162

Paiutes, 203, 204, 206
Papago (Tonoho O'odham), 134, 137, 146 n.1
Papago Woman (Chona and Underhill), 134, 137–38
Parrish, Samuel B., 218
Parry, Benita, 199
Pataki, George, 55
Pearce, Roy Harvey, 198
Pearson, Clara: 126, 129; accommodation by, to Euro-American audience, 123–25, 126, 127, 128–29; and the conventions of traditional Tillamook storytelling, 122, 125, 127; as keeper of her people's literary art, 129–30; rich storytelling style of, 125–26; stories self-translated by, 120, 121–23
Penkower, Monty Noam, 173, 175–77, 193 n.29
Penn, William, 3
Penn, W. S., 97 n.15
Pequots, 66, 213
Pequot War, 213
Peter Pan, 107, 118 n.7
Peterson, Nancy J., 12
peyote, 31
Philip, King (Metacomet), 213
Phinney, Archie, 124
Picasso, Pablo, 95 n.7
Pine Ridge SD, 18
Plantation Revue, 84–85
Playing Indian (Deloria), 18–19
Playing in the Dark (Morrison), 13
Pocahontas, 31, 101
Pocahontas: and Disney, 101; and King's *Green Grass, Running Water*, 114, 115–16; myth of, 2–3, 41, 104–06, 107, 110, 113, 115, 117 n.5
Poetry, 88
poetry, Native American, 88, 96 n.12
Pokagon, Simon, 3–4, 168
"The Politics of Primitivism" (Jacobs), 94
Pomo, 139–40, 141, 142
postcolonialism: 23, 28; and the critic, 26, 47 n.1; and the impact of Western European perceptions of Other on both, 199, 219 n.1; and Native American collaborative autobiography, 147 n.9; subjects of, 27; texts of, 20–21

postmodernism: 27–28, 182; and the deconstruc-
tion of opposites, 56–57; fragment used in, 96
n.12; honorable, 62; viewed by Appiah, 27
poststructuralism, 183
Pound, Ezra, 12
power, 199
pragmatism, 48 n.5
Predicament of Culture (Clifford), 95 n.7
prehistory, 171
Primal Mind Foundation, 32
*The Primal Mind: Vision and Reality in Indian
America* (Highwater), 32, 33, 37, 38–39
primitivism, 87, 89
The Promise of Pragmatism (Diggins), 48 n.5
prophecy, 199, 204
Proust, Marcel, 12
Pueblo, 14, 23
Pulitzer Prize, 4, 20, 22, 23, 102
Purdy, John, 6
Pushmataha, 155

Quetzalcoatl, 201, 219 n.2, 219–20 n.3

race: 33–34, 48 n.4; arbitrary usage of, 200; and entry into mainstream American culture, 41, 49
n.12; and ethnicity, 40, 42; as historical rather
than biological, 39–40; and racism, 200; viewed
by Sollors, 40
" 'Race,' Writing and Culture" (Todorov), 200
racial essentialism, 42–43
racism: 39, 52, 83; and cultural property, 58, 76
n.6; defined, 200; double consciousness produced in, 46; and race, 200; and reservations, 21;
and sports mascots, 21
Ramsey, Jerold, vii, 6, 220–21 n.12
Rao, Raja, 19
Reagan, Ronald, 55
Recollections of a Forest Life (Copway), 207–08
*Regeneration through Violence: The Mythology of
the American Frontier 1600–1860* (Slotkin), 198
religion, 225
Remarks concerning the Ojibway Indians (Henry),
220 n.9
Remington, Frederick, 3
repatriation, 60
representation: 224; double role of, 80; indigene
lack of control over, 81–82
Reservation Blues (Alexie), 91–92, 93, 97 n.15
reservations: 18, 31; American ignorance of, 45;
conditions on, 21, 48 n.7; represented by the
WPA, 178–79
"Return: Buffalo" (Hogan), 53, 58, 70–72

Revard, Carter, 45–46
Revolutionary War, 207, 211
Rhea, 165 n.3
Rich, Adrienne, 14
Ridge, John Rollin, 20, 217
Rigal-Cellard, Bernadette, 6
Rinehart, W. V., 217, 218
Ringgold County History, 185, 186
Rios, Theodore, 134–35, 145–46, 147 n.2 n.3 n.4
Robinson, Harry, 129
Rogers, Millicent, 4
Rolfe, John, 107
roman noir: American society denounced in, 153,
154, 159; characteristics of, 153; the city in, 153;
evil evacuated through evil in, 159; goal of, 159;
and the myth of space, 153; power in, 153, 154;
sacrificial substitution in, 162; in *The Sharpest
Sight*, 152–53, 153–54; violence in, 153, 155, 156,
162; women in, 157, 158
Romanticism, 90, 96 n.12
Romeo and Juliet (Shakespeare), 159, 165 n.4
Root, Deborah, 94
Rosaldo, Renato, 27–28
Rose, Phyllis, 89
Rothenberg, Jerome, 96 n.12
Rowlandson, Mary, 116
"The Ruins of Representation" (Vizenor), 59
Runner in the Sun (McNickle), 69–70
Running Sketches of Men and Places (Copway),
208
Ruoff, A. LaVonne Brown, 6, 7, 75 n.1, 221 n.13
Rushdie, Salman, 17
Russo, Mel, 54

Sacramento Bee, 20
Sahagún, Fr. Bernardino de, 201, 219 n.2
Said, Edward, 5–6, 11, 13
Salamanca NY, 66
Sands, Kathleen, 6
Santees, 206
Santos, Paula Mota, 151
Sarris, Greg: correction of nonchronology and
repetition pointed out by, 141, 149 n.14; resis-
tance strategies recognized by, 139–41, 142–43
Sartre, Jean-Paul, 21
Scheick, William B., 198
schools, Indian boarding, 218
Scotland, 65, 77 n.17
Scott, Gail, 86
Scott County History, 186
"Second-Class Indians" (Highwater), 34
Seeing through the Sun (Hogan), 82